GREAT STORIES
OF THE
AMERICAN REVOLUTION

GREAT STORIES
—OF THE—
American
Revolution

Webb Garrison

RUTLEDGE HILL PRESS
Nashville, Tennessee

Published in Nashville, Tennessee, by Rutledge Hill Press, Inc., 211 Seventh Avenue North, Nashville, Tennessee 37219.

Typography by Bailey Typography, Inc., Nashville, Tennessee.

Library of Congress Cataloging-in-Publication Data

Garrison, Webb B.
    Great stories of the American revolution / Webb Garrison.
        p.   cm.
    ISBN 1-55853-270-6 (pbk)
        1. United States—History—Revolution,   1775–1783—Anecdotes.
    I. Title.
    E296.G25   1990   90-33127
    937.7—dc20   CIP

Printed in the United States of America
        1 2 3 4 5- 04 03 02 01 00

Contents

Never Before Did So Few Do So Much for So Many ..   9

Part One—Wide Was the Water

1. James Otis was the "Oak That Drew
   the Lightning Stroke of British Wrath".......... 17
2. Leaderless Curs Held the Lion at Bay............. 22
3. "Our Sovereign Lord the King Will
   Prosecute No Further"......................... 28
4. A Runaway Slave Led the Assault 33
5. John Adams of Braintree, Attorney for the Defense .. 38
6. "Catch Your Man before You Hang Him!" 43
7. Mountain Men Were First to Gain Independence 49

Part Two—Thirteen Pygmies Tossed Pebbles at the Giant

8. Samuel Adams Led in Forming a Loosely Knit
   Communications Network 55
9. Benjamin Franklin Leaked Letters
   That Widened the Breach 60
10. Cheap Tea Was Served at the Most Costly
    Tea Party Ever................................. 66
11. Submit Meekly—Or Unite and Resist! 71
12. First Women's Movement Urged Cider,
    Buttermilk, and Water 76
13. High-placed British Friends
    Made Up a Vocal Minority 80
14. John Sullivan's Men Smelled Gunpowder .....

Part Three—Blood in the Snow

15. Paul Revere Was In at the Start
    and Finish of Early Action 91
16. Ticonderoga Lay Eight Full Days
    Away from Philadelphia 96
17. The Queen City Is Thought to Have Seen
    the First Bold Declaration 101
18. Canada Could Be the Key! 106
19. "Our Subjects in North America Are
    in a State of Rebellion" 111
20. Daniel Boone Broke through the King's Fence 115
21. Quebec's Survivors Limped Home
    with Benedict Arnold 121

Part Four—Point of No Return

22. "There Are Things More Deadly Than Bullets" 129
23. Massachusetts Chopped the Kindling
    and Virginia Struck the Flint 133
24. Salt Marshes and Palmetto Logs versus
    His Majesty's Warships......................... 139
25. David Bushnell Launched High-tech War........... 144
26. A Magnet for Adventurers and Soldiers of Fortune... 149
27. Holiday Festivities Gave Washington
    an Unexpected Edge............................ 155

Part Five—"Loyalists of the South Will Rally behind Their Sovereign"

28. British Musical Jibes Became Patriots' Anthem 163
29. Preacher-heroes Molded Public Opinion 167
30. For Kentucky's Sake, George Rogers Clark
    Kept His Scalping Knife Sharp.................. 173
31. A Gardener's Son Gave Britain a Dose
    of Her Own Medicine........................... 178
32. Patriots Shaped an Emblem When
    All Hope of Reconciliation Vanished 184
33. Gentleman Johnny's Failed Plan Turned
    Combatants toward the South 188

Part Six—In the Valley of Despair

34. Tories Fled the Colonies Much
    as Huguenots Did from France.................. 197
35. In Paris, Franklin Scored a Mighty Triumph 201
36. In the Colonies, Franklin's Son Spoke
    and Acted for King George III 207
37. Exploits of Molly Hays and Other
    Women Boosted Morale 211
38. With Independence in the Balance,
    British Pounds Bought Treason.................. 217
39. A Creek Chieftain Played Both Ends
    against the Middle............................. 224
40. Printing Presses Worked Overtime
    Turning Out Paper Money..................... 228
41. Reputations Suffered When Things Went Awry 233
42. "Our Vaunted Allies Have Made a Great
    Display of 'French Courage'" 238

Part Seven—The World Turned Upside Down

43. De Kalb's Title Was Fake but His Zeal
    for Freedom Was Genuine 245
44. With No Holds Barred, Whigs and Tories
    Fought to the Finish........................... 249
45. Over-the-mountain Men Shot Holes
    in British Strategic Plans 254
46. Greene Resolved to Clothe His Men,
    Regardless of Cost............................. 259
47. Ex-wagoner Daniel Morgan Scrapped
    Conventional Battle Plans 263
48. A Pyrrhic Victory Pushed Cornwallis into Virginia ... 268
49. Bernado de Galvez Led the Spanish
    Offensive in the West 272
50. "My God, It Is All Over!"....................... 276

A More Perfect Union 281
Index... 285

Never Before Did So Few Do So Much for So Many

Vivid as the military action was, it alone did not constitute the American Revolution. Years of increasing political and economic tension—the prelude without which there would have been no call for men to fight for freedom—had created a climate that encouraged the colonists to pursue their independence.

At the time James Otis created a furor by protesting policies established in London, the fiery Boston attorney did not suggest that Britain's North American colonies should sever their ties with the mother country. While growing numbers of protestors voiced their complaints about colonial policies, discontent with the British-American relationship was never universal in the colonies.

On the contrary, a survey of the era that led to the American Revolution suggests that the "independence movement" never had the backing of a majority of the Americans. Patriots—often called Whigs or Colonials—won the wholehearted adherence of perhaps one-third of those who lived in the North American colonies. Tories, or Loyalists, were about as numerous. As for the rest, Major James Wright, the son of Georgia's royal governor, snorted that they "didn't care a pinch of snuff" for the issues involved in the long-drawn-out struggle.

Many of the principal battles and most of the chief figures in the American Revolution are almost universally known today. Because of that, the focus of this volume is the little-known or the surprising aspects of the Revolution. In the same spirit, some nearly forgotten but significant men and women who played important roles have been given their due.

During the American Revolution, military action was confined almost entirely to a narrow strip along the Atlantic coast. While Daniel

Boone had opened Kentucky to settlers and George Rogers Clark had mastered outposts in Illinois, virtually all engagements that deserve to be called battles were fought within less than two hundred miles of what is now our nation's eastern boundary.

Even the largest of Revolutionary War battles were little more than skirmishes when compared with later wars. Even the Battle of Yorktown—not immediately apparent even to its participants as having brought Britain's total defeat by the patriots—involved only about 25,000 men. Americans and their French allies fought the British and their German mercenaries during that watershed siege. Washington's ragged Continentals and militia from several colonies may have numbered 15,000 at Yorktown. That means that the decisive battle of the war was won by less than one-third the number of Americans who were killed, wounded, or captured at Gettysburg eighty-two years later.

Numerous armed encounters between Americans and British forces, such as those at Fort Ticonderoga in New York and the Cowpens in South Carolina, involved only a handful of men. Yet they were of tremendous significance.

A few patriots began to lay their lives on the line very early in the conflict, and they continued to do so for years. However, great numbers who are counted as having been fighting men spent ninety days or less in a colonial militia unit and never so much as smelled gunpowder! By the most generous estimate, during the years of struggle a total of perhaps 250,000 men may have taken up arms for the sake of freedom. The Vietnam War saw thirty to forty times as many men in military service as did the nation's glorious Revolution.

Not even George Washington commanded the solid support of all Americans.

Although the Continental Congress was relatively powerless, its members were stubbornly determined to make military as well as political decisions. Especially, but not exclusively, in the back country, Loyalists helped wage a struggle that often mounted to the level of civil war. Infighting and betrayal by men who called themselves patriots and soldiers were far more widespread than we may realize. Washington was plagued by harassment from members of Congress, treason on the part of a long-time comrade, and mutiny staged by thousands of hungry and ill-paid fighting men.

These facts point to an amazingly small number of Americans who somehow managed to emerge as victors after a long and bitter struggle with the most powerful nation in the world at that time. Their triumph meant that the emerging United States of America would eventually spread three thousand miles to the west and would rise to world dominance while seeing the mother country shrink in size and in military and economic power.

Yet the ideas for which the American patriots fought are what has endured. Independence and more-or-less freedom have come to countless millions as a result of the protests, boycotts, skirmishes, alliances, and battles by which America gained the opportunity to shape its own destiny.

In the epic of man, the American Revolution has no close parallel. Never before or since has so small a number of stubborn idealists done so much to change the lives of such multitudes at home and around the world.

George Washington looked the part of commander-in-chief when he took charge of largely volunteer forces with no experience. [CURRIER & IVES LITHOGRAPH]

GREAT STORIES
OF THE
AMERICAN REVOLUTION

Part One

Wide
Was the
Water

British colonies in North America were separated from the mother country by the Atlantic Ocean. That meant they were isolated in a fashion that no person today can comprehend. With good weather and luck, ten or twelve weeks might bring a reply to a letter from London to Philadelphia.

This, and the vastness of the largely unexplored North American continent, contributed to the development of a mindset quite different from that which prevailed in England. Persons of intelligence and good will tended to view the same sets of issues and events from different perspectives. Since they were far apart—in space and in the time required for communication—they inevitably developed strong differences.

Many leaders on both sides of the Atlantic wanted harmony and worked hard to achieve it. But instead of shrinking, the gap between England and the colonies grew wider. Inevitably, it led to harsh words that were followed by even harsher actions.

James Otis. [Engraving from Alonzo Chappel Portrait]

CHAPTER

1

James Otis Was the "Oak That Drew the Lightning Stroke of British Wrath"

February 1761
Old Town Hall, Boston

To my dying day I will oppose, with all the power and faculties God has given me, all instruments of slavery on one hand and of villany on the other.

A man's house is his castle, and whilst he is quiet he is as well guarded as a prince in his castle.

These writs, if declared legal, would totally annihilate this privilege. Custom-house officers may enter our houses when they please. Their menial servants may enter, may break locks, bars, and everything in their way.

Wanton exercise of this power is not a fanciful suggestion of a heated brain. What a scene does this open! Every man, prompted by revenge, ill humor, or wantoness [sic.] to inspect his neighbor's house, may get a writ of assistance. Others will ask for it from self defense. One arbitrary exertion will provoke more, until society is bathed in blood and tumult!

Barely thirty-six years old, plump James Otis spoke in this vein for what listeners insisted was at least four hours. When he had finished his impassioned oration, future president John Adams reached a watershed conclusion: "American independence was then and there born! Seeds of patriots and heroes were then and there sown!"

An estimated three score merchants, their wives, their clerks, and some of their customers had crowded into the hall. None needed an explanation. All knew precisely the meaning of the legal instrument termed a "writ of assistance."

Years earlier, authorities in England had forbidden American colonists to trade with the neutral ports of St. Thomas and St. Eustatius. Most of the French islands in the Caribbean were also off limits.

However, London was more than three thousand miles away, and the neutral ports and the French islands were close at hand. So enterprising merchants went to colonial governors and offered their services. They would function as intermediaries for the exchange of prisoners held in the forbidden places, and they would outfit their vessels to accommodate this service. Then, while in one of the forbidden ports, their crews would hustle merchandise aboard until the holds of their ships were full.

Smuggling of this sort eliminated the hated excise fees and taxes. Hence it was far more profitable than ordinary commercial transactions.

Frequent complaints from competing merchants soon reached England's lawmakers, who gave strict orders that such trade should cease. However, weeks to the west, the practice was too profitable to be suppressed.

On August 4, 1760, a new and self-proclaimed stickler to the letter of the law took office in Boston. Francis Bernard, royal governor of the Massachusetts Bay Colony, promptly issued a series of proclamations. One of them focused upon the role of customs officers. Henceforth, said the governor, these officials would work to stop the importation of goods not brought through legal channels.

Colonial opposition to this edict, which centered in Boston, was vocal—and successful. Soon customs-house officers applied to the Superior Court for aid.

A learned justice who pored over volumes of English statutes eventually found copies of legislation enacted much earlier, during the reign of King Charles II. With the approval of the sovereign, Parliament at that time had created a special security system under which a collector of dues or taxes could get a legal instrument—or writ—that would assist him in his search for smuggled or contraband goods.

In practice, the writ of assistance soon became a blank search warrant. It empowered officers of the customs service or of the court to enter and search any suspicious premises. No solid evidence of wrongdoing was required.

When Thomas Hutchinson, chief justice of Massachusetts, studied the history of these writs at length, he concluded that they were entirely lawful. What's more, he ruled, they were "essential for the welfare of Great Britain and Ireland and of our sovereign King George III."

In a move to thwart Hutchinson, leading merchants of Boston pooled their resources to hire attorneys James Otis and Oxenbridge Thatcher to represent them in legal proceedings designed to block the use of these writs. In order to accept the case, Otis had to resign his position as advocate general of the vice admiralty court.

An even more vexatious situation faced him at home. His wife, who had strong Tory sympathies, was furious at her husband for pleading the case for Colonials. Seeking to deter him, she informed him that she would not sleep with him while he was busy "undermining the authority of our king."

While Otis's impassioned speech may not have included the sentence, *A man's home is his castle,* its wide circulation in broadsides made the statement into a fighting slogan. Few who used it, however, realized that the attorney's zeal to protect his own "castle" from customs officers had caused his wife to vacate his bed!

Otis delivered his argument before the full bench of the superior court. Although it is not widely known today, many scholars consider it as one of the most important pieces of oratory in American history. Some rank it with Patrick Henry's more familiar "Give me liberty, or give me death!" speech.

James Otis and his colleague lost their case, but his fiery language was widely transmitted in print and orally. Wherever his passionate words were read or repeated, men were strengthened in their resolve to resist British oppression.

It took five years for the Boston case to reach the desk of Britain's attorney general. Pondering both sides of the question, he ruled that the act of Parliament cited by Justice Hutchinson did not authorize the use of writs of assistance in the colonies. But by then the damage created by these legal instruments was already done. The breach was far too wide to repair.

Personal attacks upon "short-necked and eagle-eyed" Otis began before Boston's town hall was empty on the day of his pleading. Soon the Boston *Evening Post* published a set of verses that derided the man whom intimates knew as Jamie or Jemmy:

> Jemmy is a silly dog, and Jemmy is a tool;
> Jemmy is a stupid cur, and Jemmy is a fool.

In England, the duke of Bedford cited a statute from the time of King Henry VII. He proposed that under this provision, James Otis should be brought to England for trial as a traitor. American Tories, who

King Charles II.

jubilantly counted Otis's wife as one of their stalwart supporters, were at least as vitriolic as his British critics.

Small wonder, therefore, that a new proverb was soon fashioned. According to it, "Otis is the oak that has drawn the lightning of British wrath." Actually, Otis was far from alone in his opposition to what he considered oppression from afar, but most who agreed with him were less articulate and less prominent than he was.

Rage on the part of British leaders in London and Tories in the colonies elevated Otis to a new role among Colonials; and he became a sought-after guest at dinners, banquets, and teas. At the urging of fellow countrymen, who did not yet call themselves patriots, he sought and won a seat in the General Court (or provincial legislature).

His wife, whose views never changed, became even more furious when Otis made the motion that led to formation of what Colonials called the Stamp Act Congress. This 1764 conclave was made up of persons who openly opposed Britain's use of revenue stamps upon documents and commodities.

Delegates who comprised the body soon confessed themselves

powerless to stop the hated new method of raising revenue for the king. Hence, James Otis launched a nonimportation movement, perhaps the first within the British empire. Merchants and consumers who supported it refused to buy goods imported from the mother country.

Otis's pamphlets were almost as widely circulated in England as they were in America. During a period of perhaps a dozen years, his influence exceeded that of any other Colonial, with the possible exception of John Dickinson.

In their official communications to their superiors in London, Governor Bernard and his officials termed Otis "a malignant incendiary." When he learned that the label was being applied to him, the attorney inserted in the *Boston Gazette* a notice that branded them as liars.

Soon after that notice was published in 1769, a group of crown officers jeered when Otis walked into the British Coffee House. He reacted furiously and in a brawl with John Robinson was struck on the head with a cutlass.

Initially regarded as unimportant, the injury proved to be serious and permanent. Mrs. Otis—described as "both beautiful and formal"—rejoiced. Her husband would strike no more blows against the authority of the king and his officers! Colonials who looked to Otis for leadership lamented that "He now rambles and wanders like a ship without a helm."

In December 1771 the probate court took unusual action that brought joy to the hearts of all Tories. Samuel A. Otis, younger brother of the injured man, was made his legal guardian.

On December 17, 1775, James Otis somehow managed to elude servants. Wielding a borrowed gun, he hurried to Bunker Hill, where he tried to take part in the fighting. Partly as a result of that incident, his guardian periodically sent him into the country.

That is how the once-brilliant attorney-orator came to be at the farm house of Isaac Osgood at Andover on the evening of May 23, 1783. There the man earlier lauded as an oak that drew the lightning of British wrath was killed by a stroke of nature's lightning.

According to the *Dictionary of American Biography,* that was exactly as it should have been: "Death came as he had always wished it would; only fire from heaven could release his fiery soul."

2

Leaderless Curs Held the Lion at Bay

"**C**olonials will bare their fangs and snarl, but they know they are a pack of curs without a leader. Soon they will turn tail and run—jostling one another to see who will be first to display the blue."

Chancellor of the exchequer George Grenville spoke to a hand-picked group of lawyers. If his proposed Stamp Act was to pass, they would have to support it. Already plans were under way to print stamps on "tobacco paper," cheap coarse-grained paper that was tinted blue.

Someone ventured to ask how much revenue the act would produce.

"We need to recover no less than one-third of the cost of maintaining His Majesty's troops in the colonies," Grenville explained. "That now runs to more than £180,000 per annum. No one knows how many Colonials there are; some say 1,600,000. If that is correct, the Stamp Act must produce no less than 15 shillings per annum from each American."

After extensive discussion in the session that today would be called a briefing, Grenville's lieutenants led the movement in Parliament. Strong opposition came from many quarters. In Parliament, a speaker invoked the memory of the great Horace Walpole who had faced a similar issue thirty years earlier and had concluded, "I will leave the taxation of America to some of my successors, who have more courage than I have." William Pitt, first earl of Chatham, who was universally revered for having planned the strategy that led to the defeat of the French in India, in Canada, and on the high seas (in the Seven Years' War that ended in 1763) rose to his feet to declare, "I will never burn my fingers with an American stamp tax."

In spite of strong and high-placed opposition, Grenville's proposal carried. In private, many lawmakers admitted that they did not like

It was a common practice to issue broadsides warning of the coming of a tea ship.

> ## To the Public.
>
> THE long expected TEA SHIP arrived laft night at Sandy-Hook, but the pilot would not bring up the Captain till the fenfe of the city was known. The committee were immediately informed of her arrival, and that the Captain folicits for liberty to come up to provide neceffaries for his return. The fhip to remain at Sandy-Hook. The committee conceiving it to be the fenfe of the city that he fhould have fuch liberty, fignified it to the Gentleman who is to fupply him with provifions, and other neceffaries. Advice of this was immediately difpatched to the Captain; and whenever he comes up, care will be taken that he does not enter at the cuftom-houfe, and that no time be loft in difpatching him.
>
> New-York, April 19, 1774.

the legislation, but no one came up with a better plan. Britain needed more revenue because the national debt had risen sharply, because of the recent war and the cost of supporting a standing army to protect the North American colonies.

King George III put his signature to the Stamp Act on March 22, 1765.

Grenville was sure he could count on the support of most Tories in the colonies, an estimated one-third of the population. Eager to reward them and perhaps win the support of some who might be inclined to balk, from the beginning he announced that all administrative jobs established to implement the act would go to Americans.

This method of raising revenue was fairly commonplace in Europe, and Benjamin Franklin let it be known that he would not be averse to serving as a distributor of stamps. That lucrative post would enable him to name numerous collectors. Henry Laurens of Charles Town, one of Carolina's most distinguished leaders, seemed eager to become a distributor.

Implementation of the Stamp Act would require an elaborate network of distributors, collectors, and inspectors. Enumeration of items to which stamps should be affixed, or on which the new tax should be paid, ran to fifty-four paragraphs.

Every skin or piece of vellum, parchment, or sheet of paper used for a plea, a declaration, or a demurrer was to be taxed three pence.

Whether the document was printed or handwritten made no difference. Duty was to be paid on any paper that carried a message.

A certificate of a degree from a university, academy, college, or seminary of learning required a stamp duty of two pounds. Duty for the material on which a franchise or grant of liberty was written was set at six pounds.

Even things normally used in games of chance were subject to the Stamp Act. One shilling was the duty for a pack of playing cards, while a pair of dice was taxed at ten shillings.

Implementation of the Stamp Act was scheduled to begin on November 1, 1765. Long before then, the colonists knew the general thrust of the measure, and multitudes reacted immediately and explosively.

Tens of thousands of revenue stamps would be clearly visible to the eye. Their presence would serve as everyday reminders that for the first time, Americans were being directly taxed from afar. Earlier indirect measures such as the Hat Act, the Wool Act, and the Sugar Act served primarily to protect the interests of British merchants, but all of these measures operated in such a way that they remained largely invisible.

James Otis raged and roared that the Stamp Act involved "Taxation without representation."

Patrick Henry, a rustic Virginian who was unaware of what the Yale-educated attorney from Boston was saying, took his seat in the House of Burgesses just as details of the Stamp Act became known. Long-time aristocratic members of the lawmaking body warned Henry, age twenty-nine, to keep his mouth shut; but instead of being silenced, he was goaded into oratory.

At the time Thomas Jefferson was a college student. He attended sessions of the House of Burgesses and took copious notes about the heated debate between Loyalists and the upstart Henry from Hanover County. According to Jefferson, at the height of the argument Henry ceased to speak firmly and began to shout, one phrase at a time: "Caesar had his Brutus! Charles the First his Cromwell! And George the Third . . ."

"Treason!" cried the presiding officer. "Treason! Treason!" echoed members of the house.

Patrick Henry paused briefly, lowered his voice, and murmured, ". . . and George the Third . . . may profit from their example. If this be treason, make the most of it!"

Henry's impassioned oratory of May 1765 led to a result that aristocrats like George Wythe and Edmund Randolph could not have predicted. The House of Burgesses fashioned, then passed, the Virginia Resolves, a set of recommendations that challenged the authority of

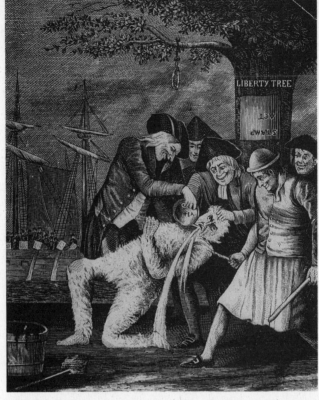

A British cartoon depicted Liberty Boys in the act of tarring and feathering a tax collector.

the British Crown. When he learned their nature, the royal governor of Massachusetts sent an urgent dispatch to London. "The Virginia Resolves," he warned, "are proving to be an alarm bell to all who are disaffected."

Benjamin Franklin changed his mind and refused all offers of a lucrative post in the stamp distribution system. Then he took steps to put distance between himself and the tax he had earlier characterized as reasonable.

In Charles Town, Henry Laurens was awakened out of bed by "a most violent thumping & confused noise." He stuck his head through a window and was greeted by jeers. Then he heard the shouted challenge, "Open your doors and let us search your House and Cellars."

Cutlass-wielding men who shouted "Liberty! Liberty!" converged upon his door. Once inside, the thinly disguised fellow Carolinians searched his house, then his cellar, his barn, and his counting room. Empty-handed after their search, they confronted the owner of the mansion. Laurens gave his solemn word that he had no stamps and would distribute none. Members of the mob then cheered him, but they warned him to have no more to do with the royal governor, Sir James Grant.

Spontaneously and almost simultaneously, angry opposition flared throughout the colonies. Liberty poles were erected in towns and cities from Boston to Savannah. Some were even thrown up in hamlets of rural New Hampshire and the back country of Virginia.

Tories struck back promptly and forcibly. One of their widely distributed handbills reproduced Paragraph 55 of the Stamp Act:

> Finally, the produce of all the aforementioned duties shall be paid into His Majesty's treasury, and there held in reserve, to be used from time to time by the Parliament for the purpose of defraying the expenses necessary for the defence, protection, and security of colonies and plantations.

Nevertheless, all attempts to justify the tax and to placate its opponents were futile.

In New York, Sons of Liberty put together an oversize cart and placed upon it an effigy of Cadwallader Colden, the lieutenant governor who supervised Fort George. Then they wheeled the cart under the guns of the fortress. After shouting jeers to armed soldiers inside, they set fire to the cart and the effigy it carried.

Newport, Rhode Island, also saw the burning of effigies, but protesters did not stop with this demonstration. They broke into the homes of known Tories, slashing pictures and smashing china. Many leather-bound books belonging to Dr. Moffat, a pioneer user of telescopes and barometers, were pulled from shelves and dumped into his well.

Boston, busiest seaport on the continent, was already aflame from the actions of James Otis. Led by shoemaker Ebenezer McIntosh, the city's Colonials went on a rampage. Leveling a brick building said to be set aside for use as a stamp office, they forced stamp distributors to flee the city. Although he was protected by British troops, Governor Bernard decided to take refuge in Castle William.

On another night Bostonians looted the home of William Story, a leading Loyalist. Then they turned to the home of the lieutenant governor. Windows and doors were smashed, furniture was burned, and paintings were ripped from the wall. Even the trees in the yard were cut down.

As November 1 approached, violence increased. While there were no reported casualties, property damage soared. Newspapers solemnly announced that they would cease publication, and business establishments draped their doors and windows in black. More than six hundred merchants put their names to public lists that pledged them

The TIMES are
Dreadful
Dolefal
Dismal
Dolorous, and
DOLLAR-LESS.

Thursday, October 31. 1765

THE

PENNSYLVANIA JOURNAL;

AND

WEEKLY ADVERTISER.

NUMB 1195

EXPIRING: In Hopes of a Resurrection to LIFE again.

Adieu Adieu to the LIBERTY of the PRESS.

I am sorry to be obliged to acquaint my readers that as the Stamp Act is feared to be obligatory upon us after the *first of November* ensuing (The Fatal To-morrow), The publisher of this paper, unable to bear the Burthen, has thought it expedient to stop awhile, in order to deliberate, whether any methods can be found to elude the chains forged for us, and escape the insupportable slavery, which it is hoped, from the last representation now made against that act, may be effected. Mean while I must earnestly Request every individual of my Subscribers, many of whom have been long behind Hand, that they would immediately discharge their respective Arrears, that I may be able, not only to support myself during the Interval, but be better prepared to proceed again with this Paper whenever an opening for that purpose appears, which I hope will be soon.

WILLIAM BRADFORD.

Late in October 1765, newspapers throughout the colonies published what editors said would be final editions.

to cease buying British goods, and in cities, towns, and villages throughout the colonies November 1 was proclaimed a day of fasting and mourning.

News of events in the colonies was slow in reaching London; but when it did arrive, manufacturers and tradesmen became so alarmed that they began registering protests with members of Parliament. In turn, lawmakers admitted that there was a spreading movement aimed at repeal of the Stamp Act.

Lord Lyttelton, who led the counterattack, hastily prepared a protest to abolition of the tax. Sixty-three members of the House of Lords, including five bishops, let it be known that they favored subduing the colonial protest with fire and sword.

But the impending boycott by nearly two million consumers was a weapon too powerful to be ignored, and on March 18, 1766, the Stamp Act was repealed. Almost leaderless though they were, the Colonials who put loyalty to their region above loyalty to the Crown had effectively defeated Parliament.

This victory relieved the Americans of a hated, but minor, form of taxation. Far more important, it sent a fearful message to Britain's leaders.

The morale of protesters in the colonies soared when crowds surged into streets and parks to shout their elation at having made a watershed discovery. It was, after all, possible for ordinary citizens to thwart faraway lawmakers and the king!

3

"Our Sovereign Lord the King Will Prosecute No Further"

"**Y**ou aboard the *Liberty!* Deliver the vessel at once, in the name of His Majesty, the King!"

Shouting from the prow of a longboat, the boatswain of the warship *Romney* was heard and understood; and sailors aboard the merchant vessel submitted without audible protest. Earlier, they had been notified that proper legal papers for seizure of the ship had been issued.

However, on the Boston wharf, matters soon got out of hand. Before the *Liberty* could be secured and warped toward the waiting ship, an ugly crowd gathered. Customs comptroller Benjamin Hallowell made the mistake of arriving to make sure that the seizure was accomplished. Joseph Harrison, chief collector of customs, came with him, bringing along his son.

Members of a small mob on the wharf threw bricks and cobblestones at sailors in the longboat, but none reached their mark. As the *Liberty* was being towed away, Bostonians turned upon the officials on the shore.

Joseph Harrison was hit with a club. When he turned and ran, he was pelted with stones. His son, who refused to flee, was thrown to the ground and then dragged along the wharf by his hair. Benjamin Hallowell, lying on the ground with his breath knocked from him, was semiconscious and bleeding profusely.

Rioters left the official lying in a pool of blood and raced toward his home, where they threw stones, shouted invectives, and drove horses from the barn. Moving to the home of the inspector general of customs, John Williams, they smashed more than one hundred windowpanes of his elegant house.

"London will take notice of Americans tonight," one member of the mob boasted to his comrades. "June 10, 1768, will not be forgotten for many a year!"

His on-the-spot verdict proved to be correct. Years later, Colonials who were present that day gloated as they told their grandchildren about their exploits.

It didn't take a man trained in law or government to realize that the case of the *Liberty* was important. Unlike some earlier protests, it meant a full-fledged Colonial test of royal power.

Tension between colonists and the British officials of Boston had simmered for months. Passage of the Townshend Acts of 1767 had caused the city to reach the boiling point. This legislation provided new import duties on glass, paints, lead, paper, and tea. These duties were far from burdensome when viewed impartially, but few Americans even pretended to be impartial. Because resistance was expected, a special American Board of Commissioners was established to implement legislation enacted by Parliament. Although the board was located in Boston, its members were directly responsible to the British Treasury Board.

Colonial merchants and tradesmen fumed. Although most citizens were not directly affected, when they learned of the new arrangements many berated them loudly.

One Bostonian, newly wealthy John Hancock, was particularly vocal. The son of a poor clergyman, he had been reared by his childless uncle, who was one of the most prosperous merchants in New England. When Thomas Hancock died in 1764, he bequeathed most of his estate—more than £70,000—to the nephew whom he had trained to take his place in business.

Through his uncle's generosity, John Hancock received a Harvard education. As the new head of the Hancock enterprises, he was sure he knew his rights, and acquaintances remarked to one another that he would "bellow at the top of his lungs" in asserting those rights.

Governor Francis Bernard arranged a grand celebration to mark the arrival of the new American commissioners. As soon as he learned of the plans to greet the officials, Hancock arranged to humiliate them. As head of the Cadet Company, an amateur military organization, he refused to let his men march in honor of the commissioners.

Smarting at the insult, Governor Bernard muttered threats that one of his subordinates relayed to Hancock who retaliated with a public statement in the House of Representatives. Neither new commissioners nor old commissioners would interfere with his business, he promised. In fact, he would refuse to allow any customs official to go aboard any of his ships in the London trade.

Matters might have ended with this war of words had not Hancock's ship *Liberty* reached Boston at the height of the verbal exchange. Its captain had hardly dropped anchor before two tidewaiters appeared. Everyone, including Hancock and his captains, knew that these minor customs officials were authorized to board ships to inspect cargoes.

"They had no writs," John Hancock later affirmed. "They wore no badges of identification. For all that my captain knew, they could have been vagrants who walked off the wharf. But they demanded to go below for what they called 'a full examination.'"

Notified of the impending search, Hancock hurried to the wharf. The tidewaiters were barely below deck when he ordered some of his sailors to seize them and tie them up. He then locked them in a compartment that they later claimed was full of bilge water. Released after about three hours, the officials proceeded with their inspection, finding the ship's hold to be empty.

The American commissioners soon registered a formal complaint that brought the attorney general of the province into the quarrel. He investigated, then filed a criminal information statement. According to it, John Hancock had deliberately interfered with the work of customs officials.

Legal action was formally initiated on June 11, and much of the prosecution's case rested upon sworn testimony of Thomas Kirk. With a companion, he had boarded the *Liberty* in routine fashion, he said, and one of Hancock's men offered him a bribe, which he refused. Immediately afterward, Hancock himself appeared and had him confined for at least three hours. While behind a locked door, he could see nothing but "heard constant sounds of unloading." As an informant, Kirk stood to gain one-third of the value of the *Liberty* and her cargo if smuggling could be proved.

British officials and colonial merchants alike admitted that smuggling was rife. Some of the newly appointed commissioners had never before set foot on American soil, and at their arrival in November 1767 they expressed "shock and dismay" upon learning that only six vessels engaged in smuggling had been seized during three years.

Some of their colleagues, better aware of the distance between London and Boston, had warned them. "Smuggling is a way of life in the colonies," Henry Hulton is reported to have said. "Keep quiet, and save your hides."

As a body, the new board had no intention of keeping quiet. More to the point, some newly arrived commissioners were eager to demonstrate the strength of the Crown and its officers. How better to do so than by making an example of a man of wealth who was known to be active in the secret society known as the Sons of Liberty?

The Massachusetts attorney general refused to be swayed by pressure from high-placed officials and ruled that there was insufficient evidence to prosecute thirty-seven-year-old John Hancock.

Red-faced commissioners decided to appeal the case over the head of the attorney general. When they forwarded their plea to the Treas-

Because he was the wealthiest man in New England, merchant John Hancock had the most to lose by opposing British regulations.

ury Board in London, they asked that John Hancock be fined at least £100,000.

For months depositions were sent across the Atlantic to London and rulings were relayed back to Boston. As tension increased, mobs prowled the streets many nights. Most customs officials and their families retreated behind the fortifications of Castle William in Boston Harbor.

No one knows how many sailing vessels were employed in the trans-Atlantic proceedings, but eleven months after the *Liberty* was seized, attorneys of the Crown gave up. In a formal dispatch, Advocate General

Sewall prayed for leave to retract all charges and reported that "Our Sovereign Lord the King will prosecute no further thereon." There had been no deaths or critical injuries, but buildings had been smashed, bodies had been bruised, and officials in both London and Boston had been humiliated.

News that the case had been closed reached Charles Town three weeks after it became known in Boston, and merchants in the southern port city cheered when they learned that Hancock and the Colonials had defeated the king and his ministers.

John Hancock's chief claim to fame today rests upon his bold signature upon the Declaration of Independence. Because he wrote "large enough for the king to read it," signatures have become known as one's "John Hancock."

During and after the long struggle between Britain and her North American colonies, merchant/patriot John Hancock prospered mightily. Only one great disappointment came to him. When war broke out between British and colonial forces, he opposed the choice of George Washington as commander in chief. He wanted the post for himself and was so furious at not getting it that he nourished his anger for years. In his ninth term as governor of Massachussets, Hancock had to be host to General Washington who he knew was about to become president of the new United States. John Hancock deliberately snubbed his famous guest.

Although he always insisted that he should have been given the post that went to Washington, Hancock took solace in being the only man ever to cause the king of England to give up an official lawsuit. Ironically, the celebrated case arising from an attempt to inspect a ship would have been trivial under other circumstances. The ship's cargo is said to have been nothing more than casks of second-rate wine!

CHAPTER

4

A Runaway Slave Led
the Assault

Court of Inquiry
Boston, Massachussets Province

The People seemed to be leaving the soldiers, and to turn from them,
when down came a number from Jackson's corner. They were crying and
huzzaing, damn them—they dare not fire, we are not afraid of them!

One of these people, a stout man with a long cord wood stick, threw
himself in, and made a blow at the officer. I saw the officer try to ward
off the stroke. Whether he struck him or not, I do not know.

The stout man then turned around and struck the grenadier's gun at the
captain's right hand, and immediately fell in with his club and knocked
his gun away, and struck him over the head. The blow came either on the
soldier's cheek or hat.

This stout man held the bayonet with his left hand, and twitched it and
cried, kill the dogs, knock them over.

This was the general cry; the people then crowded in.

—Andrew, slave of Oliver Wendell

Sworn testimony by Andrew provides the most complete eyewitness account of what has become known as the Boston Massacre. The first major bloodletting during the time when tension
between British and Colonials was mounting steadily, it contributed to
the mutual animosity and mistrust.

In the aftermath of the *Liberty* affair, officials in London took drastic steps to prevent a repetition. A member of Parliament went on
record as insisting that authorities "must stop these provinces in their
career to opulence and importance." Failure to do so, he said, would

cause "the Seat of Royal Residence to be transferred from St. James to Faneuil Hall [in Boston], and this devoted Island made a pitiful Province to its own provinces!"

Boston's fifteen thousand or so residents were clearly the worst malcontents on the North American continent. It was imperative that they be put in their place. For this purpose, the ministry ordered an additional one thousand troops to the port "for the purpose of suppressing riots."

News of the strategic move reached the colonies well ahead of the vessels carrying the British soldiers. Upon arrival, under terms of the Quartering Act, they were to be billeted in the homes of citizens, virtually all of whom labeled themselves as law abiding.

British Redcoats had already made a deep impression upon Americans during the French and Indian War. These career soldiers were widely regarded as being surly, brutal, and greedy; and no man of any sense was ready to see even one of them put into the house with his wife and daughters.

Governor Jonathan Trumbull of Connecticut ignored the unwritten code by which colonial officials did not openly question London's decision. "The Mischief, Rapine & Villainy commonly prevalent among the Troops who are kept in idleness," he warned his superiors, "are such as will be intolerable in the Colonies."

When the contingent of Redcoats arrived in September 1768, they debarked with fifes playing and drums beating. Then the veteran soldiers of four units marched up King Street behind bright silk banners on ten-foot poles. Royal Governor Bernard rejoiced, for now he had the manpower to prevent the kind of disorder that had erupted in the recent past.

When Colonel William Dalrymple made the perfunctory request that all of his men be assigned to the homes of citizens, the Boston council took a firm stand. It declared that citizens were not required to furnish quarters until all barracks space was filled, and Castle William, in the harbor, had plenty of empty berths.

Governor Bernard strongly objected to using the military base, however. He had counted upon dispersing the troops into the homes of malcontents as a way of putting pressure upon them. He declared that concentrating soldiers in a fortified installation in the harbor would thwart the decisions made in London.

James Otis and other attorneys held firm. They cited statutes that supported their position and refused to budge.

Desperate, the governor designated an empty factory building for use by the Redcoats. That meant the homeless who had crowded into it would have to vacate it at once. When an officer, accompanied by the sheriff, tried to serve eviction papers, the angry squatters seized the

Paul Revere's broadside included a highly imaginative sketch of the massacre in King Street.

sheriff and locked him up. When soldiers arrived on the double, a mob gathered and began taunting the Redcoats. After a two-day stalemate, Governor Bernard decided to disperse his troops among small empty buildings throughout the city.

Tavern fights and street brawls grew increasingly frequent. There was no serious trouble, however, until about 9:00 P.M. on March 5, 1770. Surrounded by a band of threatening colonists, a sentry stationed at the Customs House shouted for help. His message was relayed to an officer who ordered seven soldiers to fix their bayonets and advance to the rescue of their comrade.

Under the leadership of Captain Preston, the rescue squad—most of them grenadiers—advanced slowly along King Street. Although their muskets were not loaded, the bayonets enraged Colonials who saw them.

Captain Preston pretended not to hear the taunts and verbal threats. Reaching the source of trouble, he told the sentry, a man named White, to fall in with the rest of the squad. White obeyed, but a densely packed crowd quickly blocked the street, preventing him and his comrades from returning to their quarters. By this time, bells were ringing throughout the city.

Neither the governor, the Redcoats, nor members of the mob had any idea of what had taken place in London a few hours earlier. At the insistence of the prime minister, Lord North, the British Parliament had taken drastic steps. All new import duties affecting the colonies were repealed, except for a special one imposed upon tea. At the same time, Lord North pressed for immediate action designed to cause the Quartering Act to die a legal death.

Word of these actions at the center of the empire would not reach North America until weeks after the Boston Massacre, a designation that was popularized by a vivid and imaginative engraving. Published by coppersmith Paul Revere, it showed smartly uniformed soldiers firing a volley into a mass of helpless civilians.

Despite Revere's engraving, all evidence suggests that the Colonials were the aggressors. They showered the soldiers with verbal abuse, then began throwing sticks and stones. With tension mounting, a tall fellow known locally as "the mulatto" is said to have taken a leadership role. At the top of his powerful voice he yelled, "The way to get rid of these troops is to attack the main guard!"

By this time, freshly loaded muskets were being pointed at the mob. Crispus Attucks, the mulatto, may have led a physical assault, as Oliver Wendell's slave charged. It is equally possible that a nervous Redcoat precipitated the incident by firing his musket.

Whatever the triggering cause, gunfire erupted; and when it ceased, five Colonials lay dead or dying in the street. In addition, according to Paul Revere's inflammatory broadside, there were "six wounded; two of them (Christ'r Monk & John Clark) Mortally."

During legal proceedings that followed, the mulatto who led the attack upon soldiers was identified as a runaway slave. More than a dozen years earlier, a slave owner had inserted this advertisement in the Boston *Gazette* at least three times:

RAN-away from his Master, William Brown of Framingham, on the 30th of Sept. last, a Molatto Fellow, about 27 Years of age, named CRISPUS, six feet two inches high, short curl'd Hair, his Knees nearer together than common; had on a light colour'd Bearskin Coat.

Whoever shall take up said Run-away, and convey him to his abovesaid Master, shall have Ten Pounds Reward, and all necessary charges paid.

That reward was never claimed. Presumably the runaway found refuge among free blacks of Boston, who made up a substantial part of the estimated 5,214 freemen in Massachusett's population of 235,810, as enumerated in 1763.

Attucks may have found work as a seaman. That would have enabled him to be out of the reach of authorities except for brief periods when his vessel was in port. Whether that was the course he followed is unknown, but it is clear that he escaped capture. As a result, he died in a hail of bullets and became revered as "the first martyr of the American Revolution."

Along with his four fallen comrades, Attucks was interred in the Granary Burying Ground. In time, the same tract of land came to hold the bodies of John Hancock, John Adams, and other notable patriots. Decades later, Bostonians erected an elaborate monument to the men slain on King Street. Crispus Attucks headed the list.

An elaborate account of the burial, complete with sketches of four initialed wooden coffins, appeared in the Boston *Gazette* soon after the massacre. It was widely reprinted throughout the colonies, although it took weeks to circulate as far south as the Carolinas. Passed from hand to hand in company with Paul Revere's illustrated broadside, it pushed the tempers of increasing numbers of Colonials to the boiling point.

A broadside about "The Horrid Massacre" listed names of "FIVE of your fellow countrymen" who "lay wallowing in their Gore!"

AMERICANS!
BEAR IN REMEMBRANCE
The HORRID MASSACRE!
Perpetrated in King-ſtreet, Boston,
New-England,
On the Evening of March the Fifth, 1770.
When FIVE of your fellow countrymen,
GRAY, MAVERICK, CALDWELL, ATTUCKS,
and CARR,
Lay wallowing in their Gore!
Being *baſely*, and moſt *inhumanly*
MURDERED!
And SIX others badly WOUNDED!
By a Party of the XXIXth Regiment,
Under the command of Capt. Tho. Preſton.
REMEMBER!
That Two of the MURDERERS
Were convicted of MANSLAUGHTER!
By a Jury, of whom I ſhall ſay
NOTHING,
Branded in the hand!
And *diſmiſſed*,
The others were ACQUITTED,
And their Captain PENSIONED!
Alſo,
BEAR IN REMEMBRANCE
That on the 22d Day of February, 1770
The infamous
EBENEZER RICHARDSON, Informer,
And tool to Miniſterial hirelings,
Moſt *barbarouſly*
MURDERED
CHRISTOPHER SEIDER,
An innocent youth!

5

John Adams of Braintree, Attorney for the Defense

"**M**r. Adams, sir, I come on behalf of Josiah Quincy, Jr.," explained a nearly breathless James Forest. He was sure that Adams knew Quincy to be a native of his own hometown, Braintree.

"Go on . . ."

"Mr. Adams, sir, young Mr. Quincy has engaged to undertake a difficult defense of wrongfully accused men—provided that you will take the lead in the case."

Adams, age thirty-four, was reckoned among the ablest and most stubborn attorneys in Boston. He had already heard that every Crown officer in the city had refused to undertake the defense of Captain Preston and his men, and thus he did not need to ask for a detailed explanation. Forest's excited face and breathless voice made his mission clear. Adams was instantly convinced that the man known around the city as a British toady had come to persuade him to defend the perpetrators of the Boston Massacre.

By Adams's certain knowledge, Paul Revere was already at work upon a copperplate engraving. Rumor—correct as events proved—said Revere would engrave at least eighteen lines of verse under a sketch showing Redcoats firing upon defenseless civilians.

Published posthaste, Revere's broadside showed soldiers blazing away at an orderly and respectable group of citizens. "THE BLOODY MASSACRE . . . by a party of the 29th REG," as Revere titled his work, was highly inflammatory:

> With murd'rous Rancour stretch their bloody hands,
> Like fierce Barbarians grinning o'er their Prey.

Redcoats, Revere charged, might find a legal loophole that would enable them to escape punishment. But he warned:

Attorney John Adams.

Should venal courts, the scandal of the land,
Snatch the relentless villain from her hand,
Keen execrations, on this plate inscribed,
Shall reach a judge who never can be bribed.

Not even Paul Revere would have had the temerity to challenge the
integrity of John Adams. What's more, the man from Braintree had
privately expressed his opinion that British soldiers were about to be
given a taste of mob justice.

He refused to give James Forest an immediate answer. He did indicate, however, that he would seriously consider leading the defense
team in the impending trial.

"Counsel is the very last thing an accused man should be without in
a free country," he mused. "Always, the bar ought to be independent
and impartial—under every circumstance."

Reasoning in this fashion, it took him only a few hours to decide
what he would do. Although it was sure to enrage many of the people
of Boston, he, John Adams, would do his best to secure full justice for
men already labeled as cold-blooded killers.

Samuel Quincy, solicitor general of Massachusetts, headed a four-
man prosecution team. Their prestige and skill were pitted against
Adams and young Josiah Quincy. Earlier, notoriously conservative

Robert Auchinmuty had said he would help to defend the soldiers; but when bricks began to fly through his windows, he "respectfully withdrew from the affair."

It was the talk of the city that young Quincy, brother of the solicitor general, was ready to face official and family wrath, shielded only by the tiny shoulders of John Adams.

Jurors deliberated only briefly before presenting a true bill. In their lengthy document, they swore that Thomas Preston, Esq., William Wemms, and seven other males "now resident in the County of Suffolk . . . being moved and seduced by the instigation of the devil and their own wicked hearts," did "willfully, feloniously, and with malice aforethought" shoot and kill Crispus Attucks with "a certain handgun of the value of 20 shillings."

Strangely, only Attucks was named as a victim. But nine Redcoats—not seven as stipulated in many accounts of the tragedy—were put on trial for their lives.

General Thomas Gage, commander in chief of all British troops in North America, had worried a great deal about the upcoming legal contest. When he heard that a prominent Colonial would lead in the defense of his men, he was greatly relieved. The outcome of the trial would have a profound effect upon relations between the British and American subjects of the king who lived three thousand miles apart. Gage therefore personally urged John Adams to make sure that "Not only what happened on the said night should be made to appear, but also every insult and attack made upon the troops previous thereto."

While the letter from Gage was on its way to Boston, Samuel Adams and his fellow Sons of Liberty were busy. They saw to it that many eyewitnesses appeared before a justice of the peace. Their lengthy and inflammatory depositions were immediately published in newspapers. Then they were collected and issued as a special report that circulated throughout Massachusetts and gradually trickled southward into other colonies.

Legal delays kept Captain Preston and his men in their hot, damp cells until October, when a jury was impaneled.

Adams began by taking the prosecution by surprise. He moved that Captain Preston be tried separately from his men. When that motion was granted, the imprisoned soldiers jumped to what seemed a logical conclusion: they would become scapegoats, while their commander might go free. They vigorously protested the decision for separate trials, but they were unable to prevail.

Accused of "murder with malice aforethought," Preston was pale from weeks in jail. He confessed surprise when his colonial attorney presented a lengthy list of defense witnesses. No murder trial in Massachusetts history had ever lasted more than one day; already, it was

King Street, Boston, the moment after fatal shots were fired on March 5, 1770.
[INTERPRETATION BY FELIX O. DARLEY]

clear that this one could stretch out for weeks.

To the surprise of Captain Preston, events moved forward speedily. Adams called to the stand one Richard Palmes, a resident whom he had kept in the city under court order. Palmes testified in halting fashion, as though afraid, swearing that he personally heard Captain Preston say he had no intention of ordering his men to fire.

"The instant he spoke," said Palmes, "I saw something resembling ice or snow strike the grenadier on the captain's right hand. This man instantly stepped one foot back and fired. At the elbow, the nap of my surtout was scorched by the gunpowder."

After all witnesses had been heard, four justices charged the jurors and then had them locked up for the night. That precaution proved to be unnecessary. In less than four hours of deliberation, a verdict of "innocent" was reached.

Captain Preston's trial had lasted a record five days. His subordinates were then called from their cells to appear before the court.

Long arguments and detailed testimony soon began to shake what had appeared to be a simple case for the prosecution. A handful of British soldiers, fresh from the mother country and ignorant of colonial ways, had become angry. As the mob challenging them grew to two hundred or more, they became frightened. With half a dozen muskets, they faced sticks, staves, and stones, in addition to a barrage of inflammatory insults.

John Adams's closing argument focused upon the fact that a shout by a boy in the street "is no formidable thing." Then he added, "When such a cry is made by a multitude, it becomes a hideous shriek—almost as terrible as the yells of Indian warriors." Any man in the position of the surrounded Redcoats would have considered his life to be in dire danger, their attorney insisted.

John Adams's closing argument lasted for nearly six hours. He concluded by stressing that the law was clear. Every man—soldiers included—had a right to kill in his own defense.

Members of the jury had listened intently as Adams and Quincy built a careful case against mob rule. To the surprise of spectators, they deliberated for less than three hours. Then the foreman, Joseph Mayo, solemnly read the names of the accused and the verdict in each case.

Six of Preston's soldiers were found not guilty. Among them was Hugh White, the customs house sentry whose call for help triggered the riot. Two men—Matthew Killroy and Hugh Montgmery—were found not guilty of murder, but guilty of manslaughter and were branded on their thumbs. Their comrades suffered no punishment, other than the lengthy imprisonment while awaiting trial.

John Adams accepted a legal fee of less than twenty guineas for the entire proceedings. He used that money, and much more, to repair damage to his home inflicted by townsfolk who were angry at his role in the trial. Weeks earlier, he had learned that Sam Adams had warned, "This affair will end the political hopes of the little man from Braintree."

During the lengthy proceedings, some hotheads had cooled a bit. Many sober thinkers changed their minds about the "massacre" as they listened to testimony evoked by John Adams. Instead of turning upon their countryman to punish him, scores of leading citizens began to laud him for his courage.

In London, British friends of the colonies slept well for the first time in many weeks when they learned the outcome of the trials. To those who consistently railed against all Colonials, they insisted that John Adams had proved that "justice may be had, even in faraway Massachusetts."

Made bold by the decisive shift in public opinion, attorney Adams set out to prove that the prediction about him by Samuel Adams was wrong. He stood for a seat in the lower house of the General Court, or legislature, and won by an overwhelming majority. Impelled into the political arena in so unlikely a fashion, the man who defended killers of his countryman so rose in the esteem of Americans that he became the second president of the United States.

6

"Catch Your Man before You Hang Him!"

"**A** dispatch from Boston confirms our worst fears. Montagu intends to patrol Narragansett Bay."

Merchant John Brown, flanked by two of his brothers, waited for the announcement to take effect. Then he pounded the table before him and whispered to the officers of a dozen colonial vessels. "Perhaps it will afford us a chance to catch him in the trap he has set for us."

At Providence, Rhode Island, no one needed a detailed explanation. In the aftermath of the Boston Tea Party, tempers were already at the boiling point. More than half of all Rhode Island vessels were engaged in smuggling, which meant that every ship would be in danger upon the arrival of an armed British vessel.

John Montagu, destined to become the fourth earl of Sandwich, was at least as angry as were the men whose livelihoods he threatened. Huge Narragansett Bay had many coves and inlets and many of them offered ideal cover to seamen determined to thwart London's Acts of Trade and Navigation. No region in North America sheltered men more contemptuous of His Majesty's revenue measures.

John Brown's warning of the impending British move was general in nature. He did not know that the ship *Gaspee* would soon arrive to enforce the law, and he did not know of her commander, William Dudingston.

Hand-picked by Montagu, Lieutenant Dudingston was well known in the Royal Navy then stationed in colonial waters. Time and time again he had boasted that "Given the chance, I will seize smugglers and treat them for what they are—pirates!"

Oral tradition credits John Brown with a leading role in preparing to meet the impending threat. According to the same body of tradition, Dudingston was first among the British to institute a special ceremony. Having reached his New World station, he immediately let it be known that every colonial ship's master must dip his colors to salute a British gunboat. Although the Colonials grumbled and swore, most of them had complied for fear that hot lead from His Majesty's Navy would come if they did not show subservience.

John Brown was already a man of substance in the mercantile and political realms. He had helped construct the building in Providence to house Rhode Island College when it was removed from Warren in 1770. Much later the institution would become Brown University, named in honor of John Brown, the wealthy merchant who spent twenty years as treasurer of the institution.

Already important in North American waters, Brown's ships would soon move into the East India and the China trades. As a fervent, vocal opponent of the Stamp Act, he had emerged as a leader of colonists who openly opposed "taxation without representation."

By the time he learned that his own waters would soon be patrolled, Brown was engaged in a secret industrial project. An untried iron furnace of rather visionary nature had attracted his interest, and he had invested heavily, confident that Colonials could soon use the furnace to produce their own cannon.

While waiting for the furnace—the Hope—to be completed, John

Although everyone in the region knew that merchant John Brown led the burning of the Gaspee, *he was never prosecuted.* [DICTIONARY OF AMERICAN PORTRAITS]

Brown continued his widespread mercantile operations. It was from one of his packets just returned from Boston that he learned of plans to put a stop to smuggling in New Jersey.

Before moving to these waters, William Dudingston made the bold move he had threatened to take earlier. Any time the master of a vessel did not salute the British gunboat, Dudingston sent shot across its bow. Colonials later swore that he sent his men on land to cut down trees for fuel and to seize sheep so his men could have fresh meat.

Preparing for Dudingston's coming, John Brown divulged his plan to a few intimates. "Outfit the fastest packet in these waters, and man her with veterans who know every reef and cove," he is said to have urged. "On a day when the weather is right, move into the bay cautiously, as though loaded with contraband. When the master of the *Gaspee* gives orders to drop anchor for a search, let the packet take off like a sea gull. Following a zig-zag course, it can lead the gunboat into waters where she is sure to run aground."

The plan was tested on June 9 when Dudingston's lookout spied a suspicious looking vessel that was easy to follow. "Every man Jack will receive a share of the prize," the British officer promised his crew.

All seamen knew that a captured smuggler and her cargo would be sold, with part of the proceeds delivered to the master of the ship that captured her and ordinary sailors often sharing in the prize money.

With visions of bags of guineas dancing in their heads, the British tars kept close behind the suspected smuggler, never quite coming in gun range. Few of them noticed when they entered waters they had not charted.

Just as the Colonials had planned, the *Gaspee* ran aground. She hit so hard that her commander admitted to his men that they had no chance of floating her off before high tide.

Waiting in the stranded gunboat, the seamen heard the sounds of muffled oars less than an hour after dark. They prepared to resist a boarding party, but in the darkness they failed to realize that eight longboats full of Colonials were converging upon them.

John Brown was too corpulent to lead the expedition personally. One of his close friends described him as "occupying two seats in a chaise." So he delegated command of the expedition to one of his seasoned captains, Abraham Whipple.

Whipple had entered Brown's employ about 1755, and within four years he was commander of the privateer *Game Cock*. During the winter of 1759–60 he took her on a six-month cruise; at its conclusion he listed twenty-three French vessels as captured prizes. Booty from them substantially increased the wealth of his employer, who was generous in dividing the profits with him.

Led by Whipple, at least ninety Colonials managed to board the stranded *Gaspee*. Using handspikes, they nearly broke Dudingston's arm while forcing most members of his crew below decks. When the British officer reached for a firearm, a member of the boarding party shot him in the groin.

That ended the brief struggle for mastery of the gunboat. Bleeding profusely, Dudingston was taken ashore and turned over to two surgeons, and members of the crew surrendered. With hands tied behind their backs, they climbed awkwardly into longboats.

As soon as the last man was off, the Colonials set the *Gaspee* on fire. She burned to the water line while crowds in nearby Providence gathered on the wharf to cheer.

Weeks later, when word of the assault upon a naval vessel reached London, officials took swift action. They named a special investigating committee with extraordinary powers. Upon the arrest of a person suspected of being involved in the *Gaspee* affair, he was to be shipped to England for trial.

Expecting to get quick results, the Privy Council authorized a handsome reward for the capture of leaders in the "Colonial act of piracy." Any man who would inform on his comrades stood to gain immunity and a cash reward.

"Lawmakers at a distance have deprived us of yet one more precious right!" thundered John Brown. "Any man transported to London for trial will lose the ancient privilege of being judged by a jury of his peers!"

As soon as he learned of the offered reward, the lieutenant governor, Darius Sessions, hurried to Providence from Pawtuxet. He managed to secure depositions from three men, each of whom admitted to having played "a subordinate role" in the burning of the gunboat. Each of the three solemnly swore that since the operation did not begin until black dark, he had no idea who led it. No witness was able even to identify the person who stood in the bow of the longboat he helped to row.

The legal machinery created in England did not get into motion in Rhode Island until December when commissioners solemnly gathered at Newport. Their self-described task was simple: "To examine such persons as Admiral Montagu shall direct to be apprehended, who are to be sent to England to be tried for high treason."

Guns of a ship-of-war brought into Narragansett Bay served as silent warnings. Clearly, London expected to find and punish the guilty parties.

But the witnesses who had given depositions to the lieutenant governor had vanished. No one in or about Newport or Providence had any recollection of events on the night of June 9.

Through a network of informants, Sir James Wallace, commander

Although revered regionally, Abraham Whipple is seldom remembered elsewhere. [*HARPER'S ENCYCLOPEDIA OF U.S. HISTORY*]

of the warship, learned that Abraham Whipple had led the raiding party. Hence he sent the American seaman a written promise: "You, Abraham Whipple, on June 9, 1772, burned His Majesty's vessel the *Gaspee*—and I will hang you at the yard-arm."

Whipple sent an oral response: "Sir, always catch your man before you hang him!"

Special commissioners, Admiral Montagu's deputy, chief justices of three colonies, and the governor of Rhode Island met in solemn session for day after day. Any man convicted in England would be liable for the death penalty. Stipulated under the Dockyards Acts of 1772, death was the mandatory sentence for "maliciously setting afire, burning, or otherwise destroying" a vessel of the Royal Navy.

A sailor once stationed on the *Gaspee* happened to meet an indentured servant, Aaron Briggs, and immediately identified Briggs as having "absolutely and positively" been a member of the party responsible for burning the ship. Questioned under duress, Briggs admitted that he was involved but insisted that the only other man he knew to have participated in the raid was "a tall, slender man wearing his own hair, of a brown color."

The authorities' delight at Briggs's confession was short-lived. The royal governor, Joseph Wanton of New Jersey, demanded a new investigation; he was said to have been motivated by the fact that his appointment had to be confirmed by action of the provincial assembly. Whatever his motive, Wanton's fresh inquiry turned up indisputable evidence that Briggs gave his testimony only after he had been threatened with whipping and hanging if he did not confess. Ruefully, the royal commissioners threw out the testimony.

Fifty-four weeks after the burning of the *Gaspee*, the commissioners forwarded their final report to London. In it they detailed their labors and concluded that it had proved impossible to identify the offenders. John Brown, Abraham Whipple, and ninety or so stout-hearted Colonials had defied the power of the British Navy and of the government that backed it.

However, as the good news trickled through the colonies, John Brown warned, "I fear that we are not out of the woods yet. A single swallow does not signal a change of season. Across the sea, those who would use and abuse the colonies will be more aggressive than ever."

CHAPTER

7

Mountain Men Were First to Gain Independence

Williamsburg in Virginia
March 1774

His Majesty, King George III, is clearly not aware of conditions beyond the Appalachian Mountains in North America. In violation of his edicts, settlers have flocked to the region in such number that it appears nothing can stop their concourse.

A set of people in the back part of this colony, bordering on the Cherokee country, found they could not obtain the land they fancied. In defiance of the law they settled upon it and contented themselves with becoming in a manner tributary to the Indians.

Having appointed magistrates and framed laws for their present occasion, they have to all intents and purposes erected themselves into, though an inconsiderable, yet a separate State; the opposite of the other colonies.

At the least, it sets a dangerous example to the people of America, of forming governments distinct and independent of His Majesty's authority.

> *—John Murray, Earl of Dunmore*
> *and His Majesty's Governor*
> *of the Virginia Colony*

By the time Murray's letter reached London in May, America's first experiment in independent government was about two years old. Directed to the secretary of state, it did not strike him as terribly important. Land west of the Appalachian Mountains was too far away to seem significant.

Little is known about William Bean, but he was among those Virginia and North Carolina pioneers who wanted lots of land—for

49

nothing. Exploring regions few white men had seen, he found what he considered an ideal spot.

A plateau-valley situated more than three thousand feet above sea level and surrounded by peaks on every side was discovered. There was plenty of water, as head springs of four rivers lay within an area of five square miles.

Pioneers who followed Bean to the banks of the Watauga River— later called the Tennessee—were a rebellious lot. They resented the ostentatious power of the royal governors of North Carolina and Virginia, and even more, they resented the taxes that governors were empowered to collect. Those who had heard of King George III were not greatly interested in him; he and his ministers lay a great mountain range and an ocean away from them.

By the time the Watauga settlement began to flourish, its existence was known in North Carolina's capital, New Bern, and Governor William Tryon dispatched to the remote area a tax collector. Oral tradition declares that he was a Colonel Lynch, whose name entered common speech when "lynch law" came into vogue.

It was the special mission of Tryon's aide to collect taxes with which to build a new mansion. "Tryon's Place," as over-the-mountain men contemptuously called it, deserved none of their hard-earned money!

A tax revolt quickly spread through western North Carolina. Organized bands of men calling themselves Regulators seized Colonel Lynch and strung him to an oak.

The hanging of the tax collector was serious business in itself, but in New Bern it was rumored that Regulators planned an organized assault upon the capital. In anger and desperation, Tryon ordered out the militia and sent his soldiers to the west under the command of Hugh Waddell.

On May 16, 1771, a pitched battle took place at Alamance, and in spite of furious efforts, the Regulators found themselves outmanned and outgunned. No one knows how many were killed before they hoisted the white flag and asked for terms of surrender. Ordered to take a solemn oath of allegiance, many of the Regulators fled westward to the Watauga region as soon as the militia marched eastward.

Virginia-born John Sevier settled in the same region for different reasons. Son of a trader in furs and rum, he married Sarah Hawkins at age sixteen and fathered children in rapid succession. With a fast-growing family whose numbers made up a labor force, he could use a large area of land.

Watauga seemed to offer what he needed, so as early as 1771 he visited the region, which he believed to be a part of Virginia. Already a captain in the militia at age twenty-six, Sevier emerged as a leader of beyond-the-mountains settlers.

John Sevier. [TENNESSEE STATE LIBRARY]

Effectively isolated from both Williamsburg and New Bern, the Watauga settlers lived on land illegally purchased from Indians in defiance of royal edicts. Soon they decided that they wanted a government of their own. As a result, they formed the Watauga Association. Articles of the association provided for election of five commissioners, a sheriff, and a clerk of court.

John Sevier, one of the five commissioners, spoke for all of them when he declared: "We recognize no higher authority on this side of the Atlantic or beyond. We will raise and train our own militia. We will make our own agreements with outsiders—Indians, British agents, and the colonies of North Carolina and Virginia."

Articles drawn up by the Watauga men have not been preserved, but their documents clearly represented America's first step toward full independence.

Soon after that step had been taken, surveyors discovered that Watauga lay within the boundaries of Virginia (as defined in London), rather than in North Carolina. It made no difference to the mountain men; they had declared their independence of both royal colonies.

Watauga's extreme isolation led Carolina authorities to ignore the self-declared independence of the region that today lies in Tennessee. Among British authorities, only the governor of Virginia seems to have been deeply troubled. He sensed that the dangerous precedent set by the Watauga men spelled eventual trouble of serious magnitude.

Increasing danger of attack by Cherokees put Watauga in peril. Seeking protection, John Sevier and his comrades drafted a petition asking that the district west of the mountains be incorporated into North Carolina. The land they held lay beyond boundaries stipulated in royal charters, and it had been gained in defiance of the 1763 proclamation that forbade any private citizen from purchasing land from Indians. However, to officials near the coast, annexation seemed the simplest answer to a vexatious question.

Members of the colonial assembly voted to accept the petition and to give the name Washington to the Watauga district. When the provincial body met in November 1776, John Sevier, John Haile, and Charles Robertson were seated as delegates from Washington.

Ripple effects feared by the governor of Virginia did not take place. Watauga was too remote from populated centers to be influential there. Hence, the short-lived experiment looms larger today than in the 1770s. It not only demonstrated that Americans had an appetite for independence, it showed that distance from centers of power can lead to deterioration and eventual breakdown of relations.

Part Two

Thirteen Pygmies Tossed Pebbles at the Giant

The British colonies in North America were diverse and distinct, differing in origin, geography, government, and socio-economic levels. Savannah, Georgia, was as remote from Boston as was London and differed from Boston more greatly than the British capital did.

Though the rising tide of unrest affected each colony, local interests—and the influence of Tories—varied widely. This meant that London did not face a cohesive, unified movement from all North America south of Canada, but rather thirteen separate sets of grumbling protesters.

In most instances these protesters still hoped and expected to patch up their differences with the mother country.

To British officialdom, Samuel Adams spelled "big trouble."

CHAPTER

8

Samuel Adams Led in Forming a Loosely Knit Communications Network

"**H**ave no fear about the state of the colonies; one and all, they are profoundly tranquil," wrote General Thomas Gage in April 1772.

His report reached London promptly and was processed during the first week of June, but fresh news came before it proceeded through channels to reach top officials. Late word included a terse account of the unthinkable: John Brown's burning of the *Gaspee* in distant Rhode Island.

Although born in Sussex, England, Gage knew North America about as well as any British officer could. He had come to the continent with General Edward Braddock in 1755 as a lieutenant colonel. Rising through the ranks, he became commander in chief of British forces in North America in 1763. Yet after eighteen years in the colonies, he remained an outsider, an official who owed his post and his allegiance to London. Hence his ability to assess the mood of Colonials was severely limited.

From his New York headquarters, Gage tried to keep his finger on the pulse of frequently troubled Boston. There he sensed no signs of anything more than continuous grumbling and an occasional street fight. Insulated by protective circles of subordinates, Gage did not realize that Boston was about to erupt at the very time he dispatched his optimistic assessment.

Trouble—the latest trouble, that is—started in 1768 and simmered for months. London thought it wise to try to insulate Chief Justice Thomas Hutchinson, so an order was issued requiring that his salary be paid from customs revenues rather than through colonial channels.

Thomas Paine published the inflammatory booklet, Common Sense.

This device appeared to work well. As a result, a second step was taken two years later. Under the terms of a dispatch from London, salaries of the governor, lieutenant governor, and chief justice of Massachusetts were thenceforth to be paid from the duty on tea. Two years later all superior court justices of the province were added to the special payroll list.

Boston-born Samuel Adams, who graduated from Harvard College at age twenty, tried to lead a protest movement against the tea tax in 1768. Payment of a salary—any salary—from a British imposed tax or duty should be resisted, he said. He insisted that this procedure would effectively free the recipient of such a salary from colonial restraint.

Fellow citizens tended to yawn. "If anybody knows about taxes, Sam Adams should," some quipped.

In 1765 Adams had taken the job of tax collector for the port of Boston. Descended from a patrician family, he accepted the post out of necessity. Upon leaving Harvard, he had worked briefly in the counting house of Thomas Cushing, then he set up his own business. When it failed in a few months, he entered his father's brewery, which he guided to disaster after his father's death.

Adams was a conspicuous failure in business, and he was badly in need of cash. Hence he was glad to accept a Crown post, regardless of its nature. However, he was no more effective as tax collector than he had been in business. During eight years, uncollected taxes accumulated in the sum of £8,000, causing Adams to lose his post.

Once out of office, he became a fervent, eloquent critic of British taxation. His pamphlets and speeches led him to be labeled the "Great Agitator." Soon he was numbered "in the front rank of Colonials perpetually seeking to arouse sentiment directed toward London, the sovereign and his ministers."

The addition of provincial superior court justices to the list of officials paid from duties imposed upon colonists gave Adams fresh ammunition. "This is the final straw!" he shouted at a Boston town meeting on October 28, 1772.

Many of the citizens who gathered that night had already read some of Adams's newspaper articles and letters. In them he warned that the colonists should never turn loose the purse strings. To do so, he pointed out, would deprive them of any means of restraining "vassals who look to London for the food on their tables, the clothing on their backs, and the elegant carriages in which they ride."

Goaded and guided by Adams, the citizens took a vote. By an overwhelming majority, they requested from the governor additional details about plans made in London and not yet officially announced. When Governor Thomas Hutchinson accepted the written request, he made it clear that he did not intend to give a specific response.

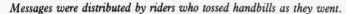

Messages were distributed by riders who tossed handbills as they went.

Like Adams, Hutchinson was a Boston native and a Harvard graduate. Unlike Adams, he succeeded at everything he undertook. With a college diploma in hand at age sixteen, he studied law for a time. Then he persuaded the town fathers that he would make an ideal agent for Boston in the capital of the British empire.

He spent seven years as Boston's representative in London, although he devoted more time to cultivating influence than in attending to Boston's business. This shaped him into a high Tory and brought his appointment as judge of probate in Boston.

Hutchinson became lieutenant governor of the province in 1758. A decade later, he was chief justice. In 1771 he became royal governor.

Viewed from London, he was an ideal officeholder. He was valued so highly that for a time he simultaneously held four high offices under the king's appointment.

Although strong willed, the American-born Tory was effeminate in appearance. Samuel Adams and other vocal critics delighted in repeating a favorite description. "He is a lap dog of the king," they said. "He was trained to come to heel during years in London, and he has been made fat by scraps thrown to him from the royal table."

When Governor Hutchinson spoke with his countrymen, he minced no words. He pointed out that he was responsible to London, not to Boston, and he would share no information concerning the revised plan for paying salaries. He had no intention of calling the provincial legislature into session to consider the issue. What's more, he was seriously considering removing the seat of the legislature from Boston to Cambridge.

Just four days after the citizens had voted to ask for specifics from the governor, they held another town meeting. At it, the "evasive words of Hutchinson" were reported by angry Bostonians. This time Adams did not need to take the lead in working the crowd into "fever heat of anxiety and anger." Most of them who attended already knew of the governor's high-handed response, and they came to the meeting hoping for action.

They got it in the form of a recommendation that every town in the province—an estimated 240 of them—be invited to join in Boston's protest. That move was adopted with huzzas. Then town clerk William Cooper was instructed to circulate a letter and statement to Massachusetts towns.

Preparation of the letter and its supporting document was entrusted to a newly created body called the committee of correspondence. Headed by James Otis, Samuel Adams, and Dr. Joseph Warren, the committee soon began work upon a statement that became known as the "Boston pamphlet." After three weeks it was officially adopted, and citizens then voted to have six hundred copies printed. That would ensure that it reach every town in the province and many in distant colonies.

Once formed, the committee on correspondence took on a life of its own. Eventually its members received replies from more than one hundred Massachusetts towns. As winter moved into spring, correspondence was received from Camden, South Carolina; Richmond, Virginia; Augusta, Georgia; and many places between.

Town after town established a committee of correspondence of their own. Since mails were slow and uncertain, committees in major towns often hired horsemen to serve as couriers. They distributed broadsides in and about the town and transmitted messages to and from other committees.

Although the new communications network was slow and cumbersome, it was unlike anything the thirteen colonies had ever seen. Sam Adams had accomplished more than he could have hoped. For the first time, Colonials who opposed London's control were in frequent contact with one another as well as with British officials.

Intoxicated by its unexpected success, the parent committee of correspondence widened its field to include all the colonies. Bostonians then made a final glorious gesture. By nearly unanimous vote, a town meeting approved expansion of the work of their body to encompass "the entire World!"

9

Benjamin Franklin
Leaked Letters
That Widened the Breach

London 12 December 1772

*There has lately fallen into my hands part of a correspondence. I have
reason to believe it laid the foundation of most if not all of our present
grievances.*

*I am not at liberty to tell through what channel I received it. I have
engaged that it shall not be printed, nor copies taken of the whole or any
part of it. Confident that you will respect these provisions, I send you
enclosed the original letters in handwriting that is well known.*

*I can only allow these letters to be seen by you, by the other gentlemen
of the Committee of Correspondence, and a few others. After being some
months in your possession you are requested to return them to me.*

> *Respectfully,*
> *B. Franklin,*
> *Agent for the Massachusetts province*

Benjamin Franklin's packet was addressed to Thomas Cushing,
speaker of the Massachusetts Assembly. Along with his explana-
tory message, it contained eighteen letters written during the preced-
ing three years. Ten were penned by Thomas Hutchinson and four by
his brother-in-law, Andrew Oliver, who was lieutenant governor of the
province.

Eight other letters sent by Franklin were written by minor officials.
All were addressed to Thomas Whately, who had recently died.

Benjamin Franklin, Deputy Postmaster General of North America, London agent for Georgia, Massachusetts, New Jersey, and Pennsylvania.

Whateley long had served as undersecretary of the treasury and as private secretary to George Grenville.

Franklin did not indicate when or how he obtained the letters, and there were no clues in his private correspondence. He divulged no details in a sensational public hearing or in conversations that were preserved. Clearly, the letters were stolen, but by whom and for what purpose indignant authorities never learned.

Also clouded in doubt are the motives that prompted Franklin to take the dangerous and costly step of sending them to Boston. He may have been eager to see Boston leaders incited to take bold action against the Crown, or he may have wished simply to bolster his own position among those Continentals—no small number—who regarded him with suspicion.

To many of his fellow Americans, Benjamin Franklin seemed to be a closet Tory. In 1753 he had accepted the post of deputy postmaster general of North America and he held on to it tenaciously. When the short-lived Stamp Act was made public, he solicited for his friends posts as distributors of stamps. Over and over, he urged hot-headed Colonials to avoid violent actions aimed at thwarting British authority.

Almost constantly in London since 1764, Franklin was known to revel in the amenities of English society. He accepted honorary degrees from the University of St. Andrews and from Oxford University, and he gladly became a member of England's prestigious Royal Society.

Written injunctions to the contrary, did he really expect the stolen letters to be held as closely guarded secrets? Was his principal motive in transmitting them his desire to be fully accepted as first an American, then a subject of the king?

No one knows the answer, but the impact of the letters he sent to Boston was immediate and explosive. Hardly anyone could have anticipated the harsh reaction.

Five months after Franklin's packet left London, the letters it contained were made public. Samuel Adams read them to the shocked and astonished members of the House of Assembly. A passage in one of Hutchinson's letters brought stunned silence when it was read:

I never think of the measures necessary for the peace and good of the colonies without pain. There must be an abridgement of what are called English liberties.

I relieve myself by considering that the most perfect state of government requires a great restraint of liberty. I doubt whether it is possible to project a system of government in which a colony three thousand miles distant from the parent state shall enjoy all the liberty of the parent state.

I am certain I have never yet seen the projection. I wish the good of the colony when I wish to see some further restraint upon liberty, rather than that the connexion with the parent state should be broken; for I am sure such a breach must prove the ruin of the colony.

That passage, more than any other in the letters secured by stealth, spurred the assembly to action. By a vote of 101 to 5, members declared their outrage that "the tendency of the letters was to overthrow the Constitution of this Government and to introduce Arbitrary Power into the Province."

Shortly afterward, the gist of thirteen of the eighteen letters was published in the Boston *Gazette*. Then newspaper and broadside publishers in most colonies excerpted them from the *Gazette*.

To Bostonians, the letters contained little that was novel. Hutchinson, Oliver, and other agents of the Crown had made oral statements much like the inflammatory passages in the letters.

But the timing of their publication was crucial. The letters became public knowledge only a few weeks before the colonists received a belated announcement. Parliament had passed another hated tax, this time upon tea.

Public transmission of the leaked documents gave disgruntled Colo-

"*A View of the Town of Boston with Several Ships of War in the Harbour.*"
[Paul Revere Engraving, Royal American Magazine]

nials a printed source from which to quote. Somehow, that seemed far more official than the same message droned from a platform in a public meeting. It was whispered—correctly, as time disclosed—that at least one of the Hutchinson letters had been approved by His Majesty King George III.

In several colonies the leaked letters led to greater activity by committees of correspondence. In at least two legislative bodies, they were the subject of debate. But only in Massachusetts was there anything approaching strong reaction.

There the assembly solemnly endorsed resolutions demanding the immediate recall of the governor and lieutenant governor. Signed and sealed, the documents were put aboard ship. It was the duty of Benjamin Franklin, as provincial agent, to receive and transmit them to British authorities.

Nearly ninety days passed before the London agent of the American province received the set of resolutions he knew to be on the way. During the fall, they slowly worked their way through the system that circulated official documents through official circles.

Banker William Whately, executor of the estate of his dead brother to whom the damning letters had been written, was incensed. He accused John Temple, a former commissioner of customs at Boston, of having stolen them. Temple hotly denied the charge. When Whately demanded honor, Temple was forced to meet him on the dueling grounds.

They fought in December 1773, but neither man was seriously injured. When William Whately let it be known that he would challenge Temple again, Benjamin Franklin realized that Temple's life was in grave danger, and he came forward. He announced that it was he, and only he, who was responsible for having secured the Hutchinson letters and having sent them to Boston.

By the time the resolution of the Massachusetts assembly was ready for presentation to the Privy Council, Franklin was widely labeled as a thief. Still, it was in his capacity as agent for the province that he had forwarded the unprecedented set of charges. Provincial lawmakers were sure that the governor was guiding a conspiracy to bring more soldiers and sailors into Massachusetts and that once there they would be used "to overthrow the system of free government established under the charter of 1691."

In late January 1774 the sixty-eight-year-old Franklin donned a suit of figured Manchester velvet. Placing his wig on his head, he made his way to the Cockpit, an adjunct of Whitehall Palace.

Alexander Wedderburn, a brilliant Scottish attorney who was a notorious Tory, poured invectives upon Franklin for a solid hour. Standing with few changes of expression, the American did not speak in his own behalf.

Charges against Hutchinson by the provincial assembly were dismissed out of hand. Said the Privy Council, "These baseless accusations are vexatious and seditious." With the issue settled, they turned to the man held responsible for having created it.

Franklin was publicly threatened with a stay in Tyburn or Newgate jail, although there was no serious effort to press the charge of sedition. On Sunday, the day after the hearing, he received a document announcing that he was relieved of his postmastership. On Monday he was ordered to give an accounting of his service as agent for Massachusetts, and a successor was named.

Soon he was stripped of his role as agent for Pennsylvania and New Jersey, and in March the royal governor of Georgia wrote a letter informing Franklin that the colony could not accept his reappointment as its agent in London. Collectively, the posts of which the American was stripped had been paying him the princely salary of £1,500 a year.

Reviled in London, he returned to America in May 1775 to receive a hero's welcome. Soon he was accepted as elder statesman among those who—for the first time—were beginning to label themselves as patriots.

Triumphant at his vindication, Thomas Hutchinson remained in office for nearly a year, but the issue of the letters would not go away, at least not in Boston. Tempers of the patriots and of the British representatives continued to mount; and, as the danger of violence grew, London named once-placid General Thomas Gage as military governor of Massachusetts. Hutchinson left the place of his birth and established himself in London, where he quickly dropped into obscurity.

Clearly, the resolution evoked by the purloined letters was a gesture of provincial defiance. But its only immediate effect was to alienate some in Britain who called themselves friends of America.

Hutchinson was formally vindicated in the presence of the archbishop of Canterbury, the duke of Queensberry, eight earls, and a house full of lawmakers, but that did not put the matter to rest. Benjamin Franklin took up his pen again in anticipation of the spirited debate he felt would be coming soon. In September 1773 he drafted for the *Public Advertiser* what was perhaps the most biting satire he ever wrote: "Rules by Which a Great Empire May Be Reduced to a Small One."

Franklin's "rules" were initially circulated in Pennsylvania. Then they spread to Massachusetts and other colonies. His argument was so persuasive that many who had considered themselves neutral were persuaded to join the Sons of Liberty.

"Suppose citizens of colonies to be always inclined to revolt," he suggested, "and treat them accordingly. By this means, like the husband who uses his wife ill from suspicion, you may in time convert your suspicions into reality.

"Choose inferior, rapacious, and pettifogging men for high posts; support them against all complaint. Reward them for handling matters badly."

When a great empire wants money from colonies, suggested Franklin, "despise their voluntary grants and resolve to harass them with novel taxes. Accept petitions for redress, but treat them with scorn. Above all, use revenue so collected to support every governor who has distinguished himself by his enmity to the people."

In Providence and in Baltimore, in Williamsburg and in Charles Town, readers instantly saw that Benjamin Franklin's satirical guidelines described the prevailing pattern of British rule. Some who read his message made a vow on the spot. "By the Almighty," many a colonist swore, "since Britain is eager to reduce a great empire to a smaller one, I will do all that I can to hasten the process!"

10

Cheap Tea Was Served at the Most Costly Tea Party Ever

"**F**ellow countrymen, we cannot afford to give a single inch! If we retreat now, everything we have done becomes useless! If Hutchinson will not send tea back to England, perhaps we can brew a pot of it especially for him!"

Pausing only when interrupted by shouts of encouragement, Samuel Adams was at his best. More than eight thousand Bostonians had gathered at Old South Church in response to his call. The church, churchyard, and streets converging upon it were jam-packed with Colonials. December 16, 1773, marked a crucial deadline. If the ship *Dartmouth* remained at Griffin's Wharf another twelve hours, citizens would have to pay the tax upon her cargo.

The roots of that dilemma lay in financial troubles far away, those of the East India Company and of England.

Old, powerful, and long very wealthy, the East India Company— almost universally known as John—held a monopoly in the tea trade. That meant that prices were easily fixed in England, where there was no competition. Matters were not so simple in the North American colonies, however. Many had stopped drinking tea, not because the price was high but because using it involved paying the small tea tax.

Fast-declining consumption in America, along with internal business problems, spelled potential disaster for John. Only a few years earlier, the company had advanced one million pounds to the British government as a loan, but by 1773 it faced financial collapse unless the American market could be recaptured.

Loss of that market stemmed from actions taken in an earlier bid to eliminate a shortfall in British taxes. Charles Townshend, chancellor of the exchequer, had warned Parliament late in 1766 that real estate

The Boston Tea Party. [EIGHTEENTH CENTURY ENGRAVING]

taxes would be reduced the following February, which would entail a revenue shortfall of £500,000 per year. He urged that corrective measures must be taken at once.

Lawmakers were virtually unanimous in telling Townshend that stouthearted Englishmen would tolerate no new taxes, which left only one potential source of new revenue: the North American colonies. So Townshend turned to them, not by choice, but out of desperation. Under his leadership Parliament passed a series of acts.

The legislation provided for new import duties on lead, paint, glass, paper, and tea consumed in North America. Plans to issue writs of assistance to help collectors enforce statutes had triggered the early and fiery wrath of James Otis.

Colonial resistance to the Townshend Acts was violent and widespread. As a result, Parliament soon scuttled all measures except that which applied to John's commodity: tea. At three pence per pound, the import duty was of trifling significance to consumers. Some lawmakers even predicted that if collected in full, it would enrich His Majesty's coffers by no more than £300 a year.

"No matter!" thundered Lord North. "Britain is honor bound to enforce its laws!"

He failed to add that the East India Company had a seven-year supply of tea on hand and that this surplus was destined to rot in warehouses if it could not be sold in the colonies. Tea taken directly to North America from India bypassed British middle men and eliminated their profit. As a result, tax-added tea could be sold to colonists at a lower price than tea consigned to the domestic market in England.

In the colonies, growing numbers of patriots had decided to pay no new tax, however insignificant, that was levied without their express consent. The conflict had reached an impasse. Britain was determined to collect the tax and to bolster the finances of John, and the patriots were equally determined to do without tea rather than pay the hated tax.

In October 1773 citizens of Philadelphia met to protest the tea tax. Simultaneously, they sought to persuade merchants to get out of the tea business.

New Yorkers took similar action the following month. There, Sons of Liberty labeled tea consignees "enemies of the colonists" and warned harbor pilots not to guide any vessel bearing tea.

In Boston the issue was especially complicated. The *Dartmouth* and two sister ships were already in the harbor when the deadline for payment of the import duty arrived. The law forbade return of the tea to England for reimportation at a later time. What's more, the salary of the governor was expected to be raised, in part, from the duty upon tea.

Governor Hutchinson had refused to permit the three tea ships to leave until the tax was paid. That decision provided the excuse that Samuel Adams and other hotheads wanted. Before the December mass meeting adjourned, plans had been made for the evening.

About 150 men, crudely and clumsily disguised as Mohawk Indians, boarded the *Dartmouth*, the *Eleanor,* and the *Beaver* at rest in the bay. Whooping with joy, they dumped into the water 342 casks of tea, mostly of the Darjeeling and Ceylon blends.

Official reaction came swiftly. Hutchinson and numerous other officials beat a hasty retreat, taking refuge in Castle William. From that fortified position they dispatched urgent letters to London.

News of the Boston Tea Party could hardly have reached the capital of the empire at a less opportune time. Officials were ready to take up the matter of the stolen Hutchinson letters and the provincial call for removal of the governor of Massachusetts.

Placed squarely in the middle of an awkward dilemma, Benjamin Franklin offered a solution to the crisis posed by the destruction of the tea. He offered to reimburse John (the East India Company) for the lost tea, estimated to be worth about £10,000. But he stipulated that his offer was contingent upon the repeal of all laws designed to subject and humiliate the colonists.

Few, if any, officials regarded Franklin's offer as reasonable. Instead of loosening the grip upon the rebellious colonies, lawmakers decided to draw the reins tighter.

Only those leaders who today would be called liberals challenged this viewpoint, which was supported by circulation of a crude cartoon.

A British cartoon purported to depict the penalty paid by a Boston collector of the tea tax.

It purported to depict John Malcomb, an exciseman who collected the tea tax in Boston. For his zeal on behalf of the Crown, Malcomb was shown in the act of receiving a coat of tar and feathers, while being forced to drink to the health of the royal family in scalding tea.

British loss of revenue was trifling, but the loss of face was of monumental importance. In swift succession, one legislative reprisal after another was enacted; and Boston's port, to which fifty or more vessels went in a normal month, was closed to all shipments except of food and fuel.

When citizens balked at providing food and shelter for new regiments of soldiers, many were quartered on Boston Common. [New York Public Library]

Upon the suggestion of Lord Sandwich, naval authorities dispatched frigates to see that the port order was obeyed. Regiments of soldiers were sent to Boston to be billeted in the homes of citizens.

Another sternly worded measure established a new restriction. Citizens of Massachusetts were forbidden to assemble for any public meeting not expressly sanctioned by the governor. Still another edict promised stern punishment for lawbreakers. In the future, any official under accusation in the province would be transported to England for trial. Finally, the Quebec Act was passed. Under its terms, civil government was established in Canada, while Massachusetts, Connecticut, and Virginia were stripped of vast western lands earlier ceded to them by charter.

Logically, the leaders of a handful of diminutive colonies should have urged their followers to come to heel. Clearly, the wrath of the gigantic British empire had been aroused. But when emotion rules, logic flies out the window.

New York sent one hundred sheep for the relief of Boston. Charles Town followed with rice and cash a few weeks later. Dormant committees of correspondence suddenly sprang into action. For the first time, great numbers of Americans reached a radical conclusion. They *must* find a way to pool the resources of all the colonies if they were to eliminate taxation without representation.

CHAPTER

11

Submit Meekly—Or Unite and Resist!

"**B**ritish oppression has effaced the boundaries of the several colonies," declared Patrick Henry in early September 1774. The more than forty delegates assembled in Philadelphia's Carpenter's Hall were clearly startled.

"Pennsylvania will never accept such a doctrine," a representative from Rhode Island is said to have muttered.

Henry was keenly aware that every man in the hall was listening, and he knew that some were shaking their heads in disagreement. Still, he put his argument in more forcible language:

"The distinctions between Virginians, Pennsylvanians, and New-Englanders is no more. *I am not a Virginian, but an American!*"

Delegates to the semiofficial gathering, or congress, were sharply divided. More than half were inclined to applaud Henry's sentiments. A minority strongly disputed his proposal that individual colonies should give up some part of their sovereignty. Two or three who listened later said, "The man's harangue bordered upon treason."

Eleven colonies, represented by forty-four delegates, came together on September 5. Partly because they had only short distances to travel, six men were there to speak for Pennsylvania. Another six represented Virginia, while only two appeared for Rhode Island and for New Hampshire. Distant South Carolina had five spokesmen in the body.

Nine days after talks began, three deputies from North Carolina made their appearance and were greeted with cheers. Not a man was there from Britain's youngest and weakest North American colony, Georgia.

Every delegate agreed that weighty issues were sure to be debated. But if some of these matters should come to a vote, in what fashion would a tally be made? Two of the colonies had three times as many spokesmen there as did some of the other colonies. Since there were

Patrick Henry, who left home at age fifteen and spent more than a dozen years as a "conspicuous failure" in business and law.

no official census figures for the colonies, it would be impossible to use population as a basis for votes.

After spirited debate, a conclusion was reached. Each colony would have one vote. To cast that vote, Maryland's three delegates, for instance, must concur. If they failed to do so, they would cast fractional votes.

The closing of Boston's port in the aftermath of the city's tea party had reactivated many dormant committees of correspondence and spurred the formation of new ones. On May 12, 1774, committee representatives had come together for a conference, rather than simply to exchange news bulletins and letters. Brookline, Cambridge, Newtown, Lynn, Lexington, and Charlestown patriots joined Bostonians in Faneuil Hall.

After Samuel Adams was chosen as chairman, delegate after delegate rose to condemn Britain's new oppressive measures. Each town represented gave assurances through its spokesmen that "every patriot will join suffering brethren in Boston by providing every measure of relief."

As General Gage began to fortify Boston Neck, committees of correspondence worked harder than ever. (Only Pennsylvania and North Carolina were without a single such body.) A printer in one committee found a cartoon issued by Benjamin Franklin during the French and Indian Wars. Depicting a severed rattlesnake, it urged separated colonies to *Join or Die.*

Suddenly the old sketch took on new meaning. As a result, it was published over and over and served to give visual impetus to the growing movement toward action. That was the most that anyone could expect; at the moment, organic unity was inconceivable.

Long established usage named any gathering or meeting as a "congress." Hence James Otis and a handful of other incendiaries who wanted a special gathering had called for a Stamp Act congress late in 1765. It convened in New York, with nine colonies represented. Resolutions of the informal body centered largely upon taxation without representation. They stirred up so much popular resentment that they were widely credited with helping to secure repeal of the hated Stamp Act.

As Britain tightened the noose around the neck of Massachusetts, many patriots thought of the Stamp Act congress. Why not call another gathering to discuss ways to resist new oppressive measures?

The idea of a new intercolonial congress seems to have been fashioned in John Brown's domain of Providence, Rhode Island. Once publicized, it was greeted with enthusiasm. Together the colonies could combat all of Britain's Coercive Acts. So on May 24, 1774, Virginia burgesses met informally at Raleigh's tavern in Williamsburg.

Designed by Benjamin Franklin in 1754, a "Join or Die" cartoon was effectively revived after the port of Boston was closed by the British.

Earlier, Governor Dunmore had prohibited all official meetings.

"Let us begin to lay plans for an intercolonial congress to meet annually in the future," one delegate proposed. His idea was met with such enthusiasm that the resolution it evoked was dispatched to legislative bodies in the other colonies.

Support among the colonies for a congress was enthusiastic, and by the time the conclave was scheduled for Philadelphia in September 1774, many were calling it—erroneously—"a continental congress."

Continental was a misnomer because few Americans ever had any hope that Canada would participate, and vast tracts along the Atlantic and the Gulf of Mexico had few ties with England's thirteen colonies. Both East Florida and West Florida were heavily Spanish in outlook, and residents of these sparsely settled regions had no interest in disputes between Britain and her older colonies. Immense tracts, largely unexplored, lay west of the settled region along the Atlantic coast. So despite its title, the Philadelphia gathering would bring together spokesmen from regions making up only a small fraction of the North American continent.

Most legislative bodies of old-line colonies south of Canada selected delegates. Some of the delegates did not go to Philadelphia, however; and lacking any official standing, the Continental Congress could do little. After having spent many hours in heated debate, delegates managed to pass some nonbinding resolutions.

Pennsylvania's delegates stressed the growing economic power of the colonies, pointing out that Philadelphia, Boston, and New York were about equal in size to England's Sheffield, Bristol, and Leeds. What's more, some of them predicted—correctly as events proved—that Philadelphia's growth soon would make it second to London in size among cities of the British empire.

Flexing their financial muscles, delegates voted on September 22 to establish a general embargo on British goods. Sporadic regional efforts of this sort had proved ineffective, but if all of the thirteen colonies would unite in economic protest, London would take notice!

As days passed, the man who dared to call himself an American rather than a Virginian was regarded with increasing respect. Unlike Boston's Harvard-educated attorneys, Patrick Henry had read law for just six weeks before taking up the vocation. Married at age eighteen to the daughter of an innkeeper, at first he had few clients and now at age twenty-eight he still was undistinguished, except for what many admirers called "his natural gift for oratory."

Henry took the floor of the Continental Congress frequently and almost always succeeded in battering arguments of conservative delegates. These "near Tories" objected to each of ten resolutions that enumerated rights of colonists.

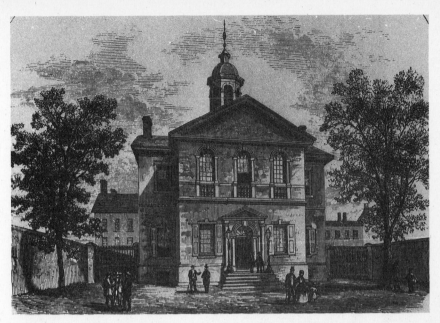

Carpenter's Hall, Philadelphia, saw the first significant coming together—or congress—of delegates elected by legislative bodies of twelve colonies.

High on the list of asserted rights was that of assembly. Trial by peers—instead of trial in England or by an admiralty court—was listed as basic. Delegates agreed that colonists had a right to be free from supporting a standing army. Still another resolution insisted that Englishmen in America had the right to choose for themselves legislative councils whose members would decide to tax or not to tax.

Although outspoken patriots, Patrick Henry included, knew that such resolutions would have little or no effect in London, it was hoped that they would persuade all Sons of Liberty to take bolder stands.

Only the nonimportation plan had anything approaching real power. Under its provisions, trade with England, Ireland, and the West Indies would come to a halt. However, to be effective, the boycott would have to be enforced by vigilant local committees willing to punish violators.

Far from having achieved anything approaching organic union, the thirteen colonies retained their individuality. Internally, all of them were sharply divided between patriots, Tories, and the indifferent.

Philadelphia had produced little except talk, hope, and a plan. Still, delegates voted to hold a second session in six months "if the grievances of the American colonies against Britain have not been corrected by that time."

12

First Women's Movement Urged Cider, Buttermilk, and Water

"Of course I know that I am putting my husband's job at great risk. That is the price that must be paid. Women have been quiet too long; it is time for us to show our strength."

Penelope Barker, vivacious young second wife of a port collector, stretched out her hand to her friend and smiled. "I can count on you to come, I know!"

Tradition says that during early fall 1774, Mrs. Barker visited more than fifty homes in and near Edenton, North Carolina. While some women firmly refused as soon as they learned what she had in mind, many listened to her argument, then gave her their support.

Situated at the mouth of the mile-wide Chowan River, Edenton was initially a haven of refuge. Debtors, indentured servants, and other fugitives gathered there, many coming from Jamestown, Virginia, to be safe from the law. Refugees were so numerous that for a time citizens of Williamsburg, Virginia, called the North Carolina community "Rogue's Harbor."

Matters changed as coastal North Carolina became more thickly settled, and eventually the village was designated as an official port of entry. Ship's papers listed it as "The Port of Roanoke." By 1770, a typical month saw ten or more two-masted schooners clear the port and sail through Ocracoke Inlet to the West Indies, England, or Europe. Most vessels carried tobacco, turpentine, salt fish, corn, or lumber.

Having been made capital of the colony, it was fitting that Edenton should pay homage to royalty by naming its two principal thoroughfares King Street and Queen Street. Before long, many residents called the place Queen Anne's Towne.

Penelope Barker. [NORTH CAR-
OLINA DEPARTMENT OF ARCHIVES
AND HISTORY]

When Thomas Barker, said to have been "absolutely mad about his beautiful wife," learned of Penelope's plan, he tried to persuade her to abandon it.

"It is unseemly and perhaps unlawful for a woman to get involved in a political issue," he urged. "Women have always stayed in the home and have avoided staining themselves with such matters."

His reasoning was as futile as his attempts at persuasion. Penelope Craven had grown up as her father's favorite, accustomed to getting her way, and marriage had subdued her only a trifle. Determined to act, she did not know that by doing so she would lead the first women's political movement in America.

At her invitation, women dressed for a party at the home of Mrs. Elizabeth King. One of them carefully dated a blank sheet of parchment: October 25, 1774. Abigail Charlton picked up the pen and reached for the parchment.

"Wait!" exclaimed Penelope Barker. "Each of you knows why we are here. Most of you have said you will pledge yourself not to conform to the pernicious custom of drinking tea.

A British cartoon mocked women who took part in the Edenton Tea Party. [NORTH CAROLINA STATE LIBRARY]

"Here and now, I propose that we solemnly engage to drink only apple cider, sweet buttermilk, or cool spring water—so long as the king insists that his special tax remain upon tea from India!"

Most heads nodded, and a few women approved verbally. Several shook their heads and refused to put their names on the parchment. However, one by one, more than forty names were signed. Then the hostess served a special "tea" to each woman present. No ordinary brew, it was concocted from the leaves of raspberry plants, mulberry plants, or both.

News of the "unseemly action by Colonial women" did not reach London until January 16, 1775, when the *Morning Chronicle* and

London Advertiser issued a public account of actions that had no precedent.

Under the urging of their wives and daughters, said the British report, provincial deputies of North Carolina last October "resolved not to drink any more tea, nor wear any more British cloth."

An unidentified letter writer may have transmitted the women's pledge across the Atlantic, or it could have been sent by a zealous agent of the British Crown. Published, it ran to fourteen lines of type and did not mention cider, buttermilk, spring water, or even tea. It simply indicated "witness of fixed intention and solemn determination" on the part of a body of women. Their set of formal resolves was described as aimed at "fostering peace and happiness of the province."

A British cartoonist seized upon the news of unheard of doings by women and executed a sketch entitled "A Society of Patriotic Ladies at Edenton, North Carolina." Published on March 25, 1775, the cartoon did not require interpretation. At a glance, anyone could see that the foreground was occupied by a dog urinating upon a chest of tea.

British indignation ran high. The women's action was a flagrant insult to the processes of law. Clearly, these women could only be a band of hussies. Under no circumstances would a lady involve herself in political matters!

The women of Edenton had given little thought to long-range consequences of their action. When they learned of its impact in London, they realized that their influence was much greater than they had expected. Closer to home, Carolinians by the hundreds were persuaded to swear off tea. Many in thinly populated Georgia followed suit.

The growing boycott of the chief product of the East India Company soon affected the judgment of officials in Charles Town, South Carolina. There a cargo of tea brought by the ship *London* was stored in a warehouse, for all practical purposes impounded until the colonists agreed to pay the three pence per pound tax. It remained there, undamaged, for many months.

Patriots eventually ousted royal agents and officials and took temporary control of Charles Town. One of their first acts was to haul the impounded tea from storage and offer it for sale. Soon the entire ship load was sold to patriots, who knew that money realized from it would be used to help finance a do-or-die struggle with Britain.

CHAPTER

13

High-placed British Friends Made Up a Vocal Minority

From the beginning of tension until the final settlement of difficulties, Colonials had high-placed friends in London. Some of England's most brilliant orators repeatedly spoke out against the king and his ministers.

Parliament, however, was heavily influenced by members of the House of Lords, where membership was by virtue of aristocratic heritage, not as a result of elections. These men were predominantly anti-American, and nearly every crucial vote saw them control a majority, even though it was sometimes small.

Very early, Irish-born Edmund Burke expressed strong views on "the American question." His outspoken opposition to colonial policies espoused by King George III propelled him into leadership of the Whig party.

Burke spoke in Parliament in the spring of 1774, urging repeal of the tax on tea. A few months later he opposed bills that called for closing the port of Massachusetts and annulling the Massachusetts charter.

Political foes charged Burke with "pocketbook influence," since he was serving as agent for the colony of New York. He ignored these accusations and made what many regard as his greatest speech on March 22, 1775.

Burke issued an eloquent call for "Conciliation with America." In it he reminded members of the House of Commons that "a fierce spirit of liberty" had developed three thousand miles from London. It was rooted, he declared, in old-fashioned English principles and virtues and could not be ignored.

British exports to the New World came to only £500,000 in 1704, he pointed out, but by 1772 they had increased tenfold. Citing this rapid growth in commerce, he called for "trade rather than taxation." Burke

Irish orator Edmund Burke won his reputation as a spokesman in favor of treating Colonials "precisely like other Englishmen."

summed up a three-hour speech in a single biting sentence: "It is not what a lawyer tells me I may do, but what humanity, reason, and justice tell me I must do."

For the most part, his plea fell upon deaf ears. An appeal that could have brought an end to tension was summarily rejected. Far away in Newport, Fredericksburg, and Germantown, few Americans of the era knew of his daring proposal.

Instead of being silenced by defeat, Burke introduced another bill a few months later, on November 10. Had it been adopted, "all offensive acts" would have been repealed. In addition, all past violators of laws concerning taxation and import duties would have been granted amnesty.

Burke had strong support, but the ministry always held the upper hand. Five days after he urged reform and amnesty, Parliament voted to prohibit all trade with the colonies for a brief period. In addition, goods, vessels, and the men who manned them in defiance of the prohibition were declared lawful prizes subject to seizure by any British gunboat.

On February 16, 1778, Burke took the floor again. This time, he spoke against the use of American Indian mercenaries by officers of the Crown.

Tempers were already at the boiling point on both sides of the Atlantic. As a result, Burke's pro-American oratory "excited such applause that the ministers—who as usual had cleared the house of strangers—were congratulated on their prudence, for it was said that had the public heard Burke's speech, lives of cabinet members would have been in danger."

Though always outvoted, the Irish orator was not alone. Charles James Fox publicly and loudly opposed the official governmental position from the time of the Boston Tea Party. He, too, voted for repeal of the tax on tea, calling it "a mere assertion of a right which could force the colonists into open rebellion."

In his early life, Fox was famous only as a great gambler. As a spokesman for pro-American views, he "discovered power for debate which his friends applauded and his enemies dreaded."

In October 1774, Fox censured the king's ministers for their role in increasing discontent in America. "The king of Prussia, nay, Alexander the Great," he said, "never gained more in one campaign than the noble Lord North has lost—for he has lost a whole continent!"

Eighteen months later the ex-gambler was still an outspoken friend of America. "If the question lies between conquering America and abandoning it," he told Parliament, "I am for abandoning it. Our advantages from America stem from trade, not taxes." That outspoken stance led fellow lawmaker Henry H. Luttrell to charge that Fox was speaking treason.

London's most influential newspaper, the *Morning Post,* always endorsed the views of the sovereign and his ministers. Hence, its editor taunted Fox because he had not challenged Luttrell to a duel. Pro-American lawmakers met informally to consider the tone of the newspaper piece. "The publication," they concluded, "was a scheme to get rid of Fox by provoking a duel."

Fox refused to be goaded. Defying good manners and prevailing opinion, he began referring to King George III as "Satan," usually using oblique language. But once he let his guard down and blurted, "Certainly things look well, but he [King George III] will die soon—and that will be the best of all."

Many governmental leaders held their posts through royal appointment or by inheritance. Naturally, such persons jeered at the friends of America in London. So did an increasing number of cartoonists and pamphlet writers.

Among those satirized, none was more colorful than cross-eyed John Wilkes. As an outspoken advocate of colonial moderation, he was three times expelled from the House of Commons. The masses retaliated by making him Lord Mayor of London. In that office, he voiced so strong a public protest that his name was cleared so that he could again debate and vote in Parliament.

"Wilkes and Liberty!" became a major political slogan on both sides of the ocean. Seeking to counter its impact, political foes used "dirty tricks" of every variety. Wilkes had once boasted of having leaked classified information to the press, so Tories retaliated by printing and circulating phony election ballots.

Through Wilkes's influence, prominent Londoners formed the Society of Supporters of the Bill of Rights. Tempers ran so high that public demonstrations in favor of the society's position led to a riot. That resulted in Wilkes's arrest on a general warrant—one in which the name of no individual appears—and a stay in jail.

While Wilkes was behind bars, the House of Assembly of South Carolina sent him £1,500. In Boston, Sons of Liberty gathered at the Liberty Tree and drank toasts to him while hailing him as "the illustrious martyr of liberty."

Wilkes learned of the Boston incident several months later. Colonists should also have toasted Colonel Isaac Barre, he said. "It was Barre," he correctly pointed out, "who was rotated home after being wounded at Quebec and who first used the term *Sons of Liberty* in a speech in Parliament."

Wilkes was a man of the people, a forerunner of today's populists. Thomas William Coke of Norfolk was at the other end of the economic spectrum, but he also laid his fortune and political future on the line for the sake of Colonials. When King George III once expressed a desire to visit Coke's palatial country estate, the pro-American owner sent a tart message to Westminster Palace. "My home," he informed the monarch, "is open to the public every Tuesday of every week."

Jonathan Shipley was equally outspoken and brilliant. Lacking Coke's fortune, he proved much more vulnerable when he, too, echoed the cry to stop badgering Englishmen who lived in America.

Because Charles James Fox opposed arbitrary ways of raising revenue, he was satirized as opposing the "pewter pot bill," which never existed.

Cross-eyed John Wilkes landed in jail as a result of his pro-American views.

Shipley had studied for the priesthood and seemed destined to head the Church of England. He developed a deep and long-lasting friendship with Benjamin Franklin and, partly as a result of this relationship, became an advocate of conciliation and moderation. As a result, the sovereign refused to name him archbishop of Canterbury when the high post became vacant.

William Pitt, first earl of Chatham, ranks as one of the English-speaking world's all-time great orators. Unlike self-schooled Patrick Henry, Chatham spoke the language of nobility. His reputation as an orator stemmed from debates in which he urged caution and moderation in dealing with the colonists.

"You may ravage," he warned fellow members in Parliament, "but you will never conquer. It is impossible. I might as well talk of driving Americans before me with this crutch as to speak of subduing them by force of arms."

A star-studded group of British leaders repeatedly begged for compromise instead of bloodshed, but they were always in a minority. Few of their actions or their speeches became known in America in less than nine to twelve weeks after the event. As a result, it was only rarely that Colonials became more than vaguely aware that pro-American Whigs were about as numerous in Britain as were pro-English Tories in the colonies.

CHAPTER

14

John Sullivan's Men Smelled Gunpowder

"It has come!" panted Raul Revere. "The British are on the move!"

Attorney John Sullivan of Durham, New Hampshire, was not surprised. For nearly a year he had been predicting that the war of words between patriots and the British would erupt into armed conflict. For that reason, he had devoted many afternoons to drilling a company of volunteers.

"Gage has two regiments on the way to Providence, even now," Revere continued. "They come to strengthen the fort and make sure that British powder stays dry."

Sullivan did not need additional information. It was general knowledge that the British had stored a substantial quantity of gunpowder in Fort William and Mary. Situated in Portsmouth Harbor, it had never seen action of any sort. Hence it was known to house only a handful of Redcoats whose presence was more symbolic than threatening.

"Your horse is nearly done," the New Hampshire leader told Revere. "Fall in here and sleep while your animal cools. For my part, I must move at once."

Alone among New England colonies, New Hampshire included numerous persons closely associated with the movement to put Bonnie Prince Charles on the throne of England. Aging cavaliers and their sons—men of Sullivan's age—still cherished dreams, hoping to change England forever by returning a Stuart to power. Practically anyone, they said, would be preferable to "the fat German pig before whom good Englishmen now bow to the ground."

Hotheads who engaged in early talk about armed rebellion in the colonies did not imagine that their success would unseat the House of Hanover in England. But men whose fathers and uncles had risked

*In hand-to-hand fighting, it was difficult to distinguish between
a man's comrades and his enemies.*

their lives for Bonnie Prince Charlie were more ready than most Colonials to accept the idea of war with the mother country.

Paul Revere's message spurred many of these men into action. At the command of John Sullivan, Micah Davis raced to Portsmouth to round up all the patriots he could find. Another aide rode to the waterfront. His mission was simple: find on the Piscataque River a vessel suitable for the undertaking that Sullivan planned for the night.

A sloop-rigged vessel suitable for use in shallow coastal waters was selected. Sullivan inspected the gondola and pronounced it satisfactory. Most of his followers came from Durham, at the falls of the Oyster River. With their aid, on the night of December 17, 1774, he hoisted the big lateen sail, and they made the nine miles to Providence in less than two hours. There they took aboard perhaps a dozen more men who had responded to the call of Micah Davis.

It was an unusually cold night and a few of the patriots huddled on the gondola complained because spray froze as it hit their faces.

Approaching dark Fort William and Mary, the gondola was halted by shallow water, and the men aboard took off their shoes and climbed out. Then they waded the final thirty yards to their objective as quietly as possible.

Inside the fortress, a sentry heard splashing and fired a warning shot. Captain Cochran, commander of the installation, knew the fort was of little or no military value. But he feared that men whom he had seen engaged in drills might try to seize the precious gunpowder he guarded.

Cochran ran to the parapet and tried to put up a fight in total darkness. His men managed to get off one cannon ball and to fire a few muskets, but no member of the assault team was hit. Sullivan's men gleefully reported the next day that they had smelled gunpowder but never were in danger of receiving a ball.

When the patriots clambered into the fortress, Cochran received a direct hit from a spar and was badly bruised; his five subordinates, uninjured, surrendered meekly. Not a drop of blood had been spilled in the first American military act of overt treason against the Crown.

John Sullivan and his men seized more than ninety barrels of gunpowder, at least a dozen cannon, and about sixty muskets. Some of the powder became damp while it was being moved to the gondola, but it could be dried and made usable. All of the weapons were in good order.

Alexander Scammel, who claimed credit for having pulled down the king's colors, laughed when he read the official report of the governor. In a letter to the earl of Dartmouth, Governor Wentworth tried to protect himself from censure:

News was brought to me that a drum was beating about the town of Providence, to collect the populace together in order to take away the gunpowder and dismantle the fort. I sent the chief justice to warn them from engaging in such an attempt.

He went to them, warned them that such a step would mean open rebellion, and entreated them to disperse. But all to no purpose. They went to the island on which the fort is situated and forced an entrance in spite of Captain Cochran, who defended it as long as he could.

They secured the captain, triumphantly gave three huzzas, hauled down the King's colors and made off with 98 barrels of gunpowder.

In many colonies, members of the militia enlisted for ninety days and left home without military training.

Anticipating armed conflict, bands of patriots earlier had collected what gunpowder they could find. The new ban upon importation meant that when their meager supply was gone, they would be unable to get more from overseas.

Sullivan's bold step was taken without consultation with the Sons of Liberty in Boston and other major centers. Their action had clear meaning: there would be less talk and more action in the future. Seizure of the king's gunpowder was a signal that some Americans were ready to use it against His Majesty's troops.

As a military engagement, the capture of a New Hampshire fort was all but meaningless. But it was an act of treason that called for swift and stern reprisal.

In a move to stamp out armed resistance before it got out of hand, authorities dispatched troops to Lexington, Massachusetts. There "the shot heard 'round the world" precipitated the first pitched battle of the American Revolution—brought about by British reaction to John Sullivan's bloodless capture of a tiny New Hampshire fortress.

Part Three

Blood in the Snow

Despite the Boston Massacre, which occurred between soldiers and civilians, there was no genuine clash between hostile armed forces until April 1775. In the battles of Lexington and Concord, the British suffered about 273 casualties against 95 casualties among patriot forces.

Much of 1775 was spent in building up strength on both sides, but armed conflicts were numerous. Most of them took place in the North during winter months.

Although patriots realized that tension was mounting, a majority of them still hoped for concessions followed by reconciliation. Those who advocated independence were in a decided minority. They made up a tiny band of self-styled radicals who, for the moment, could do little except deliver orations, print handbills, and wait for the British to commit new offenses.

Paul Revere. [Eighteenth Century Engraving]

15

Paul Revere Was In at the Start and Finish of Early Action

Brooks, a fashionable private club for Britain's men of means and leisure, was long famous for its betting books. In April 1775 a new one opened. Some members of the club thought that hostilities in the distant North American colonies would prove to be long and costly. Others were positive that untrained farmers and frontiersmen could never stand up against His Majesty's disciplined forces.

The new betting book soon gained a hasty entry: "John Burgoyne wagers Charles James Fox one pony [50 guineas] that he will be home victorious from America by Christmas Day 1777."

Earlier Burgoyne had drawn up a theoretical plan "for Conducting the War from the Side of Canada." As a result, he was awarded a top post in the army sent to subdue the rebels. "Gentleman Johnny," as intimates called him, reached Boston aboard the *Cerberus* on May 25, 1776. By then, it was clear that blood already spilled in the snow of New England was likely to cost him fifty guineas.

Dr. Joseph Warren, president of the Provincial Congress of Massachusetts, sent Paul Revere and other messengers to Lexington to warn patriots there. General Thomas Gage was now military governor of the province, and he had no intention of tolerating anything approaching a repetition of the action at Fort William and Mary. Learning that a depot in Concord held a growing store of gunpowder and arms, he sent seven hundred soldiers twenty miles from Boston to seize the military supplies.

Although made famous in Longfellow's poem, Paul Revere did not make it to his destination when sent to warn his countrymen that the British were coming. Captured and briefly detained, he was forced to walk home as the Redcoats retained his horse for His Majesty's service when they released him.

At Bunker Hill patriots literally held their fire until they could see the eyes of their advancing foes.

Commanding the British troops was Major John Pitcairn who marched his soldiers all night, arriving at Lexington at dawn. There he found a line of minute men drawn up on the village green commanded by Captain John Parker. The British halted and the major shouted, "Disperse, ye rebels, disperse!"

From behind a stone wall a shot rang out—no one has ever discovered who fired—and a skirmish ensued. Eight minute men were killed, ten were wounded, and one British soldier was wounded before the patriots withdrew.

The British continued the six miles to Concord and the Americans retreated to the North Bridge just outside the town. While the main body of soldiers accomplished their mission of seizing the gunpowder, a small contingent of Britishers skirmished again with the colonists, now numbering several hundred. Three British solders and two Americans were killed in this battle later immortalized in Emerson's poem:

> . . . the embattled farmers stood,
> And fired the shot heard round the world.

The American Revolution had begun.

The British soldiers returned to Boston, and by June they were virtually hemmed in there by thousands of Continentals. General Gage planned to fortify the one area not occupied by his opponents, but the patriots learned of this and decided to occupy this section, near Bunker Hill, first. On the night of June 16–17, they fortified adjacent Breed's Hill because it was closer to Boston, leaving reinforcements on Bunker Hill. This brought on the first real battle of the war as the British stormed the hill, and it produced the famous directive to the defending Colonials, "Don't shoot 'til you see the whites of their eyes," made by Colonel William Prescott.

The British were repulsed twice, but on their third charge won the hill because the Americans gave out of ammunition and could not get any more from their reinforcements on Bunker Hill. They had to retreat, but they had inflicted terrible losses on the British: 1,054 killed and wounded out of the 2,200 engaged. American losses were 441 out of 3,200 engaged.

Thus, although the battle was a tactical victory for the British, it was a strategic and moral one for the Americans. Writing home, General Sir Henry Clinton said, "A dear bought victory—another such would have ruined us."

Somehow, the engagement became known as the Battle of Bunker Hill, although it really took place on Breed's Hill.

Remembered today for the ride he did not complete, Paul Revere took to the saddle several times on important missions for the Colonials. In 1773, he rode to New York to notify the city's Sons of Liberty that a

Mocking American patriots, a British cartoonist sketched "Bunker's Hill, or America's Head Dress." [LIBRARY OF CONGRESS]

tea party was being planned in Boston. A few months later when Boston was made the target of the port bill, Revere rode to both New York and Philadelphia to ask help for citizens who faced great privation. Again it was Revere who rode to the home of John Sullivan to warn him that the Redcoats were headed toward Fort William and Mary.

Dr. Joseph Warren was the patriot who dispatched Revere toward Lexington. Earlier, Warren had turned down an opportunity to become physician-general to fighting men of the province, insisting he wanted more hazardous service. He was killed at the Battle of Bunker Hill.

Because Warren wore expensive clothing, the body of the patriot was stripped. In a later report Lieutenant Walter Laurie, who was in charge of the British burial detail, said he stuffed the remains of the president of the Provincial Congress into a hole with another rebel's body.

Many months later the British were forced from Boston. As soon as the city was free, relatives and admirers of Dr. Warren clamored that he be given proper burial.

Identification was made difficult by the fact that when the grave was located it was found to hold two sets of bones. The *New England Chronicle* of April 25, 1776, gives the only known contemporary account of how identification was made:

Remains of Joseph Warren were identified by Paul Revere long after Warren's death. [HARPER'S ENCYCLOPEDIA OF U.S. HISTORY]

Though the body which our savage enemies scarce privileged with earth enough to hide it from the birds of prey was disfigured, when taken up, yet it was sufficiently known by two artificial teeth which had been set for him a short time before his glorious exit.

That terse account fails to credit the man who practiced forensic medicine long before it received that title. He was the goldsmith, coppersmith, and publisher of broadsides who took to the saddle at Dr. Warren's insistence.

In an advertisement of September 19, 1768, readers of the *Boston Gazette* were told:

WHEREAS many persons are so unfortunate as to lose their Fore-Teeth by Accident, and otherways, to their great Detriment, not only in Looks, but speaking both in Public and Private:—This is to inform all such that they may have them replaced with artificial ones, that look as well as Natural, & answeres the end of speaking to all Intents, by PAUL REVERE, Goldsmith, near the head of Dr. Clarkes' Wharf, Boston.

A jack-of-all trades, Revere seems to have been careful to avoid false advertising. He did not promise that his artificial "fore-teeth" could be used in eating. Still, an advertisement that appeared in the *Gazette* made more sweeping claims:

ARTIFICIAL TEETH—PAUL REVERE

Takes this Method of returning his most Sincere Thanks to the Gentlemen and Ladies who have employed him in the care of their Teeth and he would now inform them and all others, who are so unfortunate as to lose their Teeth by accident & otherways, that he still continues the Business of a Dentist, and flatters himself that from the Experience he has had in fixing some Hundreds of Teeth, that he can fix them as well as any Surgeon-Dentist who ever came from London.

Thirty-five years of age when his second series of dental advertisements appeared, Revere typically fastened one or two false teeth to adjoining ones by means of silver wire.

Only a few weeks before the battle of Bunker Hill, Dr. Warren was his patient. Two tell-tale false teeth were then "set" for the physician. Hence it was Revere who identified the silver wire used to put the teeth in place. His testimony served to provide positive identification of the remains of the physician-patriot.

16

Ticonderoga Lay Eight Full Days Away from Philadelphia

"**S**urrender on the spot, or be prepared to die!"

Captain Delaplace, British commander of Fort Ticonderoga on Lake Champlain, stumbled to the door. Responding to thunderous knocks, he wore only his dressing gown.

Delaplace stared in bewilderment, then blinked as he recognized the intruder. Ethan Allen of Connecticut, locally noted as the leader of the Green Mountain Boys, was a well-known troublemaker. But what was he doing at Ticonderoga at this time of day, brandishing a sword?

"What is your business, sir?" the military officer demanded.

"Give up this installation at once, with all who are stationed here, and the stores you have accumulated," Allen ordered.

"Who are you to ask such a thing? By what authority do you make such a demand?"

"By the authority of the Great Jehovah and the Continental Congress!" snapped Ethan Allen. He gestured, indicating to Delaplace a motley horde of armed men who filled the outer staircase of the barracks.

Allen's scruffy fighting men, accompanied by a band from Massachusetts led by Colonel Benedict Arnold, were overwhelmingly superior in number. Except for a sentry who had been taken at the sallyport, not a man in the fort had a weapon in his hand.

May 10, 1775, is not listed in history books as the date of a battle—not even a skirmish. Captain Delaplace surrendered without resistance, and he, his wife, and forty-six others were sent under guard to Hartford, where they were released.

Ethan Allen won a lasting place among America's heroes without firing a shot. He captured 50 swivels, 2 mortars, 120 iron cannon, a

Ethan Allen's dramatic demand for the surrender of Fort Ticonderoga.

howitzer, and a warehouse full of small arms and military stores. In addition, he took possession of a cohorn, a bronze mortar mounted on wooden blocks for portability.

Meanwhile, in Philadelphia, the Continental Congress, in whose name Allen acted, seemed more eager for peace than for independence. Representatives of the middle and southern colonies were far removed from the tense situation in the North, and many of them still believed it had developed because of poor judgment on the part of Massachusetts leaders. On the floor of the second congress, delegates carefully refrained from use of the word *independence.*

Three days were spent in drafting a fresh memorial to King George III and his ministers. Its primary purpose was to demonstrate that an unidentified British soldier—not an American sharpshooter—had fired the first shot at Lexington. Numerous depositions attached to the memorial supported this conclusion.

A few months earlier, in the First Continental Congress a delegate from Virginia had spoken bluntly. In heated debate he revealed sentiments that many others held in private. "If there is a quarrel that cannot be settled without bloodshed," he shouted, "it is between Massachusetts and Britain. Therefore, let that colony be permitted to conduct by herself whatever contest she may choose!"

Except for delegates from the North, the spirit of conciliation was all but universal. Some representatives from Virginia were closely questioned by colleagues. Yes, one of them admitted ruefully, we are embarrassed and humiliated by Patrick Henry, but we can do little or nothing to keep the man quiet.

That point of view was understandable. A few weeks earlier a Richmond convention had met to organize the militia, a necessary step if the colony were to be ready to defend herself. Most who attended did not so much as consider the possibility that the colony might some day take aggressive action. Some objected even to developing a plan of defense.

Patrick Henry sat quietly as long as he could. Then, responding to those who preferred to take no action at all, he jumped to his feet and cried:

> If we wish to be free; if we wish to preserve inviolate those inestimable privileges for which we have so long been contending; if we mean not basely to abandon the noble struggle in which we have so long been engaged, we must fight!
>
> I repeat it, sir, we must fight! An appeal to arms and to the God of Hosts is all that is left to us!
>
> Is life so dear, or peace so sweet as to be purchased at the price of chains and slavery? Forbid it, Almighty God! I know not what course others may take, but as for me . . . Give me liberty, or give me death!"

That emotion-charged speech carried the day in Richmond and guaranteed Patrick Henry a place among America's immortals. But it rankled many who heard it. Henry was far, far too incendiary to please moderates in any colony.

At the second Continental Congress there was general agreement that the continental association should be strengthened, and a number of resolutions were framed and passed. Couched in respectful language, they constituted requests, not demands. One of them expressed hope that Americans would ship no more merchandise to Canada or to either of the Floridas.

While these resolutions were being shaped, news reached Philadelphia that what had been a rumor was now known as a fact: a large detachment of British troops would soon reach New York. Clearly, that meant the king meant business about putting down what he called "a trifling insurrection." In their mood of conciliation, the delegates voted to call upon New Yorkers not to resist.

When the president of the Congress, Peyton Randolph, had to leave for home, John Hancock was named president *pro tem*, even though he was known to be eager for military action, which he hoped personally to lead. His fellow townsman, John Adams, angered and humiliated

Patrick Henry (center) *angered many listeners by his "Give me liberty . . ." speech.*
[VIRGINIA STATE LIBRARY]

him when he urged that George Washington be named to command the not-yet-established army that ardent patriots envisioned.

Washington of Virginia was a man of independent means who had let it be known he would be willing to serve without a salary. Furthermore, in spite of never having won a battle, he had extensive military experience. These factors combined to lead delegates to vote unanimously for him, to John Hancock's dismay.

Thus on June 16 George Washington accepted the call of the Continental Congress to serve as supreme commander of forces raised and to be raised in defense of American liberty.

From John Adams he knew that Massachusetts had raised 20,000 volunteers, but one-fifth of them had already become discouraged and had returned to their farms. That left 16,000 untrained men encamped between Roxbury and Cambridge. Most were huddled in thatched huts and sailcloth tents. There were plenty of captains, as every man who brought in forty-nine volunteers received a commission. But neither officers nor enlisted men received regular pay or rations; they depended upon the generosity of farmers for food.

George Washington rode out of Philadelphia toward Massachusetts on a bright morning late in June. His heart was heavy as he pondered the nature of his task and the "soldiers" he would have to use. Barely a day's ride from the city, he saw dust flying in the distance. Soon he spied a rider whose horse was covered with lather.

It was as a southern plantation owner and military veteran that George Washington was named to head colonial armed forces. [PHILADELPHIA HISTORICAL SOCIETY]

"Boston is lost!" cried the courier, who was aghast to learn the identity of the tall rider who had signaled for him to stop. Panting, the messenger blurted out details concerning the battles fought on Breed's Hill and Bunker Hill.

This news from Boston jolted the Continental Congress into action. Delegates called for organization of a medical corps and made a general request for arms and ammunition. The formation of ten companies of expert riflemen was authorized. To be raised in Virginia, Pennsylvania, and Maryland, these men would use "a peculiar kind of Musket called a Rifle—a weapon having circular grooves within the Barrell in order to carry a ball to great distances."

Nevertheless, under the leadership of John Dickinson, delegates drafted a humble petition to King George III. In the preamble they stressed that they spoke for all Americans. Later ridiculed as "the olive branch petition," the document expressed fervent hope for reconciliation of differences. Many delegates rejoiced that Congress had prayerfully requested the personal aid of the sovereign in working for restoration of peace and civil order throughout the North American colonies.

CHAPTER

17

The Queen City
Is Thought to Have Seen
the First Bold Declaration

To the Hon. Earl of Dartmouth,
Sec'y of State, American Dept.

Seditious Combinations have been formed and are still forming in several parts of this Colony. Violent measures pursued in compelling His Majesty's Subjects into submission to the dictates of a tyrannical and illegal tribunal and the late most treasonable publication of a Committee in the County of Mecklenburg are audacious and dangerous proceedings.

The Resolves of the Committee of Mecklenburg which your Lordship will find in the enclosed Newspaper surpass all the horrid and treasonable publications that the inflammatory spirits of this Continent have yet produced.

—Josiah Martin, Colonel, and His Majesty's
loyal Governor, aboard the sloop Cruiser,
30 June, Year of our Lord 1775

The earl of Dartmouth was directly responsible to the Department of State for affairs in North America. That is why governors of both North Carolina and Virginia reported to him about back-country doings. To this professional soldier who had become governor of North Carolina in 1771, matters in Mecklenburg County were of far greater import than was self-government in the remote Watauga region.

About 1750 settlers had found a good spot near the line dividing North Carolina from South Carolina. Situated at "a splendid elevation," now known to be 795 feet, it had all the assets that any good inland site could boast.

In honor of their queen, lawmakers established Mecklenburg County in 1762. Charlotte Sophia of Mecklenburg-Strelitz, who had married King George III in 1761, is said to have been flattered by the tribute. Six years later, a seat of government for the county was established, and loyal subjects called it Charlotte.

Hordes of settlers flocked to Charlotte in May 1775. Most had fire in their eyes and anger in their voices.

Word had just trickled into the back country that Boston had declared her readiness to challenge London. Parliament's joint address to the king of February 9 declared a state of rebellion to exist in Massachusetts; British lawmakers had pledged their lives and property to suppression of that rebellion. Bostonians had responded by calling for organization of governments of patriots at every level in every colony and town.

Dispatches and newspapers from the North went by ship to Charles Town, then overland to the Carolina back country. As a result, it was April before Mecklenburg settlers knew of Boston's call for help. When he learned of it, Colonel Thomas Polk, commander of the county militia, was incensed. So was Dr. Ephraim Brevard, a Princeton College graduate who was regarded as the leading citizen of the region.

At Polk's suggestion, each of his nine companies of militia elected two spokesmen, or delegates. Accompanied by bands of ordinary civilians, these men converged upon the tiny court house in Charlotte.

Abraham Alexander agreed to chair the meeting of patriots, which was launched by a reading of Parliament's joint address to the king. Shouts frequently interrupted, as most people there were just learning that British soldiers had fired upon Colonials at Lexington six weeks earlier.

Debate, oratory, and discussion lasted for hours. The next morning, the session was resumed to hear resolutions prepared during the night by a committee. (If any Tories were present as spectators or spies, they kept their silence.) Once the resolutions had been adopted by a voice vote, Captain James Jack was selected to serve as a courier to deliver them to Philadelphia, 600 miles to the north.

Reaching the City of Brotherly Love, Jack rode to Carpenter's Hall where he found Richard Caswell and William Hooper. These North Carolina delegates scanned the papers brought by Jack. Almost simultaneously, they concluded that the material was "too inflammatory to be presented to the Second Continental Congress." A few of their friends, including Virginia's Richard Henry Lee, are believed to have been shown the resolutions framed in Charlotte.

Thomas Jefferson, revered as author of the Declaration of Independence, angrily resented prior claims.

Back in the colony, Governor Josiah Martin judged that the proceedings in the back country posed grave threats to the stability of all the provinces. Precisely what Martin knew about and just what Captain Jack took to Philadelphia is the focus of a controversy more than two hundred years old.

The *South Carolina Gazette* of Charles Town published a set of Charlotte's "Resolves" on June 13, 1775, but made no reference to a second document said to have been adopted at the same time as the Resolves.

Six resolutions are believed to have constituted the lost document, widely known as the Mecklenburg Declaration. It is thought to have been a bold, enthusiastic manifesto that preceded the Declaration of Independence by more than thirteen months.

Oral tradition asserts that the Mecklenburg Declaration was intended for the Continental Congress only. Therefore it was not released for publication along with the longer set of Resolves adopted at the same time.

Some critics say that there never was a Mecklenburg Declaration. According to this view, only Thomas Jefferson and his colleagues framed a call for total independence from London's rule.

Part of the support for this point of view rests upon questions of date. Some depositions of persons who were present in Charlotte refer to May 20, 1771; others refer to resolutions drawn up on May 31. "Obviously, neither set of oral traditions can be trusted, in view of such confusion," assert some historians.

The discrepancy in dates can be ascribed to the change from the Julian to the Gregorian calendar by England in 1752, whereby eleven days were dropped. Many long-established towns of England and Ireland adhered to the Julian calendar for years after the Gregorian calendar became official. Remote areas of the American colonies were even more tardy in accepting the change.

Some participants in the Charlotte meeting may have used the Gregorian calendar. Others may have clung to the Julian. If that was the case, their recollections are not in conflict. May 20 (Julian) was May 31 (Gregorian).

Many Tar Heels are sure that there was a Mecklenburg Declaration. They are convinced that it clearly called for total independence, rather than conciliation.

Grateful admirers erected a statue of Captain James Jack in downtown Charlotte. Both the North Carolina state seal and state flag bear the date of May 20, 1775. But in 1830 an angry Thomas Jefferson penned a formal statement that denounced the Mecklenburg Declaration as fraudulent.

Precisely what took place in Charlotte on two momentous days, no one knows. But a tangled sequence of events suggests that Jeffersonians succeeded in burying a significant event in our nation's founding.

Governor Martin's letter was written after he had been forced to flee from New Bern. Penned from the safety of a gunboat, it is held by the Public Record Office in London. His document enumerates three enclosures, of which two are still in the archives.

His third enclosure—part or all of a newspaper—is missing from the file. A notation on the packet indicates, "On August 15, 1835, a paper was taken out of the file by a Mr. Stevenson," who was then U.S. ambassador to the Court of St. James.

Many analysts believe they know what newspaper was borrowed by Stevenson and never returned. According to their theory, it was the Cape Fear *Mercury* of Friday, June 23, 1775. This newspaper was taken by the high-ranking diplomat, they believe, because it included part or all of the lost Mecklenburg Declaration that included ideas and language used by Thomas Jefferson in preparing the document adopted on July 4, 1776. It was in response to charges of plagiarism that Jefferson wrote a fiery letter denouncing the Mecklenburg Declaration.

In modern times, fraudulent copies of the Cape Fear *Mercury* have been printed and circulated in an effort to bolster the case for North Carolina's priority in stating open defiance of the king and his armies.

The likelihood that the contest between Jeffersonians and Tar Heels will be resolved to the satisfaction of all is remote. Just what words and phrases were used in the Mecklenburg Declaration—if it ever existed—is unknown. Its disappearance, more easily understood than the theft of a newspaper from official British records, underscores a basic fact of life in the 1770s.

At its best, communication between widely separated American cities was little better than that between Boston and London. At its worst, it broke down completely. That made it difficult for people to know with certainty what took place outside their own experience— and impossible for persons today to unravel all the mysteries.

CHAPTER

18

Canada Could Be the Key!

"**J**oseph Reed is vital," mused George Washington. As president of Pennsylvania's second provincial convention in 1775, Reed did his best to prevent arming the colony. Now as military secretary to the commander in chief, it was essential that he face reality. So far he had shown little inclination to do so.

At his headquarters at Cambridge, Massachusetts, Washington gestured for his subordinate to sit. According to memoranda he later dictated, the commander in chief spoke eloquently and at length:

> The reflection on our present situation, and that of this army, produces many an uneasy hour when all around me are wrapped in sleep.
>
> I have often thought how much happier I should have been, if instead of accepting a command under such circumstances, I had taken my musket on my shoulder and entered the ranks, or, if I could have justified the measure to posterity and to my own conscience, had retired to the back country and lived in a wigwam.

For more than an hour, Washington detailed the sad state of colonial forces. Reed already knew the situation but failed fully to appreciate it. Much of what his commander said was summarized in a letter to Congress:

> My situation is inexpressibly distressing. Winter is fast approaching upon a naked Army, the time of their Service within a few weeks of expiring, and no provisions yet made for such important Events.
>
> Add to this the Military Chest is totally exhausted. The Paymaster has not a single Dollar in Hand, and the greater part of the Army in a State nor far from mutiny. I am of the opinion, if this Evil is not immediately remedied, the Army must break up.

No one knew better than Washington that his role had been narrowly defined. His orders were to lead armed men of the colonies in "the maintenance and preservation of American liberty." Then and later, he repeatedly stressed his certainty that his commission did not give him freedom to struggle for independence from the British Crown. His task was to lead in a loyal protest of such magnitude that London would sit up and take notice—and then initiate reforms.

Thinking aloud to Reed while pausing in his devastating summary of the state of the army, Washington pointed out, "Many British leaders clearly do not wish to make matters worse. We saw that in New York."

Reed had not been present in the city on June 25, but he knew what had taken place. Royal Governor William Tryon was due to make his official entry—coming by ship from London. Commander in chief George Washington expected to reach the city on the same day—coming by land from Philadelphia.

Only Broadway was wide enough to serve as a route for a line of march. If the two parties should meet on that street, the encounter would be embarrassing, if not much worse.

To the surprise of his subordinates and of patriots alike, Tryon acted like a British officer and gentleman. He agreed to postpone his arrival for four hours, to prevent the possibility of a confrontation.

Journeying from New York to Cambridge, Massachusetts, to take formal command, Washington was appalled at what he found there. He described the New Englanders, who made up the majority of the troops, as "an exceedingly nasty and dirty people." That verdict applied to officers and to enlisted men, for to the casual observer there were no significant differences.

Washington's men were entirely too democratic to suit their new commander. Few of them wore even partial uniforms, and enlisted men treated officers as comrades. Standing nearly a head taller than most whom he commanded, Washington barked orders. He must at once transform a motley rag-tag band of militia into a genuine fighting force!

Women, accustomed to staying close to husbands or sweethearts, were banned from sod huts and the buildings of Harvard College and the Episcopal Church. Absence without official leave and fraternization with the enemy would cause a man to feel the lash upon his bare back, warned Washington.

His imposing size made him instantly recognizable. Still, the commander in chief secured a light blue ribbon and wore it across his breast. He provided purple ribbons for his major generals, while brigadiers got pink ones and aides de camp wore green. Washington carefully recorded in his now-famous expense account his outlay of three shillings and four pence for his personal insignia.

Cockades were sent to field officers. Captains got yellow ones, and subalterns wore green. Sergeants had to settle for shoulder knots of red cloth, while corporals donned green ones.

Washington's symbols of rank were crude by comparison with the splendid insignia used by his foes. Yet his system of ribbons, cockades, and knots helped transform a motley horde of volunteers into a structured army with a functioning chain of command.

Organized companies varied in size, from about thirty to more than ninety men. Regiments and divisions were even more ragged. That meant the commander had to peruse a roster before he could know how many men he was sending to perform a maneuver. Standardization of units reduced regiments from more than forty to twenty-eight. Essential as it was, this radical change did nothing to improve the firepower of his men.

Most patriots who had weapons were equipped with clumsy muskets. Riflemen from Washington's native Virginia were appalled, upon arrival at Cambridge, to find that they carried the only weapons capable of hitting a target at two hundred yards. Washington studied the dilemma and came to a startling conclusion. Though rifles were splendid in guerrilla warfare, they were actually inferior to muskets in standard hand-to-hand combat.

"A musket ball weighs twice as much as that of a rifle," Washington pointed out to his aides. "That means it has more penetrating power. And most of our muskets can be equipped with bayonets, while rifles cannot. After a rifleman has fired two slow rounds, he will stand defenseless against a wave of attackers. Meanwhile, a stout fellow with a bayonet can defend himself even if he has no more powder."

Questions of pay were not so readily resolved. Most of the militia units were accustomed to being paid once a month, according to the lunar calendar. When Washington instituted the solar calendar, British leaders rejoiced. Faced with the loss of one paycheck each year, some grumbling Colonials seemed ready to desert to gain bounties offered by their foes.

Even those who seldom complained about their pay were prone to complain about the small quantities of poor food. Clothing was in even shorter supply. A British jokester warned his countrymen that Americans would surely win, if the struggle lasted for a twelvemonth. By that time, said he, His Majesty's troops would balk at going into battle against naked men!

Still, the most critical issue faced by Washington after having been in command for ninety days was that of enlistments. More than half of the eight thousand men whom he considered to be nearly ready for duty came from the Boston area. Most of their enlistments were due to

Uniformed patriots were rare, but a German cartoonist managed to see and to depict one of them.

expire at the end of the year, and many had made it clear that they would re-enlist only if offered incentives that would make their service more profitable and attractive.

Pay, food, and clothing were major issues, but so was idleness. Stout fellows who had rushed to enlist in expectation of seeing action very soon were disappointed and angry. Why sit around camp rotting? Far better to be busy in one's fields or shop than to do little except obey constantly changing orders and engage in an occasional drill exercise.

Enlisted men were made sober by seeing comrades receive thirty or forty lashes for infractions that most considered to be minor. Banding together, many of them began to clamor for a bounty as a reward for renewing their terms of service.

Washington may have felt secret sympathy for their demand, but he knew the mood of Congress. Money was so scarce that lawmakers were already being forced to issue bills of credit to have funds for the most essential operations of the fledgling government. Talk of a bounty for re-enlistment was futile. Any man who would not remain in camp without it would simply have to go home when his term expired.

One of Washington's own big expenditures was designed to establish a spy network in British-held Boston. From his informants, he learned the size of the enemy with surprising accuracy, even the sites at which heavy guns were mounted. So he pored over maps and reports many nights before reaching a verdict. It would be impossible successfully to take Boston with less than 10,500 men. With only about half that number ready for action, there was little that the commander could do except continue to whip his men into shape, wait, and hope.

Good news came in November. John Manley, commanding a schooner, had attacked and captured a British brigantine. Though the vessel itself was of little importance, its cargo constituted the most valuable prize yet seized by patriots on water. Washington learned with delight what the naval victory would add to his supplies: 2,000 muskets, 100,000 flintlocks, 30,000 round shot, 30 tons of musket shot, and one brass mortar. At Manley's suggestion, the 3,000-pound mortar was solemnly christened "Congress."

Washington chafed at having to ride his horse around his camps to inspect idle troops and wondered if he might direct his attention to some target other than Boston. Eventually he concluded that the time might be right to "make a somewhat different overture to the Canadians." Earlier, the patriots had tried to persuade the largely French-speaking settlers of the region to join forces with "the lower 13."

If diplomacy had accomplished nothing, perhaps a show of arms might lead these folk to sing a different tune! After days of planning, Washington outlined plans for a two-pronged move into Canada.

A substantial body of men would move over the Lake Champlain route. There would be no way to conceal their progress. Enemy scouts would be able to keep an eye on them from a distance.

Meanwhile, however, a second band of about one thousand men led by Colonel Benedict Arnold would use canoes to traverse the Kennebec River. With luck they would arrive at the St. Lawrence River, directly opposite Quebec, without having been detected. In a surprise attack they would swarm into the stoutly defended city and overwhelm it.

With Canada having fallen, Washington reasoned, London would readily make enough concessions to placate even the most ardent patriots. The Continental Army would disband and its commander could retire to his beloved plantation. Amity would prevail between Britain and her long-restless colonies.

There was one other basis for hope, however slim it might be. Lawmakers had not yet received an official reply from the Olive Branch petition framed by Congress. If well received by King George III, the conciliatory overture could make invasion of Canada unnecessary.

19

"Our Subjects in North America Are in a State of Rebellion"

"**G**overnor Penn is the man to smooth things over, no doubt about it," said a delegate from Connecticut. All around the room, heads nodded soberly. After all, it was one thing to put together a carefully worded petition to one of the most powerful men in the world. It was another thing to be sure that it would reach him and receive his attention.

William Penn's grandson had been born in England and educated at Cambridge University. He was said to have considerable sympathy for patriots, but as royal governor of the colony of Pennsylvania—loyal to Britain and her sovereign—he was regarded in London as being thoroughly sound.

Penn heartily approved of the measure taken by the Continental Congress. Strong language drafted by Patrick Henry had been rejected, and the delegates preferred the conciliatory tone of the document largely shaped by John Dickinson of Pennsylvania. He called it "A Loyal Address to His Majesty, King George III." John Adams contemptuously labeled it as an Olive Branch petition, a title that most patriots adopted.

William Penn arranged for a berth on a fast packet. For this mission, speed was essential. Delay in crossing the Atlantic would add to difficulties he knew he would face when he reached London.

Separated from Britain by more than six weeks, few colonists realized the king's position. In 1774, at the start of what seemed to be real trouble in the colonies, the monarch had sent a special message to his lawmakers. In it he called for them to hold firm and to resist all colonial attempts to thwart the will of the sovereign and his ministers.

Though some Colonials learned of the royal message, it had little or no direct impact. Not so the king's actions with respect to repeal of the hated Stamp Act. Possibly, but not positively, upon the advice of some

George III, Queen Charlotte, and six of their seventeen children.

of his ministers, the monarch declared that "the Repealing is infinitely more eligible than the Enforcing, which can only tend to widen the breach between this Country & America."

News of the king's position was received in the colonies with rejoicing. Bands played martial music for hours, and church bells rang. Lighted candles were placed in windows, and guns were fired. In New York, grateful citizens collected money with which to erect a four thousand pound lead statue of their gracious sovereign.

Neither New Yorkers nor others in the colonies knew the true situation in London. The sovereign and his ministers tried to remain coolly aloof from the situation in North America. By all means, collect all revenues and taxes possible; and maintain law and order, with due respect for the Crown. But keep the reins tight and make sure that all significant decisions are made in London.

Both the monarch and his ministers were aware that North America was larger than the British Isles. Wishing to control expansion of the colonies, London established a line beyond which loyal subjects were forbidden to settle. All English settlements must remain east of the Allegheny Mountains. Moreover, the powerful Indian tribes beyond the Alleghenies must be dealt with from London, not Philadelphia or New York.

George III did not initiate this policy. Neither did he reach a decision to forbid colonies to issue paper currency, desperately needed because English money was so scarce. However, he concurred in these and other measures that seemed reasonable from the perspective of

Westminster but were viewed as repressive from the cobblestone streets of Baltimore and Providence.

Norfolk, England, native Thomas Paine was successively a stay-maker, tobacconist, and excisemen. From years of observation, he was sure he knew what the king was really like. To Paine, he looked not at all like the sovereign glorified by the New York statue. As a result of friendship with Benjamin Franklin, he had become fascinated with America; so he fumed when gossip reached him reporting—correctly—that George III had said, "Every means of distressing America must meet with my concurrence."

Paine and his wife were separated in 1774, allowing him to go to Philadelphia under the auspices of Franklin. Soon the newcomer found the vocation for which he was born: that of political pamphleteer. He was impelled into that role by news that the monarch had openly gloated at the passage of the Boston port bill, a reprisal for the famous tea party. "Our German sovereign has now revealed his true colors," Paine told his American friends. Writing at a furious pace, he completed a white-hot message designed to convince all colonists that their true enemy was the king, not Parliament. Published as *Common Sense* in January 1776, it did not immediately win general acceptance.

Had it done so, the men who convened in Philadelphia for the Second Continental Congress would have wasted no time and energy with their Olive Branch petition. Only a few hotheads such as Patrick Henry agreed with Paine that George III was "a hardened, sullen-tempered Pharaoh." To many delegates, it bordered upon treason to charge, with Paine, that the monarch had embarked upon a course whose goal was suppression of cherished English liberties in every colonial region.

Patriots who had been born and reared in America lacked Paine's first-hand knowledge of affairs in London; so many of them scoffed at his charge that the monarch was the actual—not simply titular—head of the government. Taxation and other fiscal measures were the province of Parliament. Therefore, many patriots regarded it as foolish talk when they heard the proverbial saying that "the Crown has swallowed up the Commons."

Powerful men, some of whom were outspoken friends of the colonies, helped to shape actions of the House of Commons. To charge that ministers whom such people helped to select were mere cats-paws of their sovereign seemed a contradiction of the common sense that Paine claimed to offer.

George Washington did not give his approval to the Olive Branch petition. By the time it was adopted, he was on the way to Cambridge. A handful of other delegates to the Continental Congress refused to sign it as a matter of principle, but an overwhelming majority affixed

In 1778 angry New Yorkers pulled down their statue of the king and used its lead to mold musket balls. [NEW YORK STATE HISTORICAL ASSOCIATION]

their names to the document. Clearly, most of them hoped that moods would change as soon as the sovereign knew that hosts of Americans were loyal to him. Bickering and skirmishing that threatened to lead to worse could be brought to an end by the monarch.

The hopes of those who longed for compromise and peace proved to be groundless. Pennsylvania's governor received an official document on August 23, 1775. It consisted of a notice that although Penn had traveled three thousand miles to hand-deliver a humble petition from the Continental Congress, King George would not see him and would not accept delivery of the message he bore.

Devastated, the grandson of Pennsylvania's founder did not have the heart to face friends and colleagues whose hopes had been so high. He remained in England and did not return to America for many years.

News that the king had rejected the Olive Branch petition did not reach George Washington until October. By then, plans to seize Canada and bargain for concessions in return for its surrender to the Crown were mature. Matters had reached such a stage that it made little practical difference that George III had issued a proclamation on the heels of his rebuff of American moderates.

Under terms of the monarch's edict, except for Canada and the two Floridas, Britain's colonies in North America were formally declared to be in a state of rebellion. Whether in Bristol or Sheffield or Birmingham, in Boston or Philadelphia or Charles Town, every Englishman knew what this meant. His sovereign would immediately move to put down the state of rebellion by force of arms.

20

Daniel Boone Broke through the King's Fence

Alone in the Kentucke country never before in such great need of exercising all fortitude.

A climb to the summit of a commanding ridge caused all doubts to vanish. Looking around with astonishing delight, I beheld the ample plains and the beautious tracts below.

On the other hand, I surveyed the river Ohio that rolled in silent dignity, marking the western boundary of Kentucke with inconceivable grandeur.

At a vast distance I beheld the mountains lift their venerable brows and penetrate the clouds. All things were still.

I kindled a fire near a fountain of sweet water, and feasted on the loin of a buck. I laid me down to sleep and I awoke not until the sun had chased away the night.

That poetic description of Kentucky, forbidden to English settlers and later known as "the dark and bloody land," is attributed to Daniel Boone. Although the ideas were his, the words were not; self-taught, he wrote little and used phonetic spelling in describing his exploits.

Few accounts of the American Revolution summarize his accomplishments; some do not so much as mention his name. He fought in no well-known battle, wrote no pamphlets, and never went on record as opposing British tyranny. Yet he embodied the spirit of revolution. It was Boone, more than any other American, who dared to break through the legal fence erected by Parliament and the king. Carefully constructed with the goal of "containing the North American colonies," the 1763 barrier was designed to prevent fast-growing numbers of settlers from spilling over the mountains. Even in London, it was apparent that if that barrier did not hold, it would be difficult or impossible to govern effectively a population weeks away from Atlantic ports.

Romanticized in art, poetry, and prose, Daniel Boone never seems to have thought of himself as a knight in buckskin, charging against the chain mail of King George III and his ministers. He was simply a quick-witted, land-hungry frontiersman who saw an opportunity and seized it.

Boone's Quaker parents left Devonshire, England, for the uncertainties of the Pennsylvania frontier. Their sixth son was sixteen when they moved south to the Yadkin River valley in remote North Carolina. By then, Daniel was a seasoned woodsman whose annual take of deerskins and beaver pelts was envied by many older, more experienced hunters.

Marriage to Rebecca Bryan, a high-spirited young woman said to have strong Tory leanings, would have been enough to cause many a man to settle down. Not Daniel, though. Never interested in his farm, he continued to hunt and to trap, always looking for a better opportunity some place far away. He bought land near Pensacola in 1765 but abandoned Florida when Rebecca refused to live there.

With the deep South eliminated, Boone's options were reduced. He could stay on the Yadkin in his cabin, or he could do what few others had dared to do: cross the mountains into the West and try his luck in Indian country.

Indian trader John Finley accompanied Boone on a 1767 trip exploring Kentucky. Once he saw the vast, fertile land, Boone was sure that his destiny lay there. On a second trip he was captured by Shawnees but managed to escape and to live off the land for nearly two years.

Few other Americans, if any, knew as much about the region as did Boone in 1774. For that reason Virginia's royal governor, Lord Dunmore, selected him for an especially delicate, dangerous mission. Surveyors whom Dunmore had sent into Kentucky faced grave danger as a result of an Indian uprising. Unless warned and guided back to civilization, they were likely to be slaughtered. At Dunmore's urging, Boone and a companion set out to save the surveyors, covering 800 miles in just sixty-one days and bringing their men out alive. Boone was rewarded with a commission as captain of militia and was placed in command of three forts.

His "military experience" led admirers to call him Colonel Boone for the rest of his life. But a post of honor that required frequent inspection of the forts under his supervision offered neither the freedom nor the excitement on which he thrived.

A bit earlier, a North Carolina judge, Richard Henderson, had re-

Boonesborough, as it appeared about 1777.

ceived second- and third-hand reports about the country Boone had explored. His knowledge of law told him that three people would instantly object to any proposal to erect settlements there: King George III, the governor of North Carolina, and the governor of Virginia. Virginia's western boundary had recently been extended, although no one knew precisely where it lay. But the governor was sure that his colony included much of the region reserved for Indians.

Henderson pretended to be completely naive. Working through a network of agents, he managed to persuade Cherokee chieftains to come together at Watauga in 1775. There, in exchange for trading goods worth about £1,000, they solemnly ceded their lands south of the Kentucky River to North Carolina. No party to the transaction had the slightest idea how much land was actually transferred by the treaty; when surveyed years later, it measured about seventeen thousand acres.

Boone's glowing reports, conveyed to Henderson by others, had led to formation of the Transylvania Company and its subsequent treaty with the Cherokees. Hence it was logical for Henderson to select the frontiersman to build a road that would permit settlers to move into the region to buy land.

Daniel Boone chose the Cumberland Gap as the starting point. From it he cut a winding pathway that became famous as the Wilderness Road. Its completion meant that the legal fence erected from the other side of the Atlantic now included a gaping hole through which settlers were ready to pour, if only they could be sure they would not be scalped.

Again at the urging of Henderson, Boone agreed to establish a town and to build protective forts. Boonesborough, erected on the bank of the Kentucky River, was anything but elegant when Rebecca Boone and her daughter arrived in late spring 1775. Although accustomed to frontier life, she confessed awe and fear at having ridden more than three hundred miles without seeing a single church or even a wisp of smoke curling from a log cabin.

Her husband's new village consisted of less than half a dozen rough cabins strung along the bank of the river. There were a few cornfields, but no tobacco. Forts were in the planning stage, but they would not be erected for many months. A crude stockade, designed as a temporary defensive work, was only half completed. Anticipating the arrival of Kentucky's first two white women, sure to bring their fears with them, Boone arranged for a sentry to stand guard where the stockade stood open. He assured his wife, that soon it would thrive as the capital of the fourteenth colony!

Under the guidance of Judge Henderson, a government was formed, with Daniel Boone and five other men representing Boonesborough in the not-yet-established provincial legislature. Other delegates were elected in Harrodsburg and nearby settlements. Transylvania would soon take her place alongside Virginia, Massachusetts, and Maryland, it was believed.

No man to waste an opportunity, delegate Boone seems to have used his new office to encourage the processing of a land claim. Under its terms, he expressed himself satisfied with a mere 100,000 acres.

About ten days after formation of the new government was begun, the Reverend John Lythe called the settlers together under a great elm. It was only fitting, he told them, that they should remain in devout attention while he read the prescribed prayer for the health of

A heroic and imaginative lithograph showing Daniel Boone in the act of protecting his family from an Indian's attack.

the royal family in London.

Within twenty-four hours after that service of prayer for King George III and his family, a courier dashed into Boonesborough bringing sketchy but accurate word about "the big battle at Boston." No one who listened to his news with awe imagined that within three years, British officers in red coats would lead Indians in an attack upon Boonesborough.

That initial word from Boston was followed by other news pointing to the possibility of armed conflict between patriots and British. In this climate, Canadians sent emissaries into Kentucky with an offer from General Sir Guy Carleton. Any man who would join his forces, said the Canadian commander in chief, would be given equal rank and pay. Also, if the majority of Kentucky males accepted these terms, Carleton would personally guarantee that there would be no more harassment by Indians.

Boone and his comrades did not reply to the Canadian offer. They were not interested in quarrels between Bostonians and Londoners; they wanted only to build cabins, clear land, drink sweet spring water, rear huge families, and prosper in peace.

Daniel Boone and his followers had no direct impact upon the military struggle that erupted when all thought of compromise was abandoned. Yet without taking part in a single battle of consequence, they exemplified the revolutionary principle in action.

The Wilderness Road became the path followed by a constant stream of settlers. Many used it to leave Virginia for Kentucky, while others came from both Carolinas, Maryland, and Pennsylvania.

Many of these newcomers were, like Daniel Boone, land hungry, either as speculators or as farmers whose soil had lost its fertility. Some had accumulated burdensome debts which they confidently expected to leave behind when they crossed the mountains, and a minority had no clear motive except that of claiming land due to them as bounty for having spent a few months in the Virginia militia.

Regardless of what brought these restless folk to follow the footsteps of Daniel Boone, they represented the first great wave of westward movement in American history. Too far from centers of authority to be punished or even strongly reprimanded, they effectively thwarted the will of their king and of Parliament. Because they were the first to do so with impunity, reveling in the freedom conveyed by distance, they were the first truly free Americans.

CHAPTER

21

Quebec's Survivors Limped Home with Benedict Arnold

In about eight weeks we have marched near six hundred miles. With great fortitude, men have hauled their batteaux up rapid streams in which they were forced to wade most of the way, near 180 miles. They carried them on their shoulders near forty miles, over hills, swamps and almost impenetrable bogs.

Many of our cartridges are inserviceable, so that we have not ten rounds for each man. They are almost naked, bare footed and much fatigued.

To our great joy Gen. Montgomery has this morning joined us with about 300 men. We propose immediately to invest the town and make no doubt in a few days to bring Gov. Carleton to terms.

Colonel Benedict Arnold's letter of November 27, 1775, here greatly condensed, supports the view that he was more than half out of his senses. Events of the next few weeks made him a hero in Philadelphia, but many men whose blood was spilled in the snow of Canada later swore that their commander was raging mad.

Some ardent patriots favored early invasion of the region that had belonged to France until 1763. "These folks have little love for Britain; they will welcome our forces of liberation," the argument ran. "Besides, everyone knows that Redcoats are few and far between in that vast region. A small but fast-moving force can take Canada in a matter of weeks."

Delegates to the Second Continental Congress listened during May 1775 but refused to take strong steps. Instead of authorizing invasion, the body sent a "loving address" to Canadians. On June 1 this message was followed by a resolution that no expedition or invasion would be undertaken.

Within two weeks, the climate of opinion shifted. General Gage had issued a proclamation that labeled all Americans as rebels and traitors. Simultaneously, word was received that General Sir Guy Carleton was calling all Canadians to arms. His purpose, rumor said, was immediate invasion of New York and Massachusetts.

Congress had already established a chain of command. Directly subordinate to George Washington, General Philip Schuyler commanded the entire Northern Division, which included New York. Troops from Connecticut were sent to augment his forces, and he was notified that he might soon be sent to Canada.

Schuyler, like great numbers of his colleagues, was confident that many or most citizens of the region would offer help. He had broadsides printed in French and sent them to the north. They carried his assurance that Congress wished only to convey to Canadians the rights which belonged to every British citizen. Confident that his force would be swelled by recruits as he marched, Schuyler set out to take Montreal.

Colonel Benedict Arnold of Connecticut sought and got a conference with George Washington. "Montreal is easy," he insisted. "But that city, alone, will mean little. If we are to win Canada, we must take Quebec—and we must do so before winter sets in." Arnold persuaded Washington that when Schuyler's forces moved eastward from Montreal, they would be unable to take Quebec without help.

Arnold's argument was wholly sensible. Washington's intelligence reports indicated that Quebec held perhaps two hundred cannon. Situated on a high plateau and almost surrounded by massive fortifications, the Canadian city was believed to be the strongest citadel in North America. Therefore Washington agreed to send Arnold directly to Quebec to join forces with Schuyler for the assault.

At the time of their discussion in Cambridge, neither man knew that Schuyler was already seriously ill. Soon he had to turn his command over to General Richard Montgomery and return to New York.

English-born Montgomery, a professional soldier from age eighteen, had come to New York after leaving the British army in disgust. He quickly became a leader among the patriots and was made a brigadier general at the same time Washington was named commander in chief.

Montgomery's slow advance upon Montreal gave Carleton an opportunity to make his escape. By the time the city was captured without resistance, Carleton was well on the way to Quebec. There he acted swiftly and decisively.

Men from the warships *Lizard* and *Hunter*, anchored in the St. Lawrence River, were pressed into duty as soldiers. So were crew members of merchant vessels. His elite fighting force came from a regiment of Royal Highlanders, but by the time he finished conscripting Anglo-Canadian militia and French Canadians, Quebec's defender had nearly two thousand men under his command. He did not then know that remnants of Montgomery's force confidently expected to join with units led along a torturous eastern route by Benedict Arnold.

Overtly ambitious, Arnold had chafed at having to play a subordinate role at Ticonderoga, and he had fumed when he learned that Schuyler would lead the expeditionary force toward Montreal. That was when he presented to General Washington his plan for a second body of troops with which to make a two-pronged assault upon Quebec.

Washington put together a special force formed from troops of Massachusetts, Rhode Island, Connecticut, and Pennsylvania, augmented by Captain Daniel Morgan's Virginia riflemen. It would be comparatively easy to reach the mouth of the Kennebec River, known to be less than 250 miles from Quebec. For river travel, soldiers would need many clumsy batteaux, which at portage points would have to be carried. In spite of these considerations, the overall plan looked surprisingly good.

Having dispatched scouts to precede the main body of troops, Arnold pulled out of Cambridge with a strong, healthy army of invasion. One of its most colorful members was his personal aide, Aaron Burr, who brought along his Indian mistress. Called Jacatagua, the woman soon became famous throughout the expeditionary force as "the abnaki queen with Golden thighs."

Jacatagua proved more valuable than Arnold had anticipated. Legend says that it was she who solved the problem presented by stretches of river in which the current was so swift that rowing was impossible. Allegedly at her suggestion, soldiers attached ropes to each boat and then threw the ropes over their shoulders. Wading through icy water, fighting men were transformed into draft animals; and struggling mightily, they pulled their batteaux upstream, although some of the boats were damaged by striking against boulders.

That was just the beginning of their woes.

Some days, they made only three miles. As the weather became colder, food was consumed at a far greater rate than had been anticipated. Much powder became wet, and some muskets were water soaked so often that they became useless.

With 150 fearsome miles ahead, many of Arnold's men announced that they would go no farther. A vote was taken, and it was decided to permit "the ill and the timorous" to turn back. Once this decision was reached, a quarrel broke out over division of supplies. The men who had decided to pull out insisted upon having as much as those who were ready to push ahead.

As days stretched into weeks, the troops who had expected an easy march found themselves without food. They killed and devoured the only dog in the company, then made a thin paste of flour and water that they sipped while chewing shoe leather. Only an unexpected encounter with friendly Canadians who sold them food prevented starvation. By the time Quebec was within striking distance, Arnold calculated that they had waded 180 miles, hauling boats, and had carried boats on their backs across portages for a total of about 40 miles, all the while marching on half rations or less.

Because Benedict Arnold's name later became synonymous with "traitor," it is easy to forget that his march to Quebec constituted one of the all-time heroic military movements of the Western world.

While waiting for the arrival of the Montreal force now led by Montgomery, Arnold tried to estimate the odds. He calculated that Montgomery would bring at least one thousand men. Carleton, he believed, would be able to put together a ragged force comprising no more than four to five hundred. Quebec would be a pushover, and all Americans would recognize the true worth of Benedict Arnold!

When Montgomery finally appeared, his army had dwindled to less than four hundred men. Neither he nor Arnold realized the real strength of their opponents. They concurred, however, that they did not have manpower for a frontal assault in broad daylight. They would have to make good use of surprise.

The attack was planned for December 25 or 26, but the weather became so bitter it was impossible to follow the schedule. Every hour of delay increased tension, for enlistments of many men were due to expire at midnight on December 31. Enlisted men and officers alike made it clear that they were not sure they would fight after that deadline passed.

During a blinding snowstorm, the American commanders decided to push ahead on the last night of the year. When troops began to move about 4:00 A.M. on New Year's Day, Montgomery, who led one of the assault teams, signaled his men to follow him in single file. Ice had jammed in such fashion that the path they planned to use was reduced to a dangerously narrow ledge.

Not yet inside Quebec, the Americans were caught by a cannon shot. Montgomery died instantly, along with two of his officers and two subalterns. With command having devolved to Arnold, the attackers tried again from a different angle. Arnold was soon out of the action, felled by a ball that broke his knee. By now, it was clear that

750 half-naked men who had perhaps 400 serviceable muskets had spent weeks on the trail for nothing.

Soon after 9:00 A.M., the Canadians stopped firing and turned to mop-up actions. At least sixty Americans lay dead in the snow, while four hundred or so, including Daniel Morgan, were prisoners of war. The first great military venture of the thirteen British colonies had turned into disaster.

When news of the debacle trickled to Albany, Boston, and Philadelphia, John Adams put the blame upon John Dickinson. Dickinson's insistence upon compromise and his opposition to a call for independence had prevented a summer campaign that might well have succeeded, Adams accused.

Lawmakers agreed with Adams's assessment, and with Arnold still encamped before Quebec, they ordered that additional units be sent to fight under the injured hero. As a gesture of admiration and appreciation, on January 10, 1776, Congress elevated him to the rank of brigadier general.

Although forced to relinquish command to a senior general, Benedict Arnold remained in Canada until the last American unit pulled out in June. He insisted upon being in the last boat that transported his ragged veterans back to American soil.

All hope of winning Canadian support for the cause was gone. So was the possibility of using Canada as a bargaining chip. Nearly a year of violent deeds aimed at fostering reconciliation had seen the breech grow wider instead of smaller.

"God alone knows what the future will bring," many an ardent patriot admitted. "But this much is certain. Having demonstrated what he's made of, Benedict Arnold will be heard from again."

Part Four

Point
of No
Return

The rejection of the Olive Branch petition by King George III was followed by swift action on the part of his ministers. Plans for an all-out assault upon the rebellious colonies were perfected during the fall of 1775. By January, some patriot leaders knew the general details of the plan.

Clearly, reconciliation was not the goal of London. With that option eliminated, patriots had two choices: submit or wage all-out war. It was this situation that led to the Declaration of Independence. Once it was framed, colonial leaders knew that they had reached the point of no return. All hope of a peaceful settlement of differences was gone.

Lampooned by the British as dressed like a woman, Washington showed his manhood by ordering mass inocculation. [THE BRITISH MUSEUM]

22

"There Are Things More Deadly Than Bullets"

"**T**ake orders to all the regiments," George Washington directed. "Civilians who wish to enter the city are not to be impeded. But of fighting men, only those who are well pockmarked may go; all the rest are to remain in camp."

In mid-March 1776, these terse orders of the commander in chief were issued because spies had confirmed that smallpox was rife in Boston and scores of citizens were prostrate. Only men whose scarred faces labeled them as immune from the killer disease could safely enter the city they had liberated.

Eight weeks earlier, Colonel Henry Knox had reached Cambridge. His force of fighting men was not big enough to turn the tide, but he brought with him forty-three British cannon and sixteen mortars. Captured at Fort Ticonderoga, the heavy pieces had been dragged cross country for many weeks.

When they heard that they now had big guns, the patriots were infused with new fighting spirit and surged forward to capture Dorchester Heights overlooking Boston's harbor. Once that strategic point was secured, the weapons brought by Knox were pulled to the top.

General William Howe, commander of British forces holding Boston, saw what was taking place before the guns were in position. He sent couriers to warn Tories that they should join his fighting men and prepare to flee. The guns of Ticonderoga would soon make it impossible to keep a fleet in the harbor.

During a period of about ten days, one heavily loaded troop ship after another set sail for Nova Scotia. Washington remained in the liberated city for nearly a month, then led the main body of his troops to New York in a move designed to prevent Howe from using it as a base.

Smallpox raged out of control among units encamped before Quebec. Many soldiers of the ten new regiments sent by Washington became ill, boosting the roster of the critically ill. John Adams called the disease "ten times more terrible than Britons, Canadians, and Indians together." With hundreds of soldiers unable to stand erect, it was difficult to get enough men to carry the bodies of the dead from camp.

Dr. Louis Beebe, who kept a detailed journal, tried to describe the makeshift field hospital into which men were crowded shoulder to shoulder. "At any time," he wrote, "I see some dead, some dying, others at the point of death, some whistling, some singing—but many cursing and swearing."

"There are things more deadly than bullets," George Washington concluded soberly. Writing a formal letter to the Congress, he thanked its members "for their Care, in endeavoring to prevent the spread of the Smallpox in the Continental Army."

He did not say exactly what they had done. But he issued a stern order to his officers: any man caught experimenting with inoculation, a new and questionable procedure, would be cashiered. A single new case brought about by inoculation could trigger an epidemic.

In the climate of fear, even the iron nerves of the commander in chief became frayed. He exploded with anger when he learned from John Adams that Dr. Benjamin Church would almost certainly be found guilty if investigated on a charge of corresponding with the enemy.

Church had studied in London and was highly regarded by many leading patriots. They were delighted when he offered his services to the emerging fighting force of the colonies. Although he never held the title, Church was, for practical purposes, the first surgeon general of the Continental Army.

He came under suspicion in October 1775 when a letter "written by him in a curious cypher" was intercepted by James Warren, paymaster general of Washington's forces. With Church's court martial pending, damning evidence was accumulating rapidly.

Washington himself presided over the court martial and concurred in the verdict of guilty. Soon paroled, Church sailed for the West Indies and was lost at sea. Not until 1930 were the papers of British General Thomas Gage brought to the University of Michigan and carefully examined. They were found to include numerous traitorous letters from Church that gave the British leader detailed information very early, probably prodding him into the decision that led to the 1775 battles of Lexington and Concord.

Suspected traitors, smallpox, and the mounting certainty that Britain intended to wage an all-out fight created tension among the patriots. Therefore, officers listened carefully when some enlisted men

Military surgeons relied upon this illustrated manual for guidance in dealing with wounds.

who had been jailed for counterfeiting began babbling about "a Tory corps within the army."

According to them, at least six hundred soldiers were on the British payroll, receiving their funds through Mayor David Matthews of New York. It must have been Matthews, they charged, who arranged to send a dish of peas to Washington as a good will gesture. Fortunately, the commander threw the peas to chickens, who gobbled them up, then died.

There was no truth to the story of the poisoned peas, but Sergeant Thomas Hickey of Washington's own guard was unable to prove that he was innocent of trying to arrange for a drummer to stab the commander in chief. Hickey faced a court martial, was found guilty, and was hanged before a crowd estimated at 20,000 persons.

Treason, General Washington wearily concluded, was a disease that spread as silently and as fatally as smallpox. Exhorting his soldiers at the time of the execution, he piously told them that they could escape being tempted into mutiny and treachery "by avoiding lewd women who, by the dying confession of this poor criminal, first led him into practices which ended in an untimely and ignominious death."

Having dealt thus with treason, the commander in chief turned his attention to disease. Washington's own face was deeply pitted from a bout with smallpox at age nineteen. He rejoiced at the presence of the scars because they meant he could make contact with an active case of smallpox with impunity. Only a fraction of his men were so fortunate, and his spies informed him that the British were considering the use of smallpox as a weapon.

Writing to General Horatio Gates, the commander in chief admitted that as a last resort he knew of no way to defeat smallpox except by the risky course of inoculation. Thus he ordered that all troops under his command submit to "the necessity of Inoculation."

Officers who learned of the decision were warned to treat it with "the greatest Secrecy, because a moment's reflection will inform you, that should the Enemy discover our situation, they can not fail taking advantage of it."

Washington's general order requiring inoculation seems to have been the world's first attempt at mass immunization against a killer disease. Throughout the Continental Army men bared their arms, gritted their teeth, and submitted to the dreaded procedure.

As expected, there were serious consequences. Especially in the hospitals of Virginia, medical officers reported "much ill success." How many fatalities and how many crippling illnesses lay behind those words, no one knows.

Nevertheless, to the delight of George Washington, the majority of his soldiers became immune from smallpox without serious side effects. That meant he had, in time, a fighting army no longer susceptible to the killer disease, the scourge of the time.

Not knowing that he anticipated future programs for eradication of polio, measles, and other contagious diseases, Washington turned his attention to civilians. Disturbed by news that "the small pox has got into my family," he insisted that the three hundred or so persons at Mount Vernon be inoculated. Then he unsuccessfully urged that Virginians enact "a law to compel the masters of families to inoculate every child born."

Danger from British bullets remained high, but Washington was confident that he had reduced, if not eliminated, two great plagues that threatened to undo the patriot cause: treason and smallpox.

23

Massachusetts Chopped the Kindling and Virginia Struck the Flint

RESOLVED, That these United Colonies are, and of right ought to be, free and independent States: that they are absolved from all allegiance to the British Crown; and that all political connection between them and the State of Great Britain is, and ought to be, totally dissolved.

Richard Henry Lee of Virginia, an aristocrat of aristocrats, read in a clear, cool voice. Wearing a silk suit, he struck a splendid figure as he stood before members of the Continental Congress. John Adams later reported, "With 50 pairs of eyes fixed on him, not a delegate but knew perfectly what was coming when he rose to speak." No man present would ever forget Friday, June 7, 1776.

Adams jumped to his feet the instant Lee ceased to speak. Having carefully prepared to do so, he seconded the resolution before it could become mired in a mass of challenges and objections.

Speaking on behalf of the Virginia convention of May 15, Lee presented two other resolutions. Highly inflammatory at the time, they are largely overlooked today. Under their terms he proposed that the several colonies—which he called states, or political entities—should form a confederation. Furthermore, he urged that each state prepare to enter into foreign alliances.

Massachusetts had chopped the kindling with which to start a bonfire hot enough to roast all of London. Virginia struck steel against flint to light that blaze.

Carefully and methodically, the resolution that Lee presented to fel-

The Declaration of Independence was read to Continental soldiers standing at attention. [HOWARD PYLE PAINTING, *HARPER'S MAGAZINE*]

low Virginians indicted King George III. Rejecting widely held views that made the British ministry responsible for "our present Miseries," Lee called for giving up allegiance to the Crown. In doing so, he was confident that many in the Continental Congress would oppose such a step.

Richard Henry Lee was right.

Debate raged for the rest of the day and throughout Saturday. A powerful band of conservatives led by John Dickinson of Pennsylvania shouted that delegates from Pennsylvania and New York were bound by instructions of their assemblies and could not vote for independence, even if they personally wished to do so.

With matters at an impasse, delegates agreed to wait three weeks to take a vote upon Lee's resolutions. Meanwhile, it seemed prudent to move toward preparation of a statement to be presented if the resolutions passed. Even moderates from the middle states, who had threatened to walk out of the Congress, were eager to see that any statement offered should not be "huddled up in a hurry by a few Chiefs."

According to minutes prepared by Charles Thomson, secretary of the Congress, a committee of five was named in unusual order: Mr. Jefferson, Mr. J. Adams, Mr. Franklin, Mr. Sherman, Mr. R. R.

Livingston. Under normal operating procedures the name of the oldest member, Benjamin Franklin, would have headed the list. But this was no normal time; the youngest member, a Virginian, was listed first.

Elder statesman John Adams declined to draft the proposed statement. He proposed, instead, that Thomas Jefferson be instructed to prepare a declaration that the former colonies were now independent political powers, or states. Whether or not the emerging Declaration of Independence was in any way affected by the Mecklenburg Declaration claimed by North Carolina remains a matter of conjecture.

As drafted, Jefferson's document underwent drastic changes. At least twenty sections were modified, cut, or eliminated. One passage that did not survive laid the blame for the growing problem of slavery in America upon the doorsteps of a man far away:

He [King George III] has waged cruel war against human nature itself, violating its most sacred rights of life and liberty in the persons of a distant people who never offended him, captivating and carrying them into slavery in another hemisphere, or to incur miserable death in their transportation thither. This piratical warfare, the opprobrium of infidel powers, is the work of the Christian king of Great Britain.

By His EXCELLENCY

GEORGE WASHINGTON, ESQUIRE,

GENERAL and COMMANDER in CHIEF of the FORCES of the UNITED STATES OF AMERICA.

BY Virtue of the Power and Direction to Me especially given, I hereby enjoin and require all Persons residing within seventy Miles of my Head Quarters to thresh one Half of their Grain by the 1st Day of February, and the other Half by the 1st Day of March next ensuing, on Pain, in Case of Failure of having all that shall remain in Sheaves after the Period above mentioned, seized by the Commissaries and Quarter-Masters of the Army, and paid for as Straw

GIVEN under my Hand, at Head Quarters, near the Valley Forge, in Philadelphia County, this 20th Day of December, 1777.

G. WASHINGTON.

By His Excellency's Command,

ROBERT H. HARRISON, Sec'y.

LANCASTER: Printed by JOHN DUNLAP

Food became so desperately short that Washington was forced to seize grain from farmers.

Writing to his wife, Abigail, John Adams expressed certainty that the Lee resolutions and the declaration that stemmed from them would eventually pass. "Great Britain has driven America to take the last step," he wrote, "a complete separation from her; a total absolute independence, not only of her Parliament, but of her Crown."

Under intense public pressure, members of the Pennsylvania Assembly adopted a new set of instructions for their delegates to the Congress. Far from radical, the fresh orders simply permitted them to join with other delegates "in adopting such measures as shall be judged necessary for promoting the liberty, safety, and interests of America."

Richard Henry Lee's resolutions were adopted on July 2. After two days of furious debate, all opposition collapsed and the document largely drafted by Thomas Jefferson won approval.

A manuscript went immediately to printer John Dunlap, who ran off broadsides that were distributed by couriers. With his men standing at attention, George Washington read a broadside to them as soon as it was received at Cambridge. On July 19 Congress directed that an engrossed copy be prepared on parchment so that it could be signed as the official copy.

In later years Thomas Jefferson mistakenly affirmed that on July 4 the Declaration of Independence was signed by all members of the Continental Congress except John Dickinson. Paintings that depict the signing are based upon his faulty recollections. No one actually put his name to the document until August 2.

On that day, the engrossed copy was carefully compared with Jefferson's original. As man after man filed to the table to affix his signature, the air was electric with tension. It was clearly an act of treason against the sovereign to be identified with the call to renounce allegiance to him. Every signer's career—and his fortune—was at risk.

Charles Carroll of Maryland lived on a vast estate that he modestly called Carrollton. By far the wealthiest of the signers, he was the subject of wry humor as he approached the table. "There go a few millions!" a fellow delegate quipped as Carroll signed.

Broadsides and other printed copies were circulated without names affixed. For security reasons, names of the signers were kept secret.

When news of the Declaration of Independence reached London, it was at first treated casually; editors gave it only six lines in a newspaper. Soon, though, the mood of the British capital turned ugly. Authorities offered a substantial reward to anyone who would provide a list of signers. By royal edict, the men whose names were affixed to the damning parchment were branded as traitors subject to execution if apprehended.

In a retroactive move aimed at protecting them from royal wrath,

Richard Henry Lee.

the names of Richard Henry Lee and John Adams were deleted from journals of the crucial sessions of Congress. Names of the signers of the Declaration of Independence, although well known to an inner circle of leaders, were not made public for many months.

Reverence for the document that symbolizes the fire lighted by Virginia is modern in development. Today the engrossed copy with signatures—not Jefferson's original manuscript—is a national treasure and it is permanently housed in the National Archives Building in Washington. There it rests inside a Thermopane glass case that contains inert helium gas and a trace of water vapor. Special filters have been installed to protect it from light, and both temperature and humidity are constantly monitored.

In 1776, and for many years afterward, the document was treated almost casually. Troubles began for the parchment as soon as signatures began to be affixed. Numerous delegates were absent from the ceremonies of August 2. Thereafter, Charles Thomson had to unroll and then re-roll the Declaration every time a signature was added. By the time fifty-six names were written with several kinds of ink, some parts were showing signs of wear.

That was just the start of physical problems encountered by the document. During a period of 176 years, it was moved at least twenty-six times.

When the British threatened Philadelphia, patriots moved the Declaration to Baltimore. Then it went to Lancaster, Pennsylvania, for a twenty-four-hour stay before proceeding to York, Pennsylvania. There the document, along with other official papers of the emerging nation, was stored in the county court house. No one, not even Thomas Jefferson, seems to have worried over its possible loss.

Later it was stored in Princeton, New Jersey; Annapolis, Maryland; and Trenton, New Jersey. These stops antedated the period during which U.S. secretary of state Thomas Jefferson had charge of it, probably keeping it in his temporary office on lower Broadway, New York City.

Transfer of the seat of government to Philadelphia meant another journey for the document. After a few years it went to the new permanent site of government in a swampy wilderness along the Potomac River at Federal City, not then generally known as Washington.

When the British reached Washington, D.C., during the War of 1812, important papers were hurriedly taken away by a departmental clerk, Stephen Pleasanton. Pleasanton had no containers except bags of coarse linen, which he stuffed full of documents in time to get them out before the British burned many public buildings.

While in Pleasanton's care, the Declaration traveled by wagon over rough roads to Leesburg, Virginia, where it was for a time stuffed under the front steps of a clergyman's home. When it was returned to Washington, it was shifted from one building to another for years. While in the Patent Office, the parchment was badly damaged by sunlight.

Subsequently, it spent years in a room with an open fireplace. Heat and smoke added to the damage from handling, aging, and sunlight. "Because of rapid fading of the text and deterioration of the parchment," it was retired from public view in 1894.

Later placed between sheets of sealed glass and shielded from direct sunlight, it was shipped to the Library of Congress in an ordinary mail truck.

During World War II it was placed in a vault at Fort Knox for fear that the Japanese might bomb the nation's capital. Later, after it spent another decade in the Library of Congress, it went to the newly opened National Archives Building, this time transported in an army tank.

At least one specialist on the much-traveled charter of American liberty thinks that "The older the Declaration has grown, the more formal and ceremonial we have become about it, and its present shrine may be regarded as a sarcophagus within which it lies embalmed."

Clearly, an "embalmed parchment" is not what Richard Henry Lee, Thomas Jefferson, or John Adams had in mind during fateful weeks of 1776. They wanted—and got—fuel to feed the blaze ignited when the steel of mighty Britain was struck by the flint of a band of dissident colonies who, for the first time, were beginning occasionally to be termed the United States of America.

24

Salt Marshes and Palmetto Logs versus His Majesty's Warships

Preparing to move land forces against Charles Town, South Carolina, Sir Henry Clinton sent a courier to deliver the customary gentleman's offer:

> Whereas a most unprovoked and wicked rebellion has for some time past prevailed, I do most earnestly entreat and exhort [His Majesty's] subjects to return to our common Sovereign and to the blessing of a free government. In His Majesty's name, free pardon is offered to all such as shall lay down their arms and submit to the laws.

Having sent that message, Clinton moved his men to Charles Town's Long Island (now the Isle of Palms) and waited for naval forces to appear. Once big guns were ready to pound rebel installations, he planned to move his units through salt marshes and across a shallow trough that separated his base from fortified Sullivan's Island.

Plans for the greatest expeditionary force in British history had been developed and perfected during the fall of 1775. According to London's best estimate, the rebellion should be crushed no later than early fall 1776.

Sir Henry Clinton was named to head the land and sea operation aimed at smashing opposition in the southern colonies. Because Tories were most numerous and powerful there, it was deemed wise that Clinton and his force strike the first hard blow.

Afterward, General John Burgoyne was selected to head an army whose task was to put Canada under tight control, then sweep into the St. Lawrence River valley. Since the middle colonies were the most vexatious sources of trouble, the biggest force was to occupy New York and spread out from that base. William Howe and Robert Howe, brothers who held the rank of general and admiral, respectively, were named to accomplish this central task.

Trouble began early, although London was not aware of it for weeks. In northern waters, patriots captured a packet bearing diplomatic dispatches. When opened and read, they revealed that in late December at Whitehall, British leaders had formally adopted the three-pronged plan of action. Initially suspected as being part of a ruse to cause havoc in America, the seized documents were known to be authentic after Thomas Corbett of Charles Town seized a mail packet. In it he found letters addressed to royal governors from East Florida to Virginia. They detailed the British plan and stressed that the southern colonies would be the target of the first major action.

Warned in this fashion, Carolina leaders mustered into the militia all the men they could find. A secret citizens' committee was formed under the leadership of Henry Laurens, who insisted that every possible defensive step be taken.

It was Laurens who sent a vessel into Florida waters with the hope that a store of munitions might be found and taken. Even he did not expect that his expedition would yield nearly 15,000 pounds of powder seized at St. Augustine.

Alarmed at the prospect of having one-third of the colonies battered into submission, George Washington pondered before selecting a subordinate to go south. He chose General Richard Lee and ordered him to take charge in Charles Town. Lee dawdled for weeks, arriving just in time to pronounce the city's defenses deplorable. An attack was expected momentarily.

Lee was especially scornful of the installation that natives of the region called Fort Sullivan. Named for the island on which it stood, it was the work of Colonel William Moultrie. Having no other building materials, Moultrie had utilized palmetto logs to create a defensive post he believed big enough to hold one thousand men.

Fort Sullivan's size was not the issue, Lee said haughtily. He pointed out that it "consisted entirely of palmetto logs and sand— incapable of withstanding big naval guns for half an hour."

Moultrie's men had used no other building materials than those underscored by Lee. They had cut palmetto logs into twelve-foot lengths and with them erected two rows of palisades about sixteen feet apart. Sand was hauled to the spot and poured between palisades until it reached nearly to the tops of the logs. Cannon were stuck through embrasures to aid a sister fort on James Island in closing Charleston's harbor to hostile vessels.

Lee considered Fort Sullivan to be a pushover, a verdict shared by Clinton and relayed to Admiral Parker as he came closer to his objective.

Early in January, Parker began assembling a flotilla at Cork. Even-

Because British warships were unable to subdue Fort Sullivan, it was re-named Fort Moultrie in honor of its commander.

tually it included about thirty vessels to transport supplies and 2,500 troops led by the earl of Cornwallis. Eleven warships, whose combined firepower was known to exceed that of all artillery in North America held by rebels, were expected to make short work of Charles Town's defenses.

On February 13, 1776, Parker's huge command set sail, Clinton having left Boston a few weeks earlier. Tories of the Carolinas who had received word that they would have a major role in military action had formed numerous companies and regiments to aid the invading forces.

Quick action by patriots of North Carolina saw Tories defeated so decisively that they no longer constituted a reserve force. Meanwhile, Charles Town leaders brought in militia from outlying points and took every possible precautionary move. Under the direction of Laurens, churches and residences were stripped of their leaden window sashes—then very common—so the metal could be melted down and made into bullets.

At Fort Sullivan, Moultrie and his men were under no illusions. Only two sides of their installation were completed, and if the British should succeed in coming at them from a landward position, their only hope lay in the riflemen brought from Virginia by Lee.

Admiral Parker was surprised and angry to discover that his intelligence was faulty. Approaching Charles Town in mid-May, he expected to pass over the bar easily, drop anchor, and make leisurely preparations for launching a deadly barrage of gunfire. Instead, he found the bar to be so high that his two largest vessels could not pass over it. Forced to break down their big guns to lighten the ships, then to re-mount them after having passed over the bar, he lost two weeks.

Early on the morning of June 28, vessels of the British squadron began to take up positions inside Charles Town harbor. Parker's fifty-gun flagship, the *Bristol*, headed the first line at a distance of about two hundred yards from Fort Sullivan. With this vessel in the front line were the *Solebay*, the *Experiment*, and the *Active*. A second line was formed by the *Acteon*, the *Syren*, and the *Sphynx*. To the rear lay the twenty-eight-gun *Friendship* and a ketch, the *Thunder Bomb*, that was equipped to launch powerful ten-inch shells from its mortars.

Once he saw that his warships would soon be ready for action, Clinton ordered his men to cross the marshes and shallows that separated them from Fort Sullivan. Only a few units had moved into action when he received news that, unlike similar waters along Britain's coasts, the bottom of the narrow waterway he expected to cross was anything but uniform. Holes created by the tides were deep enough to cause an entire squad to drop out of sight in a matter of seconds.

Hastily revising his plan, the British general put many of his men into boats, but soon they found that numerous spots of very shallow water made the boats useless. A few men climbed out of them and ran toward Fort Sullivan, calling for its surrender. Instead of raising a white flag, defenders gave signals to riflemen, who released a volley of deadly fire.

Aware that he could not perform as he had planned and fearful that his career was damaged, Clinton called off the attempt to reach Fort Sullivan from the landward side. So he ordered the warships to open fire, assuming that they would reduce the rebel installation to splinters with a few good volleys.

Balls from the *Bristol, Experiment,* and *Active* hit their target almost immediately. But the soft palmetto logs did not splinter, and most of the missiles that penetrated them were stopped by sand behind the palisade. One lucky shot entered through an embrasure and killed half the members of a gun crew, but these unlucky fellows were the chief casualties inside Moultrie's structure that Lee refused to call a fort.

For a time the installation was without an emblem, for a British ball cut down the staff that held it. Sergeant William Jasper dashed into heavy fire in order to retrieve the flag and fasten it to a palmetto tree, an exploit that made him regionally famous.

Gunners inside Fort Sullivan were ordered to take their time, aim carefully, and try not to waste a single shot. Firing at comparatively close range, they raked the flagship of Admiral Parker so effectively that within two hours half of his officers were dead or wounded. Although British officers did not know it, by then Moultrie and his men were practically out of powder. After holding their fire until five hundred more pounds of powder could be brought from Charles Town, they resumed their deadly fire at the crippled ships.

In a move designed to draw fire away from their flagship, the captains of three frigates moved toward Sullivan's Island, only to run aground. After several hours, crewmen managed to get the *Sphynx* and the *Syren* off what natives of these waters called the Middle Ground, a hidden sand bar, but the *Acteon* was stuck fast.

As sunset approached, Admiral Parker's signal sent most of his warships lurching toward the open sea. They had used more than 100,000 pounds of iron and at least 30,000 pounds of gunpowder. Rebels under Moultrie had employed at most 15,000 pounds of powder and not a single shell such as those launched from the *Thunder Bomb*. Yet the attackers counted about 250 dead and wounded against 12 defenders dead and 24 wounded.

Official reports of the stunning and humiliating failure said little about palmetto logs, salt marshes, and sand. Patriots everywhere rejoiced when they learned that firepower of mighty battleships had been made futile by an improvised fortress. George Washington and his aides discussed Charles Town at length, after which they agreed that any combined land and sea operation directed from a distance of three thousand miles was likely to fail to take topography and other local factors into account.

When word of the fiasco reached London, it served only to harden the stance of leaders who had approved the operation. Tradition has it that at least one subordinate in the State Department was glad to learn that the expedition against the southern colonies was being put on hold for an indefinite period. "A man such as Lord Cornwallis never should have been sent to Charles Town," he reputedly said. "He's far too good a soldier for such a puny operation. Now that he is free to move into the middle colonies, we shall hear from him again soon, and rebels will be whistling out of the other side of their mouths."

25

David Bushnell Launched High-tech War

Writing from New York in October 1775, Samuel Osgood confided a military secret to John Adams: "The famous water machine from Connecticut is every Day expected in Camp; it must unavoidably be a clumsy Business, as its Weight is about a Tun. People say it will take a year to put it into action against the enemy."

Clumsy or not, the device conceived and built by a man just out of Yale College was North America's first piece of high-tech military equipment. David Bushnell of Saybrook, Connecticut, confessed to having been obsessed with it for many months:

"My education was long deferred, due to my father's ill health," he is reported to have said many times. "Only after his death did I secure a tutor, who prepared me for entrance into Yale College. It was there, during my first year, that I accidentally discovered that gunpowder can be exploded under water. Once I knew this hitherto undiscovered fact, it became a controlling force in my life. Somehow, I knew that I was destined to put this to awesome use."

By the time he graduated at age thirty-three, he had completed the design for a machine that he confidently expected to employ against the British.

Nothing remotely like it had ever been seen. Affectionately called "my turtle" by the inventor, it looked a bit like a huge animal floating on the surface of the ocean with its head held high. As envisioned by Bushnell, it would operate under water to blow vessels of His Majesty's navy sky high.

Connecticut's leader of the provincial council of safety, along with several of his subordinates, turned out for a demonstration in February 1776. They were so impressed with the potential of the "turtle" that they gained the ear of George Washington. He reputedly managed to find money needed for perfection of the invention but was doubtful

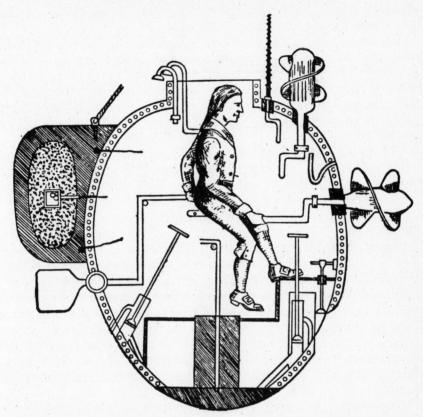

David Bushnell's one-man water machine was propelled by its operator's muscles.

that it would make big naval guns obsolete. According to Washington, the complicated device meant that "too many things were necessary to be combined, to expect much from the issue against an enemy who are always on guard."

Washington's skepticism was not shared by leading patriots to whom its secret was revealed. Many were certain that clashes in Boston would soon be obscured by much larger battles in or near New York. That city made an obvious target; with a population of 20,000 it was second only to Philadelphia in size on the continent. Also, its spacious harbor practically invited use by troop transports and warships.

What London expected would be the central campaign to bring a swift end to rebellion in the colonies began in July 1776. Sir William Howe, fifth viscount of Howe, had been in command at Bunker Hill, but despite his poor showing in that engagement, he was named to command the second of three thrusts against the rebels. His brother

Richard, whose sailors admiringly called him "Black Dick," headed naval forces attached to the expedition.

Unlike British leaders who were so eager to capture Charles Town that they failed to secure proper information about the locality, the brothers Howe were intimately acquainted with New York and her harbor. They selected Staten Island as a point of debarkation and began pouring troops into the colony as fast as transports could bring them. In about sixty days, General Howe assembled a force of at least 32,000 men.

Howe's only real complaint stemmed from more than nine thousand of his soldiers not understanding his orders until they were translated into German. Unable to assemble from their own citizens an army strong enough to crush the rebellion quickly, London's leaders reluctantly decided to hire mercenaries. Manpower was plentiful in the impoverished German state of Hesse, and it was natural to turn to the region from which the royal family came. Hessian mercenaries were poorly trained, generally dirty, and slow to obey orders; but they were considered essential to a speedy victory across the Atlantic.

In late August the decisions made in London brought results. Howe's forces, Hessians included, delivered a series of sledge hammer blows at Continental forces led by General Israel Putnam. The patriots were so out-manned and out-gunned in the battle of Long Island that they suffered a crushing defeat. Accordingly, General Washington hastily withdrew his entire force from Brooklyn Heights to Manhattan.

City streets offered poor protection to the Continentals; the British advanced slowly and methodically, and Washington decided to evacuate New York. Having withdrawn to a strong position on Harlem Heights, on September 16 he managed to repulse wave after wave of Redcoats who tried to storm his defenses.

It was during this time that David Bushnell sent the "turtle" for its first swim against the enemy. His target was the sixty-four-gun *Eagle*, flagship of Black Dick Howe's vast fleet anchored in New York waters.

Sergeant Ezra Lee, hand-picked to operate the one-man water machine, was familiar with its novel devices. He had practiced many times with the vertical and horizontal screw propeller and rudder and knew that in calm water he could easily make three knots an hour. Having descended several times, he was familiar with the depth gauge, lighted by phosphorus.

Lee had full confidence in the vessel's explosive device, or torpedo. Also fashioned of heavy oak, it sat above the rudder. Loaded with 130 pounds of gunpowder, it was designed to be detached as soon as the operator fastened it to a target by means of a hand-operated screw that under test conditions readily bit into the hardest wood. A clock, which could be set for twenty or thirty minutes was rigged to fire the tor-pedo's warhead when the "turtle" was safely away from the blast.

Late in the evening of September 7, Ezra Lee crawled into the "tur-tle" and set out to blow up the *Eagle*. After slowly working his way to the side of the battleship without being observed, the cautious Lee waited until midnight to make physical contact with his target.

It was an easy matter to maneuver the "turtle" into a suitable posi-tion at the proper depth. But when he began to turn his auger to penetrate the side of the warship, he soon found that he faced an unex-pected obstacle. Failure of the bit to enter the side of the *Eagle* con-vinced him that the British must have equipped the ship with expensive copper sheathing. He moved to another spot, and tried again without success. After a third futile attempt to penetrate the hide of the *Eagle*, Lee decided that it was useless. He cut his torpedo loose and let it drift until it exploded, meanwhile working his way under water back to his starting point.

The initial failure simply fired David Bushnell's enthusiasm. He sent the "turtle" swimming again a few nights later, this time in the Hudson River. Sergeant Ezra Lee gave a detailed account of his experi-ences in later years. His story makes it uncertain, however, whether or not it was a second failure that persuaded Bushnell to launch his tor-pedo against the frigate *Cerebus* from a whale boat. At Black Point Bay, near New London in the inventor's home colony, the successful explo-sion of his novel device killed three workmen and injured another. That seems to have ended the career of torpedoes built for the world's first killer sub.

Only a few days after Lee's initial failure, Captain Nathan Hale ven-tured beyond enemy lines dressed as a civilian. Detected, he was sum-marily condemned as a spy and hanged in an apple orchard. His famous last words, "I regret that I have but one life to give for my country," may have inspired David Bushnell to experiment again. Soon he devised another set of mechanisms that, for their day, con-stituted state-of-the-art technology.

Blacksmiths and gunsmiths of Bordentown, New Jersey, worked under his direction to manufacture twenty barrels made of heavy oak banded with iron. To avoid arousing the suspicion of Loyalists, empty containers were moved in a series of short hauls made only at night.

Bushnell himself described his new assault against ships of the Royal Navy: "I fixed several kegs under water, charged with powder to explode upon touching anything as they floated with the tide. I set them afloat in the river, above the English shipping at Philadelphia, to fall with the ebb upon the shipping."

These never-before-seen explosive devices might have accomplished their purpose had it not been for the weather. Soon after Bushnell's

Captured after having gone behind enemy lines as a volunteer, Nathan Hale was executed without a trial.

floating bombs hit the water on a night in late December, winter winds began to howl fiercely. Ice that formed in the river impeded the movement of his powder-filled kegs, and the oak barrels, which today would be called floating mines, did not reach their objective until well after daybreak.

British tars who spotted several of them were curious and alarmed, so a longboat was dispatched to pick them up. While hauling one of Bushnell's powder kegs out of the water, the sailors caused it to explode. A man of few words, the inventor tersely reported, "Several persons who imprudently handled it too freely were killed or injured."

Thoroughly alarmed, ships' captains issued hasty orders; and for hours, guns fired at any object floating down the Delaware River. It took days for red-faced British officers to discover the nature of the infernal machines that had been launched against them. The poet Francis Hopkinson celebrated the unmanned attack in twenty-two stanzas of verse that he called "The Battle of the Kegs."

Washington and his generals decided to stick to muskets and artillery, rifles and bayonets for the duration of the conflict.

CHAPTER

26

A Magnet for Adventurers and Soldiers of Fortune

"**I** have come to fight, a victim of love," Thaddeus Kosciuszko said to George Washington through an interpreter.

Naturally, the continental commander in chief assumed that his new Polish volunteer was motivated by love of freedom. He failed to ask questions that would have revealed that Kosciuszko fled from his native country after an unfortunate love affair. Reputedly having won the heart of Ludvika Sosnowska, he incurred the wrath of the girl's father, whose retainers nearly killed the young nobleman and caused him to flee to Paris.

It was in the French capital, he explained to Washington, that he heard of "the glorious revolution that was about to erupt 3,600 miles away." Borrowing money on an impulse, he purchased passage to America and reached Philadelphia about thirty days before Bushnell's water machine was first used against the enemy.

As a man of noble birth who had been educated at the military academy in Warsaw, he naturally expected to be given high rank. After perusing a letter of recommendation written in France by Benjamin Franklin, General Washington reluctantly made him a colonel of engineers. America's commander in chief was not enthusiastic about using an officer who spoke only a smattering of broken English.

Always cautious, Washington said nothing to suggest to his new recruit that he might be coming aboard a sinking ship. Disaster had dogged the Continentals ever since General Howe had brought his enormous contingent of men to the colonies. Seemingly always on the retreat, General Washington had abandoned New York to Howe and withdrawn to White Plains. There he decided to make a stand, but he was forced to flee once more, leaving a great number of casualties behind.

On Lake Champlain, Benedict Arnold's fleet that mounted eighty-

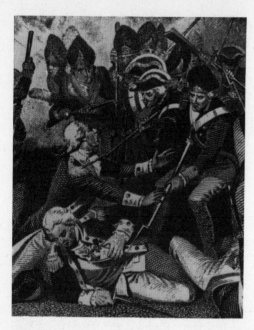

Mortally wounded, DeKalb was made a prisoner of war.

three guns was thoroughly trounced by a British fleet that had only four more guns. When 13,000 Redcoats overwhelmed Fort Washington in mid-November, they reduced the size of patriot forces by the men killed plus 2,818 prisoners. This victory cost the British less than 500 men. Another ominous development was the assignment of Lord Cornwallis to head the expedition ordered to seize Fort Lee, New Jersey, from Colonials under General Nathanael Green.

Kosciuszko was assigned to design defensive works in the region below Philadelphia. During this period of gloom for the patriots, in a matter of months the Polish volunteer built a semicircular series of breastworks that stretched for half a mile without a break. Once this lengthy installation was completed, tiny forts on the Delaware River, held by colonial forces, were in a position to defend themselves.

Washington was so delighted with what Kosciuszko had accomplished that he later sent him to erect fortifications to guard West Point on the Hudson River. During four years of experience in the field and in combat, Kosciuszko rose to the rank he had aspired upon reaching America, brigadier general. Years later, Congress rewarded him with fifteen thousand dollars and a tract of five hundred acres of land in Ohio.

Meanwhile, a soldier of fortune who had taken refuge in Paris became acquainted with Benjamin Franklin and Silas Deane, emissaries sent to the French capital by Congress. "I am Baron de Kalb," he informed the Americans, "and I visited your land nearly a decade ago."

Actually dispatched to the colonies to determine popular sentiment concerning Great Britain, far the most formidable military foe that France then faced, the man born in Huttendorf, Germany, had sent detailed reports to Paris.

Franklin and Deane failed to ask him for certified credentials, and they seem never to have discovered that their new friend was a peasant who had elevated himself to the nobility. Highly impressed with de Kalb, Silas Deane drew up for him a commission as major general and urged him to hurry to Washington's side.

Some members of Congress, delighted to have another member of European nobility in the armed forces, persuaded their colleagues quickly to ratify Deane's unauthorized action. As a result, "Baron de Kalb" saw action in a new attempt to invade Canada, then went south for the duration of the conflict, when he fought gallantly against Cornwallis during the siege of Charleston. Afterward at Camden, South Carolina, he received eleven wounds in a single battle. Barely able to mumble his name and rank when captured by the British, the bogus nobleman bled to death under the medical care of his captors.

Kalb, as he is usually listed today, performed one feat that made all of his battlefield exploits seem insignificant. Once he had won the confidence of Silas Deane, he proceeded to recruit other Europeans who said they were willing to fight in America against the British. When the German soldier of fortune reached Washington's camp, he had with him more than a dozen additional volunteers.

Although the names of most of them are now forgotten, one of Kalb's recruits had the indefinable but magical charisma that Americans later associated with John F. Kennedy. Barely past his twentieth birthday, Marie Joseph Paul Yves Roch Gilbert du Motier, the marquis de Lafayette, instantly won the heart of George Washington. Treated almost as though he were an adopted son, the wealthy French nobleman eagerly offered to serve the Continental army without pay.

Beginning to be wary of foreign adventurers, Congress hesitated to accept Lafayette's services. His willingness to serve without pay caused many members to take a second look at the young Frenchman. After checking his credentials and finding him to be a genuine nobleman, the lawmakers voted to make him a major general but refused to assign him to an active command.

Hence it was as a major general that young Lafayette joined Washington's staff. His conduct in battle soon brought him active command of a division of Virginia light troops. After the dreadful winter at Valley Forge, he was selected by Congress to carry out yet another invasion of Canada. Like Benedict Arnold, he had only a handful of men and was expected to move forward during the dead of winter. Nothing came of the proposed "irruption into Canada," but, instead of waning,

Lafayette, as portrayed by Alonzo Chappell.

the popularity of the handsome young foreigner waxed.

Kalb's recruit fought throughout the long conflict between Britain and her colonies, never with notable distinction but always gallantly. Perhaps it was his gallantry that in time caused him to symbolize the contributions made to the Revolutionary cause by foreign volunteers. Few other men whose primary allegiance was to a European power have won the hearts of Americans as did the marquis de Lafayette.

His countryman Marduit de Plessis is seldom remembered. Yet it was Plessis who taught Americans to build stout fortifications from felled trees. Trimmed to thrust three iron-tipped projecting limbs forward and placed at intervals of about fifteen feet, trees formed protective chevaux-de-frise that were strong enough to stop anything but a massive assault. So effective were these crude-looking installations that they were widely used by American military engineers for nearly a century.

Dozens of other Europeans, drawn to the American conflict, fought under Washington for months or years. Some proved acutely embarrassing to the commander in chief, but others played significant, though subordinate, roles in the lengthy struggle.

Cheshire, England, native Charles Lee may have profited most from his Continental army years. A professional soldier who never rose above the rank of lieutenant colonel in the British Army, Lee first came to America during the French and Indian War. He later became a major general in Poland and served under the czar of Russia before returning to the American colonies.

Despite his outspoken opposition to American independence, or perhaps because of it, many members of the Continental Congress were elated when he offered his service, with a thirty-thousand-dollar price tag attached.

Congress made him a major general, but he never got along well with his commander in chief. Strange tactics during the Battle of Monmouth led to a court martial and suspension from command, and he whiled away much of his time during suspension by writing insulting letters to lawmakers. These documents created so much hostility that he achieved an unusual distinction: he was the only soldier of fortune of high rank to be dismissed from the Continental army.

Frederick William Augustus, baron von Steuben, did not get a financial arrangement like that of Lee. Neither did he vie with Lafayette for the affection of his commander in chief and that of colonists in general. He shared a major quality with de Kalb: his credentials were false.

Some scholars believe that Benjamin Franklin forged papers brought to America by the veteran who had fought under Frederick

Count Pulaski.

the Great. Presenting himself as a lieutenant general in Frederick's service, Steuben was actually a half-pay captain.

If Benjamin Franklin had a hand in preparing the documents that Steuben presented to George Washington, that may have been Franklin's most notable wartime achievement. For it was the Prussian sponsored by Franklin who set up a professional training program for Continental soldiers.

Cadres meticulously drilled by Steuben were returned to their units to teach their comrades, and the new tactics spread rapidly throughout the Continental fighting forces. It was at Steuben's instigation that George Washington issued his famous "Regulations for the Order and Discipline of the Troops of the United States," a manual that for thirty-three years served as the "bible" of U.S. Army drill masters.

Elevated to the rank of major general in 1778, Steuben fought with distinction at Yorktown. At war's end he was rewarded by Congress with a pension of $2,500 per year, and New Jersey gave him sixteen thousand acres of worthless wild land.

A genuine count was one of the last foreign volunteers of significance to report for duty in America. Count Casimir Pulaski, who briefly had been commander in chief of the Polish army, became an outlaw when a revolutionary movement led by him failed. Like Lee, he spent a period in the Russian army before deciding to cast his lot with the freedom fighters in America.

After conducting himself bravely at Brandywine, he was placed in command of cavalry and made brigadier general by a grateful Congress. Fighting constantly for more than two years, he was mortally wounded during the siege of Savannah. Grateful citizens of the southern city erected an imposing monument to his memory.

With the possible exception of Lafayette and a handful of men whose names are now forgotten, foreign volunteers did not come to fight for freedom. Most were running from their past and trying to secure their future. Regardless of motives that brought scores of them here, they played a significant part in what initially seemed to be foolhardy defiance of the world's most powerful nation by a handful of rebellious colonists.

27

Holiday Festivities Gave Washington an Unexpected Edge

Above Trenton Falls
23rd December, 1776
To Joseph Reed, Esqr.

The bearer is to inform you that Christmas day at night, one hour before dawn, is the time fixed upon for our attempt at Trenton. For Heaven's sake, keep this to yourself as the discovery of it may prove fatal to us. Our numbers, sorry am I to say, being less than I had any conception of; but dire necessity, will, nay must, justify our attack.

I have now ample testimony of their intention to attack Philadelphia, as soon as the ice will afford the means of conveyance. We could not ripen matters for our attack before the time mentioned in the first part of this letter, so much out of sorts, and so much in want of everything are the troops.

Your obedient servant,
George Washington

Most units of the Continental army had been in retreat during the months since Washington took command. Now with the end of the year almost at hand, the commander in chief faced crucial decisions.

Having moved toward Trenton, New Jersey, he knew himself to be in an awkard position. The Redcoats were aware of his presence and had brought out all available forces to defend their hold on the city.

Far better equipped than were the patriots, the British would surely bring more troops by boat from New York very soon, weather permitting.

Practically all defenders of Trenton were hated Hessian mercenaries brought over by General Howe. Colonel Johann Gottleib Rahl, their commander, was reputed to be "a good fighter," and his effective force of about 1,550 men was made up of three full regiments, some twenty light dragoons, and about fifty chasseurs. Two pieces of artillery were stationed in front of Rahl's quarters, and four more big guns had been mounted at what Rahl considered to be strategic points.

British scouts, reporting daily about Washington's presence in the region, persuaded the Hessian to post two picket guards. Both were stationed on roads leading into Trenton. To the surprise and delight of the patriots, their scouts reported that the river front in general and the ferry in particular seemed to be unguarded.

For Washington, it was a classic case of "now or never." The short enlistments of many of his soldiers would expire on December 31. That meant that on January 1, his effective strength would be cut by at least one-fourth. In an unusually despondent mood, he made an entry in his diary shortly after having dictated the letter directed to Adjutant General Joseph Reed. Writing for his personal record, the commander in chief tersely concluded that "New Year's Day may see the end of our effort."

The predawn hours of Christmas Day brought a surprise. Riding close to the head of his 2,400 men as they moved toward Trenton, Washington suddenly noticed moving silhouettes. Spurring his horse into a gallop, he found himself confronting a group of ragged strangers.

"We, too, are Virginians!" an officer shouted. "We have been sent across the Delaware River on a scouting mission."

General Washington, who knew nothing of such an expedition, demanded additional details and was thunderstruck at what he heard. "We stumbled into Trenton by chance," explained the officer. "When a sentry ran out, we shot him. Then we began the retreat that has brought us to this point."

Wordless, the commander in chief pondered briefly. Clearly, the enemy would be on guard as a result of accidental interference with his plan of operation. But since there was no other target within marching distance, he must proceed or lose what appeared to be his best opportunity for a victory. Waving his sword, Washington shouted, "On to Trenton!"

Trenton had been selected for his offensive because Washington considered Hessians to be less disciplined than English-speaking Redcoats. He knew that for Germans, Christmas was likely to be a day of eating and drinking. By debarking after the sun set, his troops would

An early woodcut depicted Washington's crossing of the Delaware River in an oar boat. A later and much better known painting, full of errors, portrayed him standing proudly in a boat of a quite different type.

be safely across the Delaware River by midnight. They would then march five or so miles, divide into columns, and surround the place.

As plans go, it seemed to be the best that could be devised under the circumstances. Without a victory soon, the entire American movement for independence was likely to collapse.

Washington commandeered a flotilla of ore barges designed to carry heavy freight when propelled by poles that pushed against the river bottom. Crossing the Delaware at a point well above their target, the first contingent of Continentals got across without incident.

Then the weather turned extremely bitter. Air and water temperatures dropped below freezing and continued to drop. Soon chunks of ice began forming, and within half an hour they were large enough to impede the movement of the clumsy boats. To make things even more difficult, sleet began to fall in sheets, cutting visibility to near zero.

At about 4:00 A.M., Washington calculated that at least two thousand of his men had crossed the river. He could not wait for more to follow. Unless he reached Trenton by daylight, it would be useless to strike. So men with less than a week of military service remaining slogged through frozen mud toward the enemy. Many of them had learned that the accidental contact by the stray band of Virginians had put the Hessians on the alert. Still they moved ahead, prodded by their commander.

In New York, General William Howe had doubted the wisdom of placing Trenton under the command of a man who spoke no English. But at the urging of subordinates he yielded and said, "The colonel earned it by his courageous action at White Plains and Fort Washington—where rebels took a terrible beating."

Rahl's fellow officers, and many of his fighting men, were less concerned about the language problem than the habits of the professional soldier. "He is a heavy drinker," one contemporary noted, "who is prone to get into barroom brawls when off duty."

Born in the Prussian state of Hesse-Darmstadt and from boyhood determined to spend his life in the army, Rahl came to America with the first contingent of mercenary troops sent by Britain. An acquaintance described him as "a big, noisy bully of a man."

Firmly entrenched in Trenton and separated from Washington's forces by the Delaware River, he knew that he had an important strategic advantage. Also, British intelligence reports indicated that "rebel forces are fast running out of food; clothing of many is in tatters; most dreadfully disorganized, it would appear that troops are on the verge of mutiny."

Rahl's men were well fed and had plenty of warm clothing. In contrast with the Continentals who had only tents and other temporary shelters, the mercenary troops were quartered in a two-story stone barracks and several brick houses. Their commander occupied a large frame house, the property of a tannery and iron works owner who insisted upon being host to the Hessian leader.

Colonel Rahl made the most of his situation. Frequently he stayed up much of the night, then slept late. He liked military music, so every day he followed the ceremonial parade of troops about town to listen to the music of his bandsmen.

Until Christmas Day, the German-speaking commander remained jittery. When he saw snow on the ground early that morning, he rejoiced. Even if "the barbarian called Washington" would not honor the sacred day, surely the weather would halt him in his tracks!

Rahl spent part of the morning playing checkers with Stacy Potts, then went to the home of Abraham Hunt for a Christmas party. Since Hunt was a wealthy merchant, he would be sure to have plenty of liquor for his guests.

Tipsy by late afternoon, the Hessian challenged fellow merrymakers to meet him at the card table. "Skat! Skat!" he insisted, according to his host, employing one of the few English words he knew.

When leading an assault, Hessians preferred the sabre to the musket.

Skat is a three-handed game played with thirty-two cards, of which two constitute the "skat," or "widow." Long popular in Europe, it never gained a wide following in the colonies. Rahl loved the game and played with gusto. Although clumsy from drink, he was beaming from a streak of winning hands when there was a knock on the door.

Traditions dating from that evening assert that a Tory farmer came to the Hunt mansion, asking to see Colonel Rahl. Turned away by a servant who answered his knock, the visitor scribbled a few lines on a piece of paper, a warning that rebel troops were massing in preparation for an attempt to cross the Delaware. Handed the note by a servant, the Hessian commander slipped it into his pocket without glancing at it, obsessed by his card game.

While Rahl continued to win at skat, Washington and his men completed their icy crossing of the Delaware River. Writing to his wife about their entrance into Trenton, Henry Knox said that the patriots "arrived by two routes at the same time. The hurry, fright, and confusion of the enemy was not unlike that which will be when the last trump shall sound."

Caught completely by surprise, the Hessians offered little resistance. Too late, Rahl climbed into his saddle and advanced to meet the enemy, only to catch a ball that inflicted a wound from which he died a few hours later. Within forty-five minutes, token attempts at self-defense by the Hessians came to a halt.

In his official report to Congress, George Washington exulted that "not one American died" in the engagement that saw British losses of "a little over one hundred killed and wounded, with more than nine hundred taken prisoner."

The patriots seized six brass field pieces and about one thousand muskets. In addition, they took three ammunition wagons, four wagons of baggage, twelve drums, and fifteen flags. James Monroe was seriously wounded, along with five comrades, all of whom survived.

No one knows what happened to the warning that Rahl reputedly thrust into his pocket. Since it came from someone who had general knowledge about the military situation, it was presumably written in German. The failure of the carousing Hessian to read the urgent message is widely credited with having been crucial to the first decisive victory won by the Continental army. In the aftermath of the dramatic triumph at Trenton, Washington moved on to Princeton for another victory.

The Declaration of Independence was re-issued and re-circulated, this time with the names of its signers appended. Trenton and Princeton were omens of hope that the struggle would soon come to a glorious end; but even if it did not, every patriot realized that the cause he espoused had reached the point of no return. There were now only two alternatives: more and greater battlefield victories or ignominious defeat swiftly followed by harsh punishment.

Part Five

"Loyalists of the South Will Rally behind Their Sovereign"

Nine months after Washington's surprise victory at Trenton, the Continentals defeated the army of General John Burgoyne at Saratoga, New York. Although casualties were light, it meant that 5,700 men who laid down their arms would not fight again.

British strategists then turned toward the South where weather conditions were favorable. Also, "Gentleman Johnny" Burgoyne was confident that Loyalists of the region would rally behind their sovereign.

This abrupt change in the plan of attack altered the course of the struggle. For its duration, most engagements of significance were fought in the South rather than in the ice and snow of the North.

When patriots stood firm at Old North Bridge in Concord, "Yankee Doodle" took on a different meaning.

28

British Musical Jibes
Became Patriots' Anthem

"**C**ome, my merry comrades, and listen to my ditty," Dr. Richard Shuckburg may have said to men gathered in the mess hall at Albany, New York. Fellow British soldiers, who knew the physician's penchant for barbed humor, presumably roared with laughter before he began to sing. Borrowing a melody from an old English children's game, he is said to have belted out derisive lines based upon having watched members of the Colonial militia stumble through drill exercises nearby.

Widely circulated accounts, including some in standard reference works, insist that the mocking lines written and first sung by a British army surgeon constituted the earliest version of the song "Yankee Doodle." There is no documentary evidence to support this tradition, whose survival is due in part to the fact that scholars have been unable to show precisely when and where the song originated.

This much is certain: by the time Redcoats fired upon Colonials at Lexington and Concord, the melody and numerous sets of words were widely familiar. Believed originally to have been sung in nasal form, one set of lilting lines stemmed from the French and Indian War and labeled all colonists as cowards:

> Brother Ephraim sold his Cow
>   And bought him a Commission,
> And then he went to Canada
>   To fight for the Nation;
> But when Ephraim he came home
>   He proved an arrant Coward,
> He wouldn' fight the Frenchmen there
>   For fear of being devour'd.

Redcoats are known to have sung these lines, or variants of them, early in their occupation of Boston, long before the start of outright hostility. According to the New York *General Advertiser* of October 13, 1768, the British fleet was brought to anchor near Castle William, a fort on an island in Boston harbor, on the evening of September 29. Once the vessels were in position, "there was throwing of Sky Rockets, and those passing in boats observed great Rejoicing, and that the Yankey Doodle Song was the Capital Piece in their Band of Music."

By March 1769, British army musicians were giving weekly "court concerts" for the entertainment of their officers. According to the Boston *Evening Post*, one such gala turned sour when tipsy Redcoats demanded "Yankee Doodle." For reasons never explained, the band failed to respond. Angry officers then "grew noisy and clamorous, the candles were extinguished, and the old honest music master was actually in danger of being throttled when rescued by one who soon threw an officer on lower ground than he at first stood upon."

As in the case of any easily sung tune to which a refrain may be added, singers probably improvised as they went. As a result, long before the patriots openly broke with their mother country, dozens of versions of "Yankee Doodle" were being sung. Most or all of them poked fun at the colonists, who were mocked as being so ignorant that they thought a feather in a fellow's cap turned him into a "macaroni," or fop.

At the time, it is doubtful that singers or listeners knew that the "macaroni" quip originated during the seventeenth century. Cavaliers who derided Oliver Cromwell and his followers had applied that label to Puritans. Much earlier, children used the same tune to chant:

> Lucy Locket lost her pocket,
> Kitty Fisher found it;
> Nothing in it, nothing in it,
> Save the binding round it.

Musicologists have searched to discover where the melody originated. Possibly, but not positively, of Dutch, German, Spanish, or Hungarian origin, the "Lucy Locket" song was already very old by the time it reached North America with soldiers who came to fight against the French and the Indians.

Dr. Shuckburgh or some other unidentified wordsmith transformed the old song by combining *Yankee* with *doodle*. American Indians, stumbling over the word *English* or the French equivalent, *Anglais*, may have coined the term *Yankee*. A Cambridge, Massachusetts, farmer, Jonathan Hastings, is often credited with having used it with Harvard students, who boosted it into wide currency.

Many Redcoats scoffed at New Englanders as "Yankees" by the 1750s, and *doodle* was a hoary title for a half-witted fool. That meant the finished composition was an open insult to all colonists, not simply those of Massachusetts and adjoining regions. A Yankee Doodle was a bumpkin who was awed and mystified by so simple an experience as his first encounter with a military drum:

> There I saw a wooden keg
> With heads made out of leather;
> They knocked upon it with some sticks
> To call the folks together.

After having smarted under the insulting message of "Yankee Doodle" for many years, Colonials abruptly seized upon it as a way to retort. Redcoats allegedly sang the ditty as they marched to Lexington and Concord, and when they retreated—so the story goes—the patriots mocked them by singing it as a taunt. Tradition says that once he reached the safety of Boston, General Gage exclaimed, "I hope that I shall never hear that tune again!"

Though Gage may have been spared from repetition of "Yankee Doodle," other Redcoats were not. It was sung and whistled throughout the Continental army and militia units of the thirteen colonies. By the time the names of the signers of the Declaration of Independence were widely known, the song was being hummed by riflemen as they squatted behind stone fences or perched in trees to pick off British soldiers at a distance.

After the Battle of Saratoga—a major turning point of the struggle—British officer Thomas Anburey was interned at Cambridge. Writing there, he lamented that "'Yankee Doodle' is now their paean, a favorite of favorites." According to his diary, it was "played in their army, esteemed as warlike as the 'Grenadier's March.'" Anburey confessed, "We held the Yankees in great contempt," then as an afterthought admitted, "it was not a little mortifying to hear them play this tune, when their army marched down to our surrender."

Since it was now time for patriots to sneer to the meter of "Yankee Doodle," they produced satirical lines that depicted Lord Cornwallis as a nursemaid and his mistress as a soldier. As for Burgoyne, who had confidently expected to sweep to quick victory from Canada, the Continentals poked fun at him and his men in an eleven-stanza version that ended:

> In vain they fought; in vain they fled,
> Their Chief, humane and tender,
> To save the rest, he thought it best,
> His Forces to surrender.

Thus may America's brave Sons,
With Honor be rewarded;
And be the Fate of all her Foes
The same as here recorded!

Until "The Star Spangled Banner" was written during the War of 1812, "Yankee Doodle" was regarded as the embodiment of the American spirit. Seldom, if ever, has another band of outnumbered rebels so successfully turned contemptuous lines of an enemy into a triumphant victory taunt!

29

Preacher-heroes Molded Public Opinion

John Peter Gabriel Muhlenberg called a committee of freeholders to order on June 16, 1774. "We are here to consider the best mode to be fallen upon to secure our liberties and properties," the moderator said solemnly.

Both the pastor and the colonists who met with him knew that as a priest of the Church of England, he was risking his "living," or ecclesiastical post, by becoming involved in secular affairs. But the tall, twenty-eight-year-old clergyman was determined that Woodstock, Virginia, should register her opposition to the act of Parliament that closed Boston Harbor. Once his name was linked with that protest, Muhlenberg's career was doomed.

Six months before the Declaration of Independence was signed, he announced that he would preach his farewell sermon. Visitors and friends crowded the village church to hear him speak on Ecclesiastes 3:1, "To every thing there is a season, and a time to every purpose under heaven."

When he finished, the pastor threw off his clerical gown and stood before the citizens of Woodstock in the uniform of a militia officer. George Washington had persuaded him to accept a commission as a colonel.

On the spot, the Reverend Colonel Muhlenberg signed up volunteers; eventually he led nearly three hundred of his parishioners into battle. Although he was too far from Canterbury for officials to bother revoking his ordination, he became a full-time soldier for the duration of the struggle.

"There is a time for all things," he said repeatedly, "a time to preach and a time to pray; but there is also a time to fight, and that time has now come."

Muhlenberg fought at Brandywine, Germantown, Monmouth,

Stony Point, Suffolk, and Petersburg. He was in the thick of battle at Charles Town and at Yorktown. Made a brigadier general in 1777, he won promotion to major general, highest rank held by any clergyman on either side of the conflict.

Clergymen of all faiths were among the unsung heroes of the American Revolution. Some wore round collars; others dressed in ordinary homespun clothing. A few distinguished themselves in combat, while several played key roles in the political process.

More than in any other area of activity, however, preacher-heroes helped to mold public opinion. Many regions were almost equally divided between patriots and Loyalists until it became evident that the rebellion might succeed. Even then, it was often dangerous and costly to espouse the cause of freedom in the fashion that many clergymen did.

Pierre Gibault, a Roman Catholic priest, was serving as vicar-general for the Bishop of Quebec at the outbreak of hostilities. He had sole responsibility for what was then called "the Illinois country."

George Rogers Clark and a small band of patriots captured the frontier town of Kaskaskia exactly two years after the Declaration of Independence was adopted. That put them in striking range of a great target: Vincennes, center of French colonial government of the Illinois country.

When Clark did not have the manpower or the weapons to make a frontal attack upon Vincennes, Gibault volunteered to ride on horseback 150 miles. After two or three days of preparation, he called householders of the frontier settlement together in the Catholic church. There he led 180 of them in taking an oath of allegiance to American leaders. As a result, Clark later took possession of the place without firing a shot.

Far more important than mere occupation of the town, the American victory was crucial when boundaries of the United States were determined for the 1783 Treaty of Paris.

Presbyterian pastor James Caldwell of Elizabethtown, New Jersey, is probably more widely known than Gibault in spite of the fact that his role in the conflict was less significant.

Very early labeled "one of the fiercest rebels in Jersey," he became chaplain in Colonel Elias Dayton's regiment and was nicknamed "the soldier parson."

In 1780 British forces burned the church where Caldwell was pastor and the house in which he lived. His family took refuge near Union, New Jersey; Caldwell stayed with patriot troops. A stray bullet from a raiding party killed Mrs. Caldwell while she was in a room praying with their two children.

The Reverend Mr. Caldwell was on duty at Morristown when his

The April 19, 1775, battle of Lexington inspired many sermons and tracts. [ENGRAVING BY AMOS DOOLITTLE]

wife was killed. Shortly afterward, he distinguished himself in the defense of Springfield, New Jersey. During the engagement he supplied patriots with hymn books from a neighboring church to use as wadding for their guns. Because many hymns were written by Isaac Watts, Caldwell urged fighters for freedom, "Now put Watts into them, boys!"

At Elizabethport, New Jersey, an American sentinel shot and killed the soldier parson late in 1781. Found guilty of murder by a court martial, the sentry was hanged. Many folk were positive—without evidence—that the man had been bribed by the British to kill Caldwell to silence him.

The Reverend Naphtali Daggett, also Presbyterian, graduated from Princeton and served for a few years as a pastor before becoming the sixth president of Yale College. When the British attacked New Haven in July 1779, "patriotism impelled him to take up a musket and join in the attempt to repel the attackers."

As a soldier, he was not a conspicuous success. Captured by the British and compelled to act as a guide for them, he was so brutally prodded by their bayonets that his health broke and he died in 1780.

Known to students as "Old Tunker," the clergyman-hero wrote an account of the affair that suggested he was treated especially harshly because he resisted. One British soldier, he said, gave him four gashes on his head to the skull bone. Another beat him with the barrel of his gun, stripped him of his shoes and knee buckles before making him march five miles "in a near daze from pain and loss of blood."

When he gained a little strength about a month after he was ex-changed, his first act was to buy a second-hand sword "for use of one of the boys in the Continental Army."

The Reverend Charles M. Thruston, a priest of the Church of En-gland, reacted much like Peter Muhlenberg. At the outbreak of hos-tilities, he "raised a company of volunteers" from his parish in the Shenandoah River valley and himself served as their captain. Badly wounded at Trenton, he rose to the rank of colonel.

Numerous clergymen who never commanded troops in battle went with them into combat as chaplains.

The Reverend William Emerson, pastor of the First Congregational Parish of Concord, Massachusetts, used his pulpit to urge resistance to invasion. Concord tradition has it that on the famous April 19 when the Battle of Concord was fought, "Emerson, gun in hand, was the first to answer the alarm and take his stand in the square under the Liberty Pole."

Emerson became a chaplain in the Continental army. When local troops began making plans to march on Canada, he received permis-sion from both church and town officials to go along. At Ticonderoga, he found himself tired but exhilarated. Later he found his black gown "an inconvenience in the woods," so asked his wife, Phoebe, to "shorten up the blue one, face it with black, and send it up." Like many other fighting men, he had a severe bout with the malady they knew only as "camp fever."

Fields of battle were not the only places of conspicuous service by preacher-heroes; several won distinction in legislative halls.

Frederick Muhlenberg, pastor of Lutheran churches in Pennsyl-vania, served in the state house of representatives, the Continental Congress, and the state constitutional convention. Later he was sent to the newly formed Congress of the United States. Twice chosen as speaker of the House of Representatives, he is thought to be the only clergyman who ever held that post.

Presbyterian John Witherspoon, born in Scotland and destined to become president of Princeton University, identified himself with the cause of liberty from the time he arrived in America. Citizens of New Jersey elected him to the convention that framed the state constitu-tion; and on the overthrow of the last Tory governor, he was elected to the Continental Congress.

Witherspoon was publicly impatient at delay in passing the Declara-tion of Independence. To fellow lawmakers he declared that he would rather have his gray hairs "descend into the sepulchre by the hand of the public executioner than to desert at this crisis the sacred cause of my country."

After erecting a Liberty Pole, patriots gathered at its base for news, sermons, and mutual encouragement.

His name is familiar because he was a signer of the Declaration of Independence. Not so well known is that he played a major role in financing the Revolution and served as one of the American commissioners responsible for arriving at a treaty of peace.

Abraham Baldwin, a Yale College graduate distinguished for having established the University of Georgia, was a chaplain from 1777 onward. During 1785–88 he was a delegate to the Continental Congress, where he served as an active member of the convention that drew up the U.S. Constitution.

Samuel Spring, an army chaplain during 1775–76, took part in Benedict Arnold's expedition into Canada and the attack on Quebec. Father John Carroll, a Jesuit, went to Canada during the same period in an attempt to persuade French-Canadians to throw in their lot with American rebels. Bishop Jean Brian, ruling Catholic prelate in Canada, "instantly suspended" any priest who received Carroll.

Great numbers of clergymen who did not march, fight, or debate legislation lent their influence to the cause of freedom through sermons and tracts. Especially where constituents were about evenly divided between patriots and Loyalists, it could be as dangerous and costly to talk and to write of freedom as to take up arms.

The Reverend Jonas Clark of Lexington, Massachusetts, let patriots use his house as a meeting place, and Samuel Adams and John Hancock took refuge there at one period. So did Paul Revere, a bit later. Clark preached a famous sermon entitled simply "April 19, 1776." Printed as a broadside and widely distributed, it condemned British atrocities so vigorously that it "did much to fan the fires of patriotism throughout the colonies."

The Reverend John Brown of First Congregational Society, Cohasset, Massachusetts, acted promptly when he heard about the battle of Lexington. "He gathered the militia under a great elm," according to a contemporary account, "and preached a sermon they never forgot."

John Cleveland of Ipswich, Massachusetts, wrote a public letter to British General Gage in which he dubbed him "a profane, wicked monster of falsehood and perfidy."

So it went throughout the colonies: Samuel Eaton of Franklin, Pennsylvania; Joseph Fish of Stonington, Connecticut (who identified the Loyalist cause with that of the devil); Unitarian pastor Jonathan Mayhew, who began preaching anti-British sermons in 1766 and never stopped until liberty was won; John Humphreys of Philadelphia, who preached and at his own expense published in July 1775 a sermon "On the Present Situation of American Affairs."

Names of a few preacher-heroes have found their way into the record. Most of them, including even Father Gibault, are often overlooked when the story of daring resistance to England is told to inheritors of hard-won freedom. As much as members of any other vocational group—perhaps more—largely forgotten clergymen molded public opinion and helped persuade thousands to renounce their king and espouse the cause of independence.

CHAPTER

30

For Kentucky's Sake, George Rogers Clark Kept His Scalping Knife Sharp

Terse diary entries followed in quick succession at Harrodsburg, Kentucky, during March 1777:

Mar. 6—William Ray and Thos. Shores surprised at Shawnee Spring, killed.
Mar. 7—Skirmish cost us 4 men wounded. We killed and scalped an Indian and wounded several of their party.

Virginia-born George Rogers Clark, age twenty-five, had been fighting Indians for half a dozen years when he noted these events. Oral tradition asserts, however, that he relied only upon weapons of the "long knives," or white men, until the fateful spring in which Kentucky's doom appeared certain. It was at this point that he adopted the use of the tomahawk and the scalping knife, then took them with him on a death-defying expedition aimed at saving the region for Virginia.

It was as an employee of the Ohio Company that Clark first entered Kentucky as a surveyor. Quickly enamored with the region, the adolescent learned that its ownership was debatable. In a rash moment, he swore to "make this into good Virginia soil and keep it that way."

Constant fear of Indian raids kept Kentuckians wary. When they saw their supply of gunpowder almost exhausted, Clark volunteered to get more. Virginia governor Patrick Henry was not enthusiastic, but he yielded to persuasion and turned five hundred pounds of the precious compound over to Clark. A few months later, in December 1776, Virginia extended her territorial domain by adding to it Kentucky County.

Settlers in the region made famous by Daniel Boone had been hope-

173

ful of living in safety, until Lord George Germain, English secretary of state for the American colonies, ordered British officials in the colonies to recruit Indians to augment British power in the frontier country. Britain's strongest western outpost, Detroit, was headed by Lieutenant Governor Henry Hamilton. Noted for his readiness to obey orders and no doubt prompted by eagerness for advancement, Hamilton implemented Germain's order at once. By early 1777 he boasted that he had won over the Shawnees, led by Chief Blackfish, and that with their help he had fifteen raiding parties on the move.

Typically led by one or two British officers, such a band would include twelve to twenty-five warriors. Living off the land, burning isolated cabins, and killing or taking captive their residents, they terrorized the frontier. Fearful Kentuckians fled back through the Cumberland Gap, and, as 1778 neared, the whole of Kentucky County included just over one thousand fighting men.

Lawmakers who were assembled in Philadelphia knew little about what was taking place and showed no concern. Even in Virginia, patriots concentrated their energy and resources upon meeting the British in old, established centers. Clark, now a major in the Kentucky County militia, gloomily confessed to comrades that he believed the end of Kentucky was in sight—barring a miracle.

Reluctant to abandon the region, Clark decided that if a miracle were to take place, he would have to perform it. If he could drive the British from the Ohio River region north of Kentucky, he believed a handful of men in a few forts could hold it against the Indians.

Although far from optimistic about such a grandiose plan, Patrick Henry managed to find about one thousand men for the defense of Kentucky County. He authorized Clark to raise a fighting force of 350 men, gave him badly depreciated currency, and told him to start at once.

That proved impossible. Henry's tall, redhaired major was persuasive, but most who heard his story shook their heads and told him they were needed elsewhere. So he was not ready to begin his planned invasion until October 1777.

The slender leader stressed the urgency of secrecy to every man whom he succeeded in enlisting. To have any chance of success, the expedition must get under way without arousing the suspicions of British leaders.

Always sending scouts ahead of his force that was barely half its authorized strength, Clark moved slowly. By May 1778 he reached the Falls of the Ohio, where he decided to build a base and teach his men how to fight Indian style. Then in late June the Americans shot the rapids and entered the Illinois country.

Barely two days after penetrating this immense region that was vir-

British officers who recruited Indian warriors usually led them in their forays.

tually unknown to English-speaking settlers, the sun began to grow dark at mid-day. Some of his recruits warned Clark that an eclipse was a very bad omen. "You are wrong," he assured them. "It is a bad omen for the enemy and hence a good omen for us; we push forward!"

Kaskaskia, the largest town in the Illinois country, might prove too formidable for the small force of Virginians unless seized by surprise. To avoid the risk of being seen, Clark led his men into the forests and swamps for an overland trek of 120 miles that required every man to give his best for six punishing days. During the last two days, with food they had brought along gone, they lived off the land as the Indians did.

On the second anniversary of the adoption of the Declaration of Independence, mud-covered men from the south filed into Kaskaskia. The settlers there, who were predominately French speaking, gaped in surprise, a reaction shared by the British commandant. He was too startled to resist and turned over to Clark official papers that gave valuable information about other posts.

From Kaskaskia the invasion force of slightly over 100 men marched 150 miles to Vincennes. Although smaller than the post already captured, it was of greater strategic importance. To Clark's surprise, a French-speaking Catholic priest persuaded the townspeople to yield without a fight. His mission apparently accomplished, George Rogers Clark headed back to Kentucky in triumph.

But in Detroit the man whose employment of Indians caused him to be called "Hair-buyer" Hamilton got news of what had taken place far to the west. Hurriedly assembling a band of about sixty-five Indians, with British officers and other whites, he marched toward Vincennes on the double. Hamilton pushed 600 miles during October and November 1778, recruiting many Indians as he went. He found Vincennes to be defended by a single rusty cannon, presided over by an aging Indian fighter who was drunk much of the time.

Once Vincennes, which had been largely inhabited by French settlers for decades, became a British outpost, Hamilton strengthened Fort Sackville by adding a dozen heavy pieces of field artillery. His boastful reports to London sent by way of Detroit indicated that His Majesty could sleep soundly. The Illinois country was in safe hands.

Hamilton failed to take into account the fiery temper and tenacity of George Rogers Clark. When he learned what had happened at Vincennes, Clark outfitted a second expedition. This time he had two barely functional cannon, which he put on a river boat with almost forty men. Leading nearly two hundred others, he set out for the Wabash River on foot.

Advancing slowly through desolate water-logged country, Clark worried more about desertion than British guns. He appointed Captain Joseph Bowman head of a company of twenty-five selected riflemen to bring up the rear, with orders to shoot any man who attempted to slip away from the company. From a captured Frenchman, Clark learned that Henry Hamilton knew nothing about the approaching force.

Vincennes came in sight late on February 24, 1779. Instead of attempting a surprise attack, Clark formed his men into two companies and sent them boldly marching up and down the streets to announce their presence. The British defenders entrenched behind the walls of Fort Sackville were confident their heavy guns could hold off any number of men with small arms. Hamilton was so complacent that he barely paused in his card game to laugh at the notion of an attack that would prove suicidal.

Clark sent Hamilton a message demanding the immediate surrender of the fort. When it did not come, he stationed his sharpshooters at strategic points and began picking off British gunners one by one. With his losses mounting, Hamilton agreed to a parley.

To the consternation of Hamilton, he was forced to meet Clark, who was sitting on the edge of a river boat, or batteau, washing his hands.

Having ambushed an Indian raiding party, Clark had personally seen to it that four warriors—some accounts say five—were scalped after having died under tomahawks wielded by white men.

The scalping of enemy dead by Americans was not limited to Clark; other frontiersmen, including Daniel Morgan, followed the same practice. Although Hamilton cheerfully hired Indians to fight and scalp for him, he was horrified that a white man would do such things; and he recorded in his notes of the occasion a description of his enemy "washing his hands and face still reeking from the human sacrifice in which he had acted as chief priest."

On February 25, 1779, the American flag was again hoisted at Vincennes. After an epic march that rivaled Benedict Arnold's ill-fated Quebec expedition, twenty-six-year-old George Rogers Clark knew that Kentucky was safe at last. He did not foresee that his exploit would in time bring to the United States the immense Northwest Territory, a prize gained as a result of a military invasion that did not cost the Americans a single life in combat.

CHAPTER

31

A Gardener's Son Gave Britain a Dose of Her Own Medicine

Whitehaven,
28 April 1778

Last night 30 armed men landed at this place from an American privateer. Men of the vessel set fire to the Thomson, a new vessel in the harbor, and it appeared that the whole world would soon be in a blaze.

The scene was too horrible to admit of further description; we shall only add to this part of this alarming story that, by an uncommon exertion, the fire was extinguished before it spread to other vessels anchored alongside.

One man from the privateer remained on shore, though it is not known whether this was through accident or designed escape. When exampled by magistrates, he gave an affidavit:

The Ranger privateer is commanded by John Paul Jones, fitted out at Piscataque in New England. Pierced for 20 guns, the vessel mounts 18 6-pounders and 6 swivels. With a crew of between 140 and 150 men she sailed for Brest in November 1777 and took in passage two brigs.

Here greatly abbreviated, that account appeared in newspapers throughout Britain during the spring of 1778. Everywhere, but particularly in Ireland, fear of armed attack by persons "attached to the American rebellion" mounted.

Common folk had long been vaguely aware that there was fighting in North America. They knew that lawmakers debated colonial policies in Parliament and that professional soldiers and foreign merce-

John Paul Jones.

naries were in action far away. But for most of them, their everyday lives were untouched until the son of a Scottish gardener led daring raids that gave Britain a dose of her own medicine.

Rumor—correct as events proved—had it that the man called Jones was a fugitive from justice who offered to fight for America because he saw that as a way to keep his pursuers at bay. Hasty investigation by British leaders turned up information that at age twelve he had become a cabin boy on a merchant vessel. The London authorities fumed that they had not discovered the man's identity earlier.

Records indicated that his vessel, the *Friendship*, was regularly engaged in triangular trade between home ports, the West Indies, and Virginia. At Fredericksburg he was said to have visited his brother William, a tailor, two or three times a year.

Documents showed that Jones, as he called himself, had been in serious trouble. Rising gradually in authority, he became master of his own vessel. Soon afterward he had ship's carpenter Mungo Maxwell flogged so severely that he died. Maxwell's father brought a charge of murder, and Jones may have been briefly imprisoned before being cleared.

A second lethal incident revolved about an alleged mutineer. This time, there was no doubt that the captain was responsible for the man's death. Near Tobago, he ran him through with a sword. Uncer-

A British caricature depicted Jones as a pirate. [THE MARINERS MUSEUM]

tain that he would be able to prove that mutiny triggered the assault, the captain abandoned his ship and took refuge in Virginia. Although born plain John Paul, in Virginia he added Jones in what was believed to be an attempt to make it more difficult to trace his identity.

Hazel-eyed John Paul Jones knew a good thing when he saw it. To the young veteran of the seas, Continental Congress delegate Joseph Hewes of North Carolina looked extremely good. As chairman of the marine committee of Congress, he was likely to have a decisive voice in the naming of officers should the delegates decide to establish a Continental navy. Jones carefully cultivated the friendship of the lawmaker and waited.

The patriots already had a number of small vessels in active service. Many were commissioned by George Washington, who for a time directed their activities. As privateers, they were instructed to make all possible captures of British ships, especially those believed to be transporting muskets, gunpowder, and other articles of war.

In June 1777 the fugitive from English justice was commissioned as a captain and given command of the privateer *Ranger*. Aging Ezek Hopkins, who had been named commodore of the fledgling Continental navy, could not lead a fight personally; Colonel Henry Knox described him as "easily mistaken for an angel, except that now and then he swears a little."

What role Hopkins and landlubbers like Joseph Hewes played in the ensuing sea drama is unknown. In all likelihood, they simply told Jones to take his ship to a French port, arrange a consultation with Benjamin Franklin, and do whatever he could to embarrass the enemy.

As chief American representative in Paris, Franklin had access to top-level French officials, both military and civilian. It seems to have been Franklin who encouraged an obviously rash and ambitious young officer to carry the war into British waters.

For four months beginning in February 1778, Jones and the *Ranger* prowled around the British Isles. His April 24 capture of the *Drake* marked the first time that an enemy warship had surrendered to an America vessel. Even though he triumphantly took the *Drake* and about two hundred British prisoners to Brest, this triumph had little impact upon London or public opinion in Britain. Comparatively few persons learned of what had taken place.

His foray directed at Whitehaven and reported extensively in news-papers was a different matter. Not only did he come close to setting fire to anchored ships and to the town itself, he managed to spike thirty-eight cannon in the fort that protected the place.

According to Jones's own account—perhaps exaggerated—he directed that tar be poured over his target. After it was set afire, while his men spiked cannon, he single-handedly held off residents who rushed to extinguish the blaze. As he modestly reported the incident in a letter, John Paul Jones faced a mob of angry townsfolk with no weapon except a hand gun, but he waved his foes back and prevented them from extinguishing the fire.

Since he was well acquainted with the region in which the earl of Selkirk lived, Jones developed a plan to kidnap the nobleman. Holding such a hostage, he reasoned, he could bargain for the release of every American held prisoner in England.

Had not the earl been absent from his mansion that night, Jones's plan might have worked. Only the family silver plate was stolen. Years later, Jones saw to it that it was returned to those from whom it was taken.

As a military operation, the cruise of the *Ranger* amounted to very little. It did nothing to stop the seemingly endless line of ships headed for America, crowded with troops or loaded with ammunition and clothing. But as a way of calling the war in America to the startled and frightened attention of ordinary folk, it was a smashing success.

Especially in Ireland, where many exploits of the *Ranger* were centered, there was a virtual uprising. In a matter of weeks, forty thousand men flocked to become Irish volunteers, or members of a home guard whose role was to protect against invasion. Irish lawmakers created such a commotion that Parliament reluctantly gave in to them;

after years of refusing to do so, major political and economic concessions were made.

To John Paul Jones, his accomplishments represented only a beginning. Returning to Paris, he begged for a full-size frigate with which to sail against Britain's most powerful warships. Lawmakers in Philadelphia expressed gratitude and admiration, but had no money to fund the enterprise he suggested. After nearly a year, Benjamin Franklin persuaded the French to turn over to Jones an aging merchantman that had been refitted for war. Old and clumsy as the *Duras* was, she was capable of mounting forty guns. Accepted with fervent gratitude, she was promptly renamed *Bonne Homme Richard* in honor of Franklin and his famous *Poor Richard's Almanac*.

With six smaller vessels attached to his command, Jones and the *Bonne Homme Richard* set out to stalk their prey. Sighting a line of British merchantmen, a lookout counted forty-one under sail. The capture of such a prize would help to fund the financially pressed Continental army, and the captain's share would make the gardener's son a wealthy man.

But before he could seize those forty-one heavily loaded ships, the American commander had to turn his attention to the gunboats that escorted them. By far the most powerful of these, the *Serapis*, should have made short work of the attacking ship.

During a three-hour epic battle, Jones and his converted merchantman managed to keep on fighting. The accidental entanglement of rigging brought the two vessels side by side and enabled small arms marksmen in Jones's three tops to pour withering fire upon an enemy no longer able to use his big guns.

Although Jones's flagship was sinking, he forced the surrender of the *Serapis*, thereby becoming an instant hero. Back at the French port of L'Orient, he gleefully reenacted the fight, with great pageantry, to the cheers of multitudes. King Louis XVI presented him with a ceremonial sword and made him a chevalier of France, and it appeared that he soon would be second only to George Washington in popular adulation in his adopted country.

Congress acted promptly to vote that he be given command of the seventy-four-gun frigate *America* upon its completion. But before the vessel was launched, naval leaders decided it should be presented to France as a gift. Lawmakers awarded the hero a congressional medal as a consolation prize but balked at the idea of promoting him over officers who had more seniority. Disgruntled, Jones served in European and Russian navies before returning once more to Paris, where his death was followed by burial in an unmarked grave.

Decades later, in a highly disputed claim, it was said that his bones had been discovered. By 1905, he had become to all America what he

DON'T TREAD ON ME

BON HOMME RICHARD & SERAPIS

A widely-circulated lithograph depicted an artist's conception of Jones' flagship, the Bon Homme Richard, *in action.*

believed himself to be in 1779, a true hero. Remains alleged to be those of John Paul Jones were dug up and brought back to the nation for which he fought. This time, there was another great convoy: a squadron of warships whose commanders were under orders to see that no harm should come to the precious bones of the Scot who is now revered as America's first naval hero.

CHAPTER

32

Patriots Shaped an Emblem When All Hope of Reconciliation Vanished

"**A** band of Continental leaders called upon my grandmother and asked her to undertake a special task," said eighty-four-year-old William J. Canby. "They probably selected her because George Washington was one of her patrons; she sewed many shirt ruffles for him about the time he was made commander in chief."

Although reporters listened respectfully to Canby, some were openly skeptical. One observed later, "He tells a believable story, but there are no documents to support it. Betsy Ross may have produced the first Stars and Stripes—but we'll never know positively whether or not she did it."

Part of the dilemma facing those who long ago set out to trace the story of the U.S. flag stems from the fact that the founding fathers seem to have taken it very casually. All of them were familiar with numerous flags of local or regional importance; even adoption of the Declaration of Independence didn't seem to make it imperative that a standard flag be flown by all fighters for freedom.

Canby, grandson of Betsy Ross, was an expert on colonial flags. According to oral tradition, he visited every museum in the East at which a tattered old emblem was exhibited.

"Until Bunker Hill," he said, "the famous British Jack—standard for use on warships of the Royal Navy—was the only flag familiar throughout the colonies. All the rest were known to only a small number of persons.

"One of the most beautiful early flags was in action at Concord. Because minutemen of Bedford, Massachusetts, carried it with them, it was known as the Bedford. A dark red field had an armor-clad hand superimposed—appearing to reach from the sky, and brandishing a sword. Embroidered with gold thread, the motto was in Latin: *Vincere aut mori* ('Conquer, or die')."

Boston flags with which the grandson of Betsy Ross was familiar included one with a solid blue field and the cross of St. George. A rival banner carried the same emblem, placed upon a field of red. Both included a small green pine tree because these trees abounded in early Massachusetts.

Far to the south, the flag flown at Fort Sullivan when the installation faced an early land and sea attack was dark blue with a white crescent and *Liberty* in block letters. It was this flag that Sergeant Jasper rescued during an artillery barrage, winning the admiration of Colonial leaders everywhere for his daring exploit.

The decision of the colonists to send delegates to an intercolonial congress triggered the creation of still another flag. Said to have been flown regularly at the place where the Continental Congress met, it was a simple banner with thirteen alternating red and white horizontal stripes and a miniature Union Jack. No one who saw it needed to be informed that the flag was a symbolic promise: sooner or later, the individual colonies will forget their differences and join in the common cause of resisting oppression from London.

One rare battle flag displayed, not thirteen horizontal stripes, but thirteen green hands linked to form a circle on a white field.

According to William J. Canby, "Instead of having confusion reduced when military units became larger and were joined by foreign forces, the flag situation became much worse. Every French regiment had its own colors, and to American eyes it was hard to distinguish between them. Count Pulaski made many patriots wonder when he insisted upon flying the personal emblem of his blue-blooded family."

Despite the tremendous variety of flags in use—so great that the British once thought George Washington was hoisting an offer of surrender when he lifted one of them—a few emblems were especially popular. Many displayed the beaver, symbol of colonial New York. Others showed the anchor of sea-dependent Rhode Island, and still others featured the pine tree. As tension mounted, rattlesnake flags became increasingly common. Some of them carried the warning, "Don't tread on me."

The Congress Colors, or Grand Union flag, had more than local meaning from the first. Yet this emblem took on another dimension when seamen selected it for use on privateers. John Paul Jones claimed credit for having been the first to hoist this flag above an armed vessel, the *Alfred*.

According to the grandson of Betsy Ross, "It was impossible to fail to see that the Grand Union flag and the British Union Jack were very much alike, yet quite different. Britain's emblem was pure red, and that of the colonials was varicolored. Yet they bore the same symbols. Looking at these flags from a perspective of decades, it appears that colonial leaders wanted their flag to be different from that of Britain, but not too different."

Betsy Ross, grandmother of the man who became an unofficial expert on the story of American flags, was one of seventeen children of a staunch Quaker. Her father, Samuel Griscom, was among the workmen who built Independence Hall. Marriage to non-Quaker John Ross led to the expulsion of Betsy (Elizabeth) from the fellowship.

Ross died in an explosion while trying to help manufacture gunpowder for the Colonials in 1776. His widow, though practically self-supporting as an expert seamstress, soon married Joseph Ashburn. They were together only a few weeks before he signed on as a crew member of a privateer. Captured, he was thrown into a foul British prison where he died of malnutrition and disease.

It was the twice widowed and very attractive seamstress of twenty-five who is widely credited with having produced the first official American flag. According to her grandson's recollection, she shook her head when told to place thirteen six-pointed stars upon a blue field. "Five-pointed stars look much better," she reputedly said, "and are just as easy to make. Look—I'll show you!"

Folding paper to make a pattern, the seamstress quickly cut a five-pointed star and thereby made a lasting imprint upon American life.

Despite the great diversity among flags, often leading to confusion in military engagements, Congress acted with its usual deliberation. Not until June 14, 1777, did lawmakers agree upon a terse statement:

> Resolved That the Flag of the United States be 13 alternate stripes red and white; that the Union be 13 stars, white in a blue field, representing a new constellation.

No one knows who framed that resolution, who favored it, and who opposed it. Francis Hopkinson, a delegate from New Jersey and a member of the Marine Committee, later put in a claim for payment based upon his having helped to design the flag. That lawmakers turned down his bid for remuneration means little. At a time when inflation had the former colonies in its grip, only the most pressing claims were recognized.

A tiny clue is found in the fact that the flag resolution is sandwiched between others dealing with naval matters. If Hopkinson did not personally originate the design, the Marine Committee probably processed and approved it before it was submitted to the full Congress.

One of those marine documents dealt with on the day the flag was approved was the commission issued to John Paul Jones. "That flag

Sergeant Jasper, hero of Fort Sullivan, died at Savannah. [HOWARD PYLE, FOR HARPER'S MAGAZINE, 1883]

and I are twins," the naval hero declared at a Fourth of July celebration. "We were born at the same hour. We cannot be parted in life or death. So long as we float, we shall float together."

Some of Jones's jealous fellow officers accused him of being a braggart and a show-off. Regardless of how much or how little truth there was in the charge, it was Jones who demanded and received the first official foreign recognition of the Stars and Stripes.

In Quiberon Bay near l'Orient, France, he made contact on February 13, 1778, with a fleet commanded by Admiral La Motte Picquet. Jones dispatched a message, asking if Picquet would return his salute of the French flag. Since the American was widely regarded in France as an admiral, Picquet responded that he would give the standard salute for an admiral's flagship: four guns less than that rendered.

John Paul Jones tried hard to get an assurance of gun-for-gun. Failing, he accepted Picquet's terms and saluted him by firing one gun for each of the stripes on his flag—and receiving in return a nine-gun salute.

If that deal struck on the seas seems to have been hastily arranged, it must be remembered that America's lawmakers had made no provision for international recognition of the flag. Even the emblems themselves were not uniform in appearance until 1818, when Congress stipulated that the flag should be constituted of thirteen red-and-white stripes with stars on a blue field, but did not specify how the stars should be arranged. Real standardization of the flag came only in 1912 as the result of an executive order by President William H. Taft.

CHAPTER

33

Gentleman Johnny's Failed Plan Turned Combatants toward the South

Camp at the River Bouquet
June 23, 1777

Whereas the present unnatural Rebellion has been made the Foundation of the compleatest System of Tyranny that ever God, in his Displeasure, suffered, for a Time, to be exercised over a froward and stubborn Generation,

I, by these Presents, invite and exhort all Persons, in all Places where the Progress of this Army may point, and by the Blessing of God I will extend it FAR, to maintain such a Conduct as may justify me in protecting the Lands, Habitations, and Families.

If the Phrenzy of Hostility should remain, the Messengers of Justice and of Wrath await them in the Field, and Devastation, Famine, and every concomitant Horror that a reluctant but indispensible Prosecution of Military Duty must occasion, will bar the Way to their Return.

J. Burgoyne

Had the elaborate proclamation of "Gentleman Johnny" Burgoyne not been headed by a detailed list of his manifold military titles, the document might have seemed to come from an Old Testament prophet. Let no patriot think himself safe, the British general warned in the stilted language of his time. Let every loyal Tory flock to the banner of his king and aid in driving pernicious and Godless rebels against their king into the sea!

Although not labeled as an announcement of impending invasion,

The murder of Jane McCrea by Indians in British service became one of the most effective of all incentives for men to enlist in the militia.

the proclamation was intended to pave the way for one. Pondering the situation in North America, the Redcoat commander drew up a 1776 document that embodied his personal "Thoughts for Conducting the War from the Side of Canada."

According to his grandiose plan, he would lead his troops from Canada into upper New York by way of Lake Champlain and the Hudson River. At Albany he would be joined by the army of General Howe and battalions led by Barry St. Leger. Their combined force would then smash all resistance in New England and bring the untimely rebellion to an abrupt end.

Six weeks away from the scene of action, British leaders pondered and debated. Clearly Burgoyne's plan showed the man's brilliance. It was almost ridiculously simple and could easily be put into action. True, it required tight coordination of three separate fighting forces, but that should not be too difficult. Following this line of reasoning, London gave wholehearted approval to the plan by which a Canadian invasion would see the beginning of the end of the patriots' cause.

Once Burgoyne received official approval, he began a leisurely march designed to keep him on schedule. One of his first acts was to issue the proclamation that offered amnesty to all who would join his forces and fight against the foes of their sovereign.

General John Stark commanded militia who mostly volunteered after the murder of Jane McCrea and retaliated by smashing a British force at Bennington, Vermont.

There is no record that a significant number of Americans took advantage of Burgoyne's offer. Proceeding southward from Canada, he led a force of about eight thousand Redcoats, Hessians, and Indians. Invited to meet with Indian allies in council, he readily accepted the offer; and after feasting with four hundred warriors, he rejoiced that most of them joined his force. Arriving before Fort Ticonderoga, Burgoyne took possession of the place without a struggle, then turned south to seize Fort Edward, abandoned earlier by the Continentals.

While Gentleman Johnny was camped on the trail leading to Fort Edward, a band of his Indian allies brought to headquarters a prized trophy: a scalp with luxuriant tresses. Momentarily displeased, he considered punishing the braves who had scalped a woman. When aides warned that such action might cost him the support of all Indians, he did nothing.

Patriots used the long hair of Jane McCrea for propaganda, asserting that every British soldier was a heartless barbarian, which was supported by the fact that the young woman was not in defiance of the king. Instead, at the time she was scalped in July 1777, she was the fiancée of Lieutenant David Jones, an officer in Colonel John Peters's band of loyal Tories.

There is evidence that the girl was killed by a stray bullet and scalped later, but patriots painted a grim picture of fiends who employed red men to slay defenseless women—even among their own ranks. No frontier incident of the period did more to speed the recruitment of militia units than did the seizure of Jane McCrea's long, beautiful hair.

Burgoyne's failure to act decisively in the matter greatly strengthened the hand of his foes. He then made a second costly blunder. Moving rapidly southward, he reached the village of Skenesborough in the wilderness area along the border of New York.

Philip Skene, the landed proprietor, had once been a major in His Majesty's forces. A genial and generous host, he gave Burgoyne the best that he had. The two men talked long into the night of victories that lay ahead and laurels to be won.

From Skenesborough Burgoyne should have taken a water route—Lake Champlain to Lake George, then along the Hudson River to Albany—but the overland route was a great deal shorter. Skene told Burgoyne it was just twenty-three miles to Fort Edward and civilization, failing to mention that the route would take the British army through a virgin wilderness whose trees were so thick that even skilled Canadian woodsmen could not clear a path rapidly enough to keep troops on the move.

Not until long afterward did Burgoyne learn that Skene persuaded him to take the short overland route for personal, rather than patriotic, reasons. The passage of the army through his virtually unexplored tract of forest land provided Skene with a road; but while that road was being cut, troops moved forward at the rate of just one mile a day. The consequent delay enabled the patriots to strengthen their position as they waited for the British.

Burgoyne's decision to follow Skene's advice was his own, but concurrent events took place because of decisions and actions of others.

General Howe, who was positive that the most important military target was Philadelphia, prepared to move toward that city. By the time he received from London orders to turn north to join forces with Burgoyne at Albany, he already was marching toward Pennsylvania. He had gone too far to turn back, so he pressed on toward Philadelphia.

St. Leger, also scheduled to meet Burgoyne at Albany, led a strike force comprised largely of Indians. He seemed to be invincible and was proceeding on schedule until Benedict Arnold, the hero of Quebec, devised a scheme of his own. Sending some of his Indian allies to spread a story claiming that a vast American force under Arnold was poised to strike, he threw St. Leger's Indians into such a panic that it led to mutiny. So Burgoyne was deprived of a second fighting force that was vital to the success of his plan.

He might have succeeded without Howe and St. Leger had it not been that the Continental Congress once more made military decisions that George Washington believed should have been his. In August the long-time commander of the Northern Department, Philip Schuyler, was replaced by General Horatio Gates.

Gates had joined the Continental army as a result of personal friendship with Washington. Much of his early life was spent as a career officer in the British army; but while fighting in America during the French and Indian War, he fell in love with the country. After early retirement, he became a Virginia farmer, and Washington had been responsible for his appointment as a brigadier general.

Elevated by Congress to a position of command, Gates quickly showed that he had not forgotten his years in British service. It was clear that sooner or later he would meet Burgoyne in battle, so he decided to find the best possible defensive position and fortify it strongly, then wait for Burgoyne to attack in European fashion. So far as he was concerned, there would be no foolhardy business such as trying to attack the Redcoats. Although his officers fumed at his inaction, Gates stood firm. He wanted an advantage when the two forces met.

Not far from Saratoga, New York, Gates looked over the terrain from the viewpoint of a veteran of European wars. Picking a spot that seemed just right as a defensive post, he put Count Kosciusko to work. Under orders of the Polish general, Continental soldiers took picks and shovels wherever they went, along with their muskets. Soon they completed a splendid set of earthworks reenforced with heavy logs.

Waiting behind their fortifications, the Continentals learned from scouts that Burgoyne and his men were approaching. Meanwhile, Washington and his men were retreating before the superior force led by General Howe. Congress fled from Philadelphia for the second time, just before Howe occupied the largest city in all the colonies.

Bad news for Pennsylvania was good news for New York. With his men far to the south, there was no way that Howe could come to the aid of Burgoyne.

The opposing forces met at Freeman's Farm on September 19, and during three hours of furious fighting in a tightly confined area, the Redcoats suffered a severe setback. General Daniel Morgan, whose "uniform" consisted of a hunting shirt and moccasins, guided his riflemen in their deadly work.

His face was scarred from an Indian arrow that had hit his mouth,

At all-important Saratoga, Morgan's riflemen (left) *played a vital but seldom-remembered part.*

and his back was brutally deformed by five hundred lashes given him during the French and Indian War. Morgan used the call of the wild turkey to transmit his battle orders; and while waiting for the Red-coats to reach his position, he encouraged his men by flourishing the scalp of an Indian killed just one day earlier.

Admirers of Morgan credit him with the victory won at First Saratoga. Although his role may have been exaggerated, there is no doubt that he and his Virginians played a decisive part.

News of the surprise victory spread rapidly, causing the Colonial forces in the region to rush to join the victors. When Burgoyne's scouts reported that they had seen John Stark arrive at the head of 1,100 men from the New Hampshire grants, the British leader knew that he must act quickly or not at all.

On October 7 opponents met again at Second Saratoga, a struggle in which Benedict Arnold was widely credited with playing a decisive role. Riding a huge black horse and described as "looking like the cocked hammer of a dueling pistol," the man who had been defeated at Quebec rejoiced at the quick, decisive victory won by the Americans.

Gates, who had relieved Arnold of command for insubordination, was furious when he learned what had transpired; but he rejoiced at his own wisdom in forcing Burgoyne to take the offensive. Time after time, grenadiers had formed solid ranks to launch a bayonet charge. Each time, riflemen had taken the crimson sashes of officers as targets and had demoralized the enemy before a solid charge could be launched.

Burgoyne, who lost 1,200 men in ten days, suddenly found himself outnumbered three to one as band after band of patriots reported to Gates; so he withdrew in confusion, abandoning three hundred men in a field hospital. Retreating toward the Hudson River but unable to cross it, he had only one alternative. Bitter as the pill was to swallow, he sent messengers with a flag of truce and asked for terms.

Perhaps out of consideration for a man who once had been a fellow officer, Gates agreed to a "convention" rather than a formal surrender. Under terms of the convention, Burgoyne's 5,700 survivors laid down their arms and took a pledge never to return to America once they reached Britain.

Congress refused to honor Gates's "convention," and interned the surrendered Redcoats for the duration of the war. Moved several times and with their ranks reduced by death from disease, only 2,600 of them were alive in 1781. Many of the survivors were Hessians who chose to remain in America.

Soon after his surrender Burgoyne was permitted to return to London, where he asked for but did not get a court martial to present his case. Aghast that a splendid British army had been defeated by ragged colonists, English common folk rallied behind their leaders and tried to form new regiments of volunteers.

On the continent, French leaders reacted with jubilation. On February 6, 1778, occurred the most crucial result of Saratoga, for on that day King Louis XVI gave official diplomatic recognition to the United Colonies and signed a treaty under which France pledged full military support to them.

Burgoyne circulated an impassioned plea for a radical change in strategy. "Turn toward the southern colonies," he urged. "Loyalists are well known to be stronger there than elsewhere; given the opportunity, they will rally behind their sovereign's banner and with the aid of troops will quickly stamp out the fires of rebellion in those regions. Once the South is secure, it will be an easy matter to deal with New England."

There is no certainty that Burgoyne's plea played a decisive role in decisions of the king and his ministers, but the general idea he advanced was accepted as plausible. Six months after Saratoga, the British pulled out of occupied Philadelphia and headed south. With the focus of activity suddenly altered and with France a powerful new player in the game, the nature of the conflict was profoundly altered.

Part Six

In the Valley
of Despair

Elation at the surrender of an entire British army late in 1777 was brief. George Washington was forced to lead his troops into Valley Forge, where they spent a dreadful winter.

With the fall of Savannah, the situation became desperate. Now the British had a splendid port city just right for use as their headquarters. From that center they expected gradually to crush remaining pockets of resistance.

Battlefield defeats, hunger, cold, Indians, traitors, and the financial woes of Congress combined to create what seemed to be insurmountable obstacles for their foes. Many colonists wondered—some silently, but many others aloud—why they had espoused the cause of liberty.

In regions dominated by patriots, children mocked Tories with impunity.

CHAPTER

34

Tories Fled the Colonies Much as Huguenots Did from France

"**I**, Fletcher Simms, do solemnly swear in the presence of Almighty God . . ."

Trembling visibly and turning his eyes from his accusers, Simms was sternly ordered, "Put your hand back upon the Bible, sir, and pray continue at once!"

Simms swallowed, resumed the witness posture, and said: ". . . I will bear true allegiance to the state of Georgia, and in all things do my duty as a good and faithful subject of the said state, and that I acknowledge the Thirteen United States of America, to be free and independent states; and that I will, to the best of my ability, when called upon, support and maintain the said independency: and I likewise renounce, refuse and abjure any allegiance or obedience to George the Third, King of Great-Britain, and that I have not, nor will not receive any protection from the said George the Third, or any of the officers and servants of the said King George."

Having completed his solemn oath, with left hand upon an open Bible and right hand raised, Simms was waved from the room by the inquisitorial committee of Augusta township. Chairman Condor Wilkes questioned the two "friends of Freedom" whom Simms had brought along to attest to his zeal for the cause of independence; and when the friends were sent from the room, he polled the committee of twelve and had Simms brought back.

"Young man," said Wilkes, "you are fortunate. You may remain in the township, subject of course to duty if called upon by the militia. We commend your patriotic zeal!"

Had Simms been unwilling to take the full oath, or had he been unable to produce two or more witnesses to vouch for his patriotism, all of his possessions would have been seized and he would have been banished from the newly created state of Georgia upon pain of death.

Enacted thousands of times in each of the political entities now calling themselves independent states, the drama in which Simms was central took place far from major coastal cities. General John Burgoyne was correct in thinking that the only strong Tory enclaves outside New York were in the South, but he was wrong in believing that these groups were strong enough to help invading forces sweep through the country with ease.

Prior to Bunker Hill, John Adams estimated that about one-third of all colonists opposed an open break with Britain. Some wanted only to be let alone and had no interest in the economic and political squabble that was brewing. Others were zealous Loyalists, ready to risk their lives and fortunes for their king and for England. Of the latter group, an estimated eight thousand who were born in America were in British uniforms in 1780, a time when George Washington's forces had dwindled to about nine thousand men.

As tensions began to mount, vast numbers of Tories fled. Many more were forced to leave when state after state adopted procedures much like those employed on the southwestern frontier in Georgia.

The exodus started in March 1776 when General Sir William Howe was forced to evacuate Boston. Then a city of about 16,000, this cradle of American independence included so many Tories that about one thousand of them thought it best to depart with British forces. The patriots who remained behind taunted:

> The Tories with their brats and wives
> Have fled to save their wretched lives!

England proved to be less than an ideal haven for Americans who went there as refugees. Many were able to take along only meager personal belongings, and they settled in London, Bristol, and other centers where most of them lived in abject poverty. A New England club was formed in London; yet even its members admitted to "feeling a certain unease" within a few weeks after reaching the capital. Despite this admission they would not—or could not—return to North America.

State after state passed statutes and ordinances that made it undesirable or impossible for Tories in exile to return home. Where no legal bans and confiscation acts were in force, vigilante-like groups of patriots threatened, and sometimes carried out, acts of violence against Loyalists.

Reports circulating in England after hostilities ceased said that exiles who tried to return home had been "whipt Imprisoned Fined—or Hanged." Some who attempted to come back were turned aside at state lines and refused admission. Others were arrested. A few even suffered mob violence.

For the Loyalist in haste to get out of the colonies, two routes of escape could be followed by land. One led northward to Canada, and the other led south to British-held East Florida. At least 28,000 Loyalists are believed to have passed through New York City alone en route to Canada. Of these an estimated three thousand blacks—mostly ex-slaves whom the British freed when they ran away from rebel owners—eventually went on to Sierra Leone. During one twelve-month period, East Florida gained more than seven thousand new residents. Practically all of them were penniless refugees.

Nova Scotia, easily reached by ocean-going vessels, attracted hordes of exiles. In one frenzied period a flotilla of eighteen ships crowded with Loyalists and their families left New York harbor for Halifax. Soon that safe haven harbored so many refugees that their "tent city," liberally sprinkled with old shacks, spread far along the beach.

Some who reached Nova Scotia immediately found themselves homesick. One exile wrote, "there are but a few inconsiderable spots fit to cultivate, and the land is covered with a cold spongy moss in place of grass. Winter continues at least seven months in the year; the country is wrapt in the gloom of a perpetual fog."

Abigail Adams, who was in Halifax at the time "the great Tory fleet" arrived, reported, "They are much distressed for want of houses, obliged to give six dollars per month for one room. Provisions are dear and scarce. Some of them with six or eight children round them sitting upon the rocks crying, not knowing where to lay their heads."

The wife of the future president had little sympathy for the plight of exiles. "Just Heaven has given to them to taste of the same cup of affliction which they administered to thousands of their fellow citizens," she mused in a letter to John Adams.

Additional bands of refugees turned to British-held islands in the Caribbean. Bermuda was an early and important haven. Many ex-Americans took up new lives in and about Nassau because any head of a family could claim forty acres of free land. At least six thousand one-time residents of the mainland colonies—perhaps more—stayed in Bermuda. Others went to tiny Antigua, and some settled in Jamaica, the largest British-held island in the Caribbean Sea.

Multitudes of Tories who could not or would not come to terms with the independence movement were all but nameless. However, nearly every colony saw a few notables flee.

Alexander Gardner left South Carolina for London, where he became a vice president of the Royal Society and had the gardenia named for him. Massachusetts lost the finest native painter of the time, John Singleton Copley. As a refugee, he adapted so well that his son became lord chancellor of England.

Faculty members and graduates of King's College (now Columbia University) fled almost en masse. So did some of New England's most distinguished attorneys. One of them, Jonathan Sewall, modified the spelling of his name so that he would never be confused with rebel kinsmen named Sewell.

Destined to become the most famous of those who refused to renounce England and her king, physicist Benjamin Thompson fled to London and reluctantly accepted a job in the British Foreign Office under Lord George Germain. There he experimented on the nature of heat, linked with a search for a way to end the capital's plague of smoking chimneys. Created a nobleman of the Holy Roman Empire by Bavaria, he spent nearly twenty years of his life as Count Rumford.

Thompson—or Rumford—was one of the fortunate few who prospered in exile. Most found themselves social misfits unable to hold a job. Those who knew enough to do so applied to the British government for pensions or compensation for confiscated property. At least 5,100 claims were entered, for a total of just under ten million pounds. Slightly over one-third of these claims were honored; those whose claims were disallowed received no redress or aid.

Philip Skene, who had craftily persuaded General Burgoyne to "take the short overland route" from his home, immediately gained an expensive road as a result. Yet Skene put in a claim for the loss of "56,350 acres, 950 cords of firewood, 2,000 sawlogs, 8,000 barrel staves, 20 cows, and eight Negroes." Skene was among the fortunate ones; for his losses a grateful Britain paid him £22,000.

Some present-day analysts insist that London was too far removed from the center of conflict to understand its nature. According to such a view, the American Revolution, while directed against British officialdom, was also a civil war in which native-born citizens were badly divided. According to some estimates, Tories put at least 30,000 men into British uniforms for part or all of the conflict. Failure to exploit deep divisions present in every colony was a major factor in the failure of plans drawn up in London.

At the time, few outsiders learned that substantially more than 100,000 American-born Tories left their country eagerly or under compulsion. They formed an exodus comparable only to the flight of Huguenots from France after Louis XIV revoked the Edict of Nantes and began persecution of Protestants.

CHAPTER

35

In Paris, Franklin Scored a Mighty Triumph

Philarete Chasles, a nineteenth-century professor in the College of France, became eloquent when he thought about a sixty-two-year-old American who had captured the hearts of the French people.

"Benjamin Franklin," he wrote, "came across the ocean to win liberty for his own country; and he brought liberty to us. He professed no religious creed except tolerance, and kindliness of heart. France, moved by a thousand passions and a thousand caprices, prostrated herself at the feet of a man who had no caprices and no passions. She made him the symbol and object of her adoration and an American took rank above Voltaire and Rousseau, by the side of Socrates."

That glowing assessment was wrong in at least one particular. Franklin not only had a passionate yearning for members of the opposite sex, he openly boasted of his prowess in the bedroom and recommended to his admirers that they avoid complications by seeking the favors of women beyond childbearing age. Clearly he had another passion also, a never-ceasing urge to defeat the British in America by securing France as an ally of the Continentals. That he succeeded against incredible odds has caused some analysts to rank the largely self-taught printer-philosopher as the most effective diplomat in U.S. history.

Badly divided on nearly every issue, the Continental Congress split on the question of whether or not to seek aid overseas. Isolationists such as Thomas Paine and John Adams wanted nothing to do with what they termed "foreign intrigue." Others—a working majority—insisted that without help, Washington and his generals could not long withstand the seemingly ceaseless flow from Great Britain of men, warships, and munitions.

Acting in secret, the lawmakers set up a committee of correspondence to look into the possibility of gaining help from overseas. Of the five men named to this body in November 1775, only Benjamin Franklin was an outspoken advocate of immediately seeking an alliance, preferably with France.

Congress debated and delayed for nearly a year, then established a three-man diplomatic mission. Many lawmakers considered Silas Deane to be the strongest member of the team; others insisted that because of his numerous strong ties with Congress, Arthur Lee was the man on whom the patriots should depend. A minority expressed confidence in Benjamin Franklin but admitted that his "advanced years" constituted a major handicap.

"France is eager and willing to help us," Franklin told everyone who would listen. "She has fought four recent wars with England and has always been defeated. Our French and Indian War stripped her of most of her possessions in the New World. Nothing would please France more than to see England humiliated and stripped of her colonies—and I am confident that she will pay any reasonable price to achieve this end."

Before departing for France in the fall of 1776, Franklin turned over to Congress, as a loan, his entire personal fortune of £3,000. Accompanied by two grandsons, one of whom he planned to use as his secretary, the U.S. commissioner traveled on a sloop of war with sixteen guns and made an exceptionally fast crossing of barely thirty days.

Habitually wearing spectacles and topping his long straight hair with a cap made of marten's fur, the American was conspicuously different in appearance from French officials and from diplomats representing other nations. Assigned quarters in the village of Passy, about one-half mile outside Paris, he expected to live quietly and to work in obscurity.

Instead, he immediately found himself to be a celebrity and a social lion.

His *Poor Richard's Almanac*, previously published in three French editions, was recommended reading in many parishes. His membership in the French Academy of Sciences, bestowed as a result of scientific papers widely published in Europe, gave him instant access to men of science and letters. Even his candor concerning his indulgence in sex—widely reported—added to his stature in the eyes of Frenchmen.

Soon his bust and portrait could be seen throughout the kingdom, while titled ladies carried snuff boxes and watches adorned with miniatures of his face and vied with one another to spend an evening with the famous American. Adulation was so great that common folk cheerfully paid for good seats to watch Benjamin Franklin ride by in his carriage.

Neither Silas Deane nor Arthur Lee joined in paying homage to a

Continental soldiers who survived the dreadful winter at Valley Forge formally cele-brated the French alliance on May 6, 1778.

man whom they considered their inferior in dealing with Europeans. Lee sent home letter after letter to influential compatriots complaining about both Deane and Franklin and suggesting that it would be wise to withdraw them as commissioners. Deane, who had arrived in Paris a few months before Franklin to buy munitions and supplies, seems always to have kept one ear turned toward London. His own ambitions would be best served, he felt, by working out a settlement with England. Hence he vigorously opposed any notion of a French alliance.

Initially regarded with scorn by professional diplomats, Benjamin Franklin proved himself adept at using their techniques. Through intermediaries he hinted to London that it might be wise to end the fighting in the New World. Such a course would stop the heavy drain upon England's resources and probably could be accomplished by consenting to give Canada, East Florida, and West Florida to the emerging United States!

"Let me never forget that the king of Spain is the uncle of Louis XVI," the man from Philadelphia reputedly mused many times to the seven-year-old grandson whose education he supervised while both were in France. "Spain has even more to gain from a Continental victory than does France. Still, France appears more ready to act."

That readiness stemmed in part from the intrigues of a man today remembered chiefly as the author of *The Barber of Seville* and *The Marriage of Figaro*: Pierre Augustin Caron de Beaumarchais. A full year before the Declaration of Independence was adopted, Beaumarchais had tried to persuade Louis XVI of France that he and his kingdom had much to gain by aiding the American movement for independence. Louis responded by providing a secret fund of one million livres as working capital. Spain also channeled money into Roderique Hortalez et Cie, the dummy corporation established by Beaumarchais. Eventually he handled at least forty million livres, and in one transaction one million livres disappeared without a trace.

Yet the self-serving adventurer played a vital role in supplying the armies of George Washington. Before Benjamin Franklin reached Paris, Beaumarchais claimed to have dispatched to the Continentals "about 200 pieces of brass cannon, four-pounders; 200,000 pounds of cannon powder; 20,000 excellent fusils; plus lead for musket balls, bombs, some brass mortars, bayonets, and clothing and linen for troops."

What role, if any, Franklin had played in enlisting the services of Beaumarchais is unknown; but it is significant that the French adventurer raced toward Passy to congratulate the diplomat as soon as he heard that Burgoyne's entire army had surrendered to General Horatio Gates. Repeatedly, Beaumarchais consulted Franklin about the purchase of supplies and ships that could be outfitted for use as privateers, and substantial quantities of military stores from France actually reached patriots long before Franklin achieved his diplomatic triumph.

In the world of international intrigue Franklin moved with such skill that he played as decisive a role in the American Revolution as that of George Washington. Persistently advancing the theme that it would be to France's advantage for the Americans to fight England, rather than for France to do so, he gained the confidence of the comte de Vergennes, minister of foreign affairs and key advisor to King Louis XVI.

"When news of the great victory at Saratoga reached Paris during the first week of December, it was clearly time to act," Franklin recalled afterward. "Vergennes obliged by sending his secretary to Passy." In a lengthy conversation, the Philadelphian pointed out that if France did not act at once, her opportunity could well be lost. He wanted a declaration of war against England, but Vergennes's aide would not even discuss the matter. Any French move to aid citizens in open rebellion against their sovereign would have to be made in two stages, not one, he said.

Given just one hour to ponder alternatives, Franklin agreed to the

In less than a century, Valley Forge was so romanticized by artists that the winter's horror was obscured. [BALLOU'S PICTORIAL, 1856]

Frenchman's terms. He would readily sign an initial treaty of "amity and commerce," to be followed by a secret treaty pledging France and the former British colonies to mutual defense. That hasty decision by Franklin paved the way for a formal visit to Versailles, which he described as dirty and ill-kept, and a public announcement of the commercial agreement.

Few if any diplomats, veteran lawmakers, or military leaders were deceived by the language of the pact. When news of it reached Philadelphia, Tories and their British friends exclaimed, "This means war with France!" General Henry Clinton, recently named supreme commander of British forces in North America, immediately began making plans to evacuate the city. Should a French fleet arrive, he reasoned, a blockade might make it impossible for him to withdraw.

When France named Conrad Gerarde Rayneval as ambassador to the United States, Britain simultaneously recalled her ambassador to France. Assigned to command vessels that would aid the Americans, the comte d'Estaing assembled twelve men of war and four frigates at Toulon. They weighed anchor on April 13, 1778, and sailed to the west under sealed orders. When their orders were opened on May 20, officers read to members of their crews a formal declaration of war against England.

Couriers brought news of the two treaties to Congress at York, Pennsylvania, where the lawmakers were assembled after fleeing from Philadelphia in September 1777. Most rejoiced, but some fumed at having formed an alliance with the most Catholic nation on earth, ruled by an absolute monarch. For the present, a majority agreed, the military pact should remain a closely guarded secret, not even divulged to George Washington.

During the dreadful winter he and his troops spent at Valley Forge, Washington fervently hoped for relief—from any source, of any magnitude—that would enable him again to field his army. He received two unofficial letters on April 30, 1778, describing the alliance forged by Franklin and the consequent turmoil in England. Washington dispatched an aide to York, asking Congress to give him official notification so that he could inform his troops. Although he received no reply, five days later he received a copy of the *Pennsylvania Gazette*, which included an entire supplement dealing with the treaty.

With plans already having been made to stage a grand review of units drilled by Steuben, General Washington set May 6 as the day to celebrate the alliance. When his troops had marched and the last shot had been fired, officers shouted in concert, "Long live the king of France!"

For the first time, Washington had more than fervor for independence and confidence in his men. The entrance of France into the conflict meant that the commander in chief now had an ally who might well shift the balance of power to victory.

Earlier, Benjamin Franklin had celebrated in his own fashion. Preparing for his meeting with Louis XVI, he meticulously brushed his clothing for the occasion. Still wearing his famous glasses, he appeared at Versailles in a suit of blue Manchester velvet, the same costume he had worn when he was called before English lawmakers to be stripped of his positions for sending the Hutchinson letters to Boston.

Taking delight in the symbolic thumbing of his nose at London, the sage of Philadelphia put the suit aside after his meeting with Louis and never donned it again. Clearly, he had tipped the scales in the struggle for a continent. It would be generations before the world would recognize what he had done, but standing proudly in his suit of blue velvet, Benjamin Franklin was sure that his appearance at the court of France spelled the beginning of the end for the British in the colonies.

36

In the Colonies, Franklin's Son Spoke and Acted for King George III

"Sir Henry, I have developed a new plan for distressing the rebels," William Franklin of New Jersey confided to Sir Henry Clinton. "We will organize the refugees into bands of fifty men. Then we must let them select their own officers and take an oath to obey the rules of the British army except for military punishment. That will speedily augment fighting forces of His Majesty, and hopefully bring this sad rebellion to a quick end."

Clinton pondered the suggestion but did not take official action upon it. Franklin's proposal involved setting up a company of subscribers who would supervise newly recruited rangers. More to Franklin's purpose, men brought into British service in this fashion would seek to seize from patriots property at least equal in value to that taken by patriots from Tories.

The Americans were solemnly warned not to harm jailed Loyalists, for Franklin proposed that "We Loyalists do solemnly declare that we will hang six for one, choosing head men and leaders for this purpose."

As though he expected by threats to bring all rebels to heel, the Tory leader added, "Wherever we loyal refugees find militiamen in arms against us or any of His Majesty's loyal subjects, we are fully determined to massacre them on the spot. We embody not the official British army, but full companies of men determined to save North America for our sovereign. Long live King George III!"

Born about 1731, William Franklin was the fruit of a common-law agreement that did not include a marriage ceremony. Although strangely silent about his son's birth, Benjamin Franklin wrote his famous autobiography expressly for him. William is believed to have been the son of his father's common-law wife, Deborah Read, but there is no certainty.

His influential father secured for him a captain's commission, under which he fought in the French and Indian War. Later he was made clerk of the Pennsylvania House of Assembly and comptroller of the general post office.

In the famous kite experiment of 1752, when lightning was shown to be a form of electricity, it was twenty-one-year-old Billy who got the kite into the air. Artists have usually depicted him as having been a small boy at the time. However, Oxford University conferred the M.A. degree upon him in recognition of his role in this discovery.

Through the influence of Britain's earl of Bute, whom he met while traveling in Europe with his father, William Franklin became royal governor of New Jersey in 1763. As the split between England and her colonies grew wider, New Jersey's large Loyalist party united behind their Tory governor. He reacted by issuing a January 1775 warning to members of the state assembly. They were to take no part in conduct that might lead to "afflictive calamities," meaning open conflict with England.

At this early stage of the American Revolution, William had already turned his back upon his father, whom he had not seen for many months. Benjamin Franklin said as little as possible about his Tory son, but in private castigated him as "a thorough courtier." Already it

William Franklin, royal governor of New Jersey.

Benjamin Franklin and a too-youthful portrayal of son William, as depicted on the panel of an early fire engine.

was clear that William intended to make a name for himself as a die-hard supporter of England, her sovereign, and her edicts.

Governor Franklin met the New Jersey assembly in May 1775 for the last time. Stripped of official power and declared to be an enemy of his country, he was sent by Congress to Connecticut as a prisoner.

Having refused to sign his own parole, the ex-governor, who continued to use his royal title for the rest of his life, was taken to East Windsor. There he was quartered in the house of Captain Ebenezer Grant. From Grant's house he appealed directly to George Washington for a pass that would enable him to visit his sick wife. Washington politely refused the request.

Sir Henry Clinton first reached New York in 1776. When he took over the colony, one of his first official acts was to arrange for the exchange and release of William Franklin.

As soon as he gained his freedom, the son of Benjamin Franklin launched a one-man drive to cripple the cause of the patriots. He persuaded Clinton to use two of his personal friends as writers of propaganda; the Reverend Samuel Seabury and the Reverend Jonathan Odell worked hard at this task. Through Odell, William Franklin almost certainly knew in advance about the plans of Benedict Arnold, destined to become the nation's most infamous traitor.

Clinton was cool to Franklin's leadership role, considering him to be both greedy and bloody. Rebuffed in New York, William turned to the South and found a friend in Governor Tryon of North Carolina. Tryon sent to London a proposal that a "joint stock company for plunder" be established and headed by Franklin. Once the matter was approved, the ex-governor became head of Associated Loyalists and was put on the British payroll at £500 per year.

From the start, it was made clear that Franklin's Associated Loyalists would be entitled to keep whatever plunder this force of irregular fighting men could seize. Eventually they got from London a formal commission "to make war in armed bands, under their own officers," as Franklin had originally proposed.

British leaders were told by Franklin that, for the predatory kind of raids he planned, latitude of command was essential. He also informed London that the more affluent Loyalists of America would follow him only if guaranteed a larger share of plunder than early "inferior Loyalists" had been willing to accept.

The battlefield impact of the Associated Loyalists was insignificant. Most of their raids, conducted at night, led only to seizure of sheep, poultry, corn, wood, and "an occasional Whig who resisted their predatory attempts."

In addition to such forays, the Associated Loyalists sent their ships to make repeated raids on the New England coast. Carrying out savage guerrilla warfare in Connecticut and New Jersey for many months, their activities reached a bloody climax in April 1782.

Members of Franklin's Associated Loyalists went to Governor Clinton of New York with a plea. They asked him to release to them a recently captured prisoner, Captain Joshua Huddy of the New Jersey militia. Huddy, they urged, could be exchanged for one of their own officers who was being held as a prisoner.

In a move strangely foreshadowing the activity of space-age terrorists, the Loyalists hanged Huddy as soon as they received him. To his dangling body they attached a placard warning patriots that they were ready "to hang man for man while there is a Tory refugee existing." They claimed that Huddy was murdered in retaliation for the death of Philip White two weeks earlier.

Outraged at having been deceived, Clinton denounced the hanging as "an act of atrocity scarcely to be paralleled in history." Then he personally set about stripping the Associated Loyalists of their powers. William Franklin, who still used the title of governor in signing his letters, fled to England. Refusing to believe that Britain could lose the struggle, the son of Benjamin Franklin claimed to have had war losses of more than £48,000. After years of haggling, a commission of Parliament awarded him £1,800 and a lifetime pension of £800 a year.

In 1784 William wrote to his father for the first time in a decade. His move toward reconciliation was too little, too late. Benjamin Franklin's 1789 will effectively disinherited William, who would have received the bulk of his now-wealthy father's estate under earlier wills. Exile William Franklin died in Paris at age eighty-two, totally destitute and having many of his personal belongings in pawnshops.

CHAPTER

37

Exploits of Molly Hays and Other Women Boosted Morale

June 28 was fearfully hot. Men of the 7th Pennsylvania regiment, unaccustomed to soggy air of New Jersey, were sweltering even before they went into action against the British. Soon it was clear that the wounded, panting for breath, would pass out without water.

John Hays' wife, Molly, found a pitcher and got busy. She ran back and forth to a well so that she could carry water to wounded and exhausted men of her husband's regiment.

That account, transmitted orally for generations, explains how the best-known battlefield heroine of the war got her nickname of "Molly Pitcher." Born as Mary Ludwig but called Molly from childhood, she married a barber. When he enlisted in the Pennsylvania militia, she accompanied him, a common practice at the time. When military activity was slack, Molly washed John's clothes, cooked some of his food, and tried to function as a housewife without a house. Thus she was present in 1778 at the Battle of Monmouth, New Jersey, in which patriots under Washington fought Redcoats under General Henry Clinton to a bloody standstill.

Legend has it that as Molly hurried from the well late in the day, she took a look at the artillery redoubt where poorly trained patriots were trying to return fire. While she watched, her husband fell, seriously wounded.

Too few men remained on their feet to serve the cannon. As members of the gun crew started to drag the weapon to the rear, Molly ran to the position and grabbed the rammer staff her husband had been using. She had watched him at work so often that she swabbed and loaded like a veteran and remained at her post under heavy enemy fire.

At Monmouth, New Jersey, Molly Hayes (earlier dubbed Molly Pitcher) took over her husband's cannon when he fell.

Molly was still serving her husband's big gun when Washington galloped by, leading a rally that drove the British back. "Cognizant of the singular role played by a female follower," according to a contemporary account, the commander in chief issued to Molly a warrant as a noncommissioned officer. For the rest of her life, the housewife was known as Sergeant Molly.

Originally buried in an obscure grave, her remains were later moved to West Point. There her granite headstone displays a bas-relief showing her serving her husband's cannon. A cannon now stands beside that grave, and she is also shown on the monument erected at the site of the Battle of Monmouth.

Some analysts have challenged the authenticity of the tale that was transmitted orally for generations, insisting that there is no documentary evidence to support the account. They believe that Molly Pitcher has been given more significance than she deserves.

Whether that is the case or not, many heroines really did boost the cause of the patriots by unlikely exploits. Some of them simply used their wits and risked their lives in their ordinary surroundings; others were active in combat. Much of the contest between Continentals and Redcoats was a protracted guerilla struggle that was punctuated by occasional battles. Because they typically traveled with supply wagons, in official reports women like Molly Pitcher were usually listed simply as "baggage."

Margaret Corbin, like Molly Pitcher, rode in baggage wagons for many months. When weary of sewing, washing, and making bandages, she often watched her husband as he trained. John Corbin, a matross (or cannoneer) encouraged her to learn everything from un-limbering a gun and securing side boxes that held ammunition to sponging the piece before charging it.

At the Battle of Fort Washington in northern Manhattan, Corbin was instantly killed when Hessian troops concentrated their fire upon his position. His wife pushed her way into the gun crew and took his place; and before the day's action ended, she was seriously wounded. Pennsylvania's executive council gave the heroine a cash settlement of thirty dollars for her battlefield service, and Congress later took up her case and voted her "one-half of the monthly pay drawn by a soldier in the services of these states and one complete suit of cloaths, or the value thereof in money."

Fort Henry, near what is now Wheeling, West Virginia, came under attack by a large band of British-led Indians when the frontier gar-rison mustered only forty men. By the time half of them were killed or wounded, the survivors were almost out of powder.

The defenders of the patriot installation knew that a keg of powder was hidden in the cabin of the Zane family, about ninety yards from the gate of the fort. However, the pro-British warriors had a clear view of the area that would have to be crossed to get the vital powder.

"Who will volunteer to risk his life for liberty and independence?" called the commander of the fort.

Four volunteers stepped forward: three men who belonged to the garrison and a girl of seventeen. "You can't afford to risk the life of a man who knows how to use a rifle," she insisted to the astonished commander. "My life is unimportant; you must let me go!"

Before she could be stopped, Elizabeth Zane slipped through the gate, strolling boldly toward her father's cabin as though she had no interest in the military action under way. The Indian attackers ignored her; so she hid the powder keg under a table cloth and returned to the fort, thereby giving the defenders sufficient fire power to hold out until the siege was raised.

Since the struggle between patriots and Tories was widespread and continuous on the frontier, some women performed conspicuous acts of bravery far from the site of a conventional siege or battlefield.

Zelma Schell lived with her husband and six sons in the beautiful, but sparsely settled, Mohawk Valley. Because patriots were too thinly spread to defend the region, it was a frequent center of raids by Tories and their Indian allies.

On an August day when Zelma was busy making candles and bak-ing bread, a force of sixteen Tories and forty-eight Indians converged upon her cabin. Protected by thick logs, family members were able to hold their own against fire from the vastly superior force. But as darkness fell, its attackers rushed the cabin and began thrusting weapons through the loopholes (slits made in the wall for small guns to be fired).

"God was my helper," Zelma Schell later said. "My eye fell upon an axe just as the first ball was fired from a gun thrust inside our cabin, and my men-folk were too busy firing to do anything else. I seized the axe, and smashed the barrel of the gun. Then, one by one, I did the same as others came in sight."

When "the battle of the Schells" was over, the remote cabin was scarred, but erect. The Tories and their Indian allies fell back with a casualty list of twenty-three dead and wounded. Using only an axe, a housewife had helped to achieve a victory more substantial than some that were fought by men in uniform.

In the region to which Daniel Boone took settlers and for which George Rogers Clark took the offensive against British and Indians, the cabin of John Merrill was attacked by renegade warriors. They shot and killed the Kentuckian and began hacking at the cabin door with tomahawks.

Nancy Merrill, who had been asleep in bed, was left to defend herself. She ripped open her feather bed and threw its contents upon glowing embers in the fireplace. The resulting blaze and blinding smoke confused the attackers; and while they staggered about in bewilderment, Nancy found her husband's axe. She killed two intruders and injured a third before the rest fled.

Rebecca Motte had no man about the house when she was surprised by a band of Loyalists and driven from her home at the edge of a captured village. That night, the South Carolina widow and mother of six children, crept back to familiar surroundings and set her own cabin on fire. When the flames spread, pro-British forces numbering 165 men were forced to evacuate the settlement they had planned to use as a garrison.

Pennsylvania-born Ann Morgan, who was known as Nancy after she married Benjamin Hart, moved with her husband to a farm near the Savannah River. British forces moved into the region late in 1778 and occupied Augusta, Georgia.

Nancy Hart disguised herself as a man, pretended to be "touched," or crazy, and penetrated British lines to get information about enemy activity. After several expeditions, she fell under suspicion, so six Tories rode to the Hart cabin to question her.

Nancy Hart dropped one Tory in his tracks and held his comrades until her menfolk returned and hanged them from pine trees.

She pretended submissiveness but secretly sent her daughter to get help. Then she offered the Redcoats a meal of cornbread, buttermilk, and fresh-cooked squirrel. As the Redcoats moved to the rough table to eat, she grabbed their guns. When one soldier tried to resist, he was shot. The other five surrendered to her and, at her insistence, were hanged from nearby pine trees when Nancy's husband and neighbors arrived.

Another unlikely heroine was just fifteen years old when South Carolina became a center of conflict. Since Tories dominated the region, it was easy for them to establish a camp near Dicey Livingston's home.

No one paid any attention to the adolescent girl who made herself at home wandering about the Tory camp, but her daily trips there were actually reconnaissance missions. She habitually gathered vital information and relayed it to patriots who used it to oust Loyalists from the Laurens district.

Lydia Darragh of Philadelphia was a year or two older than Dicey and seemed equally unlikely as a candidate for boosting the cause of the patriots. Because of her Quaker background, it was easy for her to convince members of the British forces occupying the city that "she didn't want anything to do with war." Once she was regarded as harmless, she was free to gather information.

Lydia learned of an impending attack upon the forces led by George Washington. Late in 1777 she penetrated enemy lines and reached Whitemarsh, not far from the city. Her warning is believed to have caused Washington to retreat in haste, saving his troops to fight another day. Without that warning, the commander in chief might have been killed or captured early in the conflict.

Lydia Darragh received no "veteran's compensation," no medal, and little recognition outside Philadelphia. Her contribution to the cause of independence was small; yet, it was significant. That was the case with a great many girls and women. Thousands of them marched and fought with their men in formal battles and in guerrilla clashes, but the names and exploits of most have been forgotten. Far more important even than taking an axe to a British-led Indian or seizing a sponge to service a cannon, courageous deeds of women patriots boosted the morale of their fighting men.

38

With Independence in the Balance, British Pounds Bought Treason

"**M**ajor André's hasty departure was a loss to the city."

"Perhaps," agreed the new Continental commander in charge of recently evacuated Philadelphia. "I know little or nothing about him."

"Why, General Arnold," responded Peggy Shippen, "I thought you knew everyone of any importance on both sides of the conflict! Major André directed our spring Mischanza at Walnut Grove, and the entertainment was the most splendid this city has ever seen."

"We are due for entertainment of another sort," grumbled Benedict Arnold. "Reliable information says that a fleet of eighteen French vessels is nearing the Delaware coast."

Margaret Shippen, known to intimates as Peggy, reputedly eyed her new acquaintance reflectively. As daughter of the chief justice of Pennsylvania, she was accustomed to the most elegant drawing rooms and ballrooms of the colonies. During the British occupation of Philadelphia—just ended—she had made friends with many officers whose loyalty to their king was unquestioned.

"Why are you unhappy?" she asked her new acquaintance. "Surely you are glad to have the aid of the French."

"On the contrary, madam. I wish that Jean Baptiste d'Estaing, his vessels, and his men, had gone to the bottom instead of making the crossing safely," Arnold replied soberly. "I have no use at all for pretensions of French Catholics. If we must go to bed with them in order to sever our ties with Britain, I fear we will find outselves with a case of clap [venereal disease] worse than any ever seen in London."

Neither the patriot leader, recently advanced to the rank he felt he had deserved much earlier, nor the socialite less than half his age, realized at this time that they soon would become man and wife. While there is no documentary evidence to support the story, the widely transmitted tale that the two immediately saw an opportunity for mutual advancement is entirely believable.

No American—not even George Washington—had seen harder fighting than Arnold. Accounts of his heroic march to Quebec were told and retold around camp fires of patriots everywhere. Many of them knew that it was Arnold who had insisted upon construction of warships upon Lake Champlain. Although lacking sufficient firepower to defeat a British flotilla, his vessels had blocked a British move to launch an early invasion from Canada. It was Arnold who captured Fort Stanwix, and without his leadership General John Burgoyne's plan to take control of New York probably would have succeeded. Saratoga, soon to become heralded as the turning point of the struggle, was credited to Horatio Gates; but men who fought there knew that it was Arnold who deserved the plaudits.

Only George Washington seemed fully to appreciate Benedict Arnold's military genius. It was the commander in chief who personally persuaded him not to resign his commission when political maneuvering in Congress caused five brigadiers—all junior to him—to be promoted ahead of him. A brilliant victory at Danbury, Connecticut, persuaded Congress to elevate him to the rank of major general, but his seniority was not restored. Again persuaded by Washington not to resign, he was placed in charge of Philadelphia in a conciliatory move.

While pleased at the opportunity to take charge of the most important city in the colonies and delighted at being in the social whirl with Peggy Shippen and other young women, the wounded veteran was far from satisfied. He wanted nothing to do with the French alliance, and he went to bed every night fuming at the way Congress had treated him. Partly because he had spent his own money freely in equipping his troops, he was forced to borrow from almost anyone who would lend to him.

No single factor persuaded Benedict Arnold to concoct with Peggy Shippen a plan designed to foster their mutual ambitions. Collectively, Arnold's troubles and grievances were viewed as an opportunity by the woman, already well acquainted with British Major John André and destined soon to become Mrs. Benedict Arnold. Some time early in their relationship—probably but not positively before their marriage—the two concluded that the British would be willing to pay handsomely for information. In order to make contact, they decided, it would be wise to use an intermediary.

Joseph Stansbury, age thirty-three, ran a small crockery shop in Black Horse Alley off Philadelphia's Front Street. Since he sold considerable merchandise to the Shippen family, he was not surprised to

Benedict Arnold (seated) *directed Major John Andre to stuff his boots with documents that incriminated both of them.*

be called to the home of the customer who had just married the major general. Years afterward, Stansbury wrote his recollections of his history-making meeting with General Arnold.

"After some trifling conversation," he recalled, "General Arnold opened his political sentiments respecting the war carrying on between Great Britain and America. General Arnold then communicated to me, under a solemn obligation of secrecy, his intention of offering his services to the commander in chief of the British forces."

To make that offer, Arnold would have to send a message to Sir Henry Clinton in New York—through patriot territory. It would be too risky to put anything in writing, Arnold concluded. If Stansbury should be caught and if he talked, even the word of a crockery merchant could damage a major general who had high-placed political enemies. So the man who had readily agreed to serve as a courier was required to memorize his message, word for word.

Stansbury reached New York without incident. There he met with the noted Loyalist, the Reverend Jonathan Odell. Formerly rector of St. Mary's Church in Burlington, Odell made contact with British leaders. He seems to have persuaded them that Major John André was just the man to conduct negotiations with a high-ranking patriot who was ready to sell out.

Although he had no training in espionage, Arnold had been making his preparations. Probably at his suggestion, the 25th London edition of *Bailey's Dictionary* was selected as a base on which to erect a cipher message. Every word in letters between Arnold and André was to have a code in three digits, indicating the page number of the book employed, the line number, and the word number.

As the correspondence progressed, some messages were encoded by use of page-line-word numbers from the 5th Oxford edition of Blackstone's legal *Commentaries*.

Writing to André on May 23, 1779, General Arnold used Blackstone to encode a letter saying that Sir Henry Clinton's conditions were agreeable to him. He provided the British with military intelligence—perhaps as a token of good faith—then came back to his basic theme. "I will cooperate when an opportunity offers," he promised, "and as life and every thing is at stake, I will expect some certainty—my property here secure and a revenue equivalent to the risk and service done." Not until considerably later did Clinton promise that Arnold would receive £20,000 for specific "cooperation."

Some messages were written in invisible, or "sympathetic," ink. Frequently a solution of cobalt chloride and glycerin was used because it became visible only when subjected to heat, as by use of a flat iron upon what seemed to be blank paper. These documents were customarily marked "F" to indicate that the recipient had to use fire.

"A" was the code letter for acid, indicating that a weak solution of acid should be brushed gently over a sheet of paper bearing a message written in an invisible compound of lead. When more sophisticated materials were not available, Arnold wrote on tiny slips of paper and sent them through the lines in hollow bullets.

"Masked" letters were also exchanged. This system required correspondents to have blank sheets of paper of the same size, with an irregular hole of identical shape at the same spot in each. Use of the hole exposed the message. With the mask removed, the message was surrounded by other words that appeared to form a complete letter. Because this system was tedious and limited, it permitted exchange of only brief memoranda.

Benedict Arnold even devised a special code based upon use of biblical names. In an apparently innocent letter from "Gustavus," as he usually signed himself, there might be a reference to Jerusalem. Only he and Major André knew that this meant Philadelphia. Pittsburg was Gomorrah, while George Washington was St. James, and the Delaware River was the Red Sea.

It was André who suggested that "the lady [Mrs. Arnold] might write to me at the same time with one of her intimates. She will guess who I mean, the latter remaining ignorant of underlining [hidden meanings] and sending the letter. I will write myself to the friend to give occasion for a reply. This will come by a flag of truce, exchanged officer, etc., every messenger remaining ignorant of what they are charged with."

Peggy Chew, who had a high place in the social life of Philadelphia, was duped into serving as an innocent go-between. As a result, her letters that appeared to be shopping lists and innocent chatter about social life in Philadelphia often conveyed military intelligence.

Couriers were a constant source of problem. Stansbury could not possibly do the job alone, and he was soon supplemented by John Rattoon, a vestryman of St. Peter's church in Amboy, New Jersey. Other messages were carried by William Moore, skipper of the brig *Charming Nancy*. Many went between the lines along with troop movements, for Odell had recruited two young ensigns—Tilton and Hulitt, for whom he had gained commissions—to serve as couriers.

Samuel Wallis, a Quaker landholder who was secretly a Loyalist, was a skilled map maker. Working under Arnold's direction, Wallis prepared two sets of detailed maps about General John Sullivan's planned military expedition against American Indians of the Six Nations.

Arnold and Wallis hoped to give Sullivan fake maps while providing genuine ones to British leaders, intending to lead American forces into a trap. While actually produced, the maps were so bulky it was impossible to put them to their intended use. Maps of the Hudson River valley were prepared for British use, but were never delivered.

After months of secret correspondence at a distance, Benedict Arnold met face-to-face with the man whom his wife had long counted a dear friend. John André was led to him at a point between British and American lines on September 21, 1780. They soon shook hands on a deal by which Arnold was to surrender West Point to the British, hoping thereby to enable the Redcoats to sweep through much of New York.

The conspirators threw caution to the wind.

Arnold gave André six documents—all but one of them in his own handwriting and not in cipher—and ordered him simply to stuff them into his boots. Then he gave the British officer a simulated pass and sent him back toward his own lines.

With a boot full of secret papers and dressed as a civilian, André set out to reach British headquarters in New York. He expected to go by water, using the British warship *Vulture*; but it proved to be extremely risky to try to board the vessel, so he decided to go by land using Arnold's pass and the name of "Mr. Anderson."

"Mr. Anderson" was stopped by Continental troops before he had gone ten miles. Interrogated, he was jailed in the cottage of Andreas Miller. Released the next morning, he took to his horse but was

The death of Major John Andre.

stopped again. After another delay, he was again released. Riding all day on September 23 and much of the following night, he reached a thirty-mile stretch of neutral territory between British and American lines and thought himself safe.

He was not aware that bands of patriot irregulars—not members of regular military units—habitually patrolled the neutral territory. Stopped and asked for identification, he said that he was a British officer in disguise before he learned that he was in the hands of patriots. The patriots turned him over to Lieutenant Colonel Jameson, commander of a nearby military post; Jameson immediately forwarded the prisoner to George Washington.

Because he was captured in disguise, André was tried as a spy and quickly condemned. He asked to be executed like an officer and a gentleman, by a firing squad, but Washington refused. While he was waiting to die, Alexander Hamilton—aide to Washington—offered to give up the prisoner in exchange for Benedict Arnold, who had managed to flee through the lines to New York. When the offer was not accepted, André rode to the gibbet on a wagon, where he adjusted the noose around his own neck and died on October 2, 1780.

Now safely behind British lines, Benedict Arnold was suddenly the most wanted man in North America. His "treason of the blackest dye," in the words of General Nathanael Greene, made patriots willing to go to almost any length to get their hands on him.

In this situation, George Washington masterminded what was perhaps the most bizarre plot of the long-drawn struggle. Since he was unable to seize Arnold by force of arms, he tried to arrange for the traitor to be kidnapped and spirited to American lines for arrest, conviction, and execution.

Enlisting the aid of Major Henry Lee, an old hand at espionage, the commander in chief soon worked out the details. Lee selected Sergeant John Champe of Loudoun County, Virginia, to execute their plan. On the night of October 20, Champe pretended to desert his unit; but, following Washington's orders, he crossed the Hudson River and reached a British gunboat, still wearing his Light Horse uniform.

Champe offered to join the British cause and got passage to New York. There he managed to enlist in Arnold's corps, recently assigned to him by the British. By December 11 he was ready to execute the plan to kidnap Arnold. With the aid of another undercover agent, Champe would seize him and rush him to waiting patriots in New Jersey.

Fate then took a hand. Just twenty-four hours before George Washington's plot was to have been executed, Arnold ordered his men— including John Champe—to embark on transports for a voyage to Virginia. Not knowing that he had saved his own life by this sudden action, the traitor decided to move against Richmond, which he found defended by only a few hundred poorly trained members of the militia.

British forces sailed up the James River to a point about twenty-five miles from the Virginia capital, entering it without opposition on January 5, 1781. Governor Thomas Jefferson's defending forces did not fire a shot before they fled. So much criticism followed that Arnold gained a special kind of revenge: Thomas Jefferson resigned as chief executive of the state without a successor having been named. Jefferson, who never had much liking for Arnold, smarted under the humiliating military victory of the traitor.

However, Jefferson and patriots everywhere gloated when they learned the eventual fate of the one-time patriot who had slipped through George Washington's hands. Although Arnold had confidently expected to receive a huge sum of money, permanent rank as a British general, and adulation of the masses, the authorities soon stripped him of his rank and gave him a token pension. Instead of lauding him as Parisians had honored Benjamin Franklin, Londoners dubbed him a mercenary turncoat, avoided his company, and helped cause his name to become a synonym for *traitor*.

39

A Creek Chieftain Played
Both Ends against the Middle

"**H**is Majesty the King is generous to those who serve him well."

"I know that well; nothing less than a colonel's commission will persuade me."

"Here in the Southern Indian Department, we have no officers of that rank," responded David Taitt. He paused reflectively and suggested, "Perhaps Alexander McGillivray can change this situation."

By 1778 McGillivray had already demonstrated his zeal for British service. At the trading post of Little Tallassie on the Coosa River, any Red Stick Creek who hinted that he might not wish to fight for the great king across the water was ordered to go into the forest alone and told to stay until he was ready to obey the rising young chieftain. According to Alabama tradition, the fiery leader of mixed blood so impressed the resident agent of King George III that he was promised the rank he demanded.

If that tale is true, there is no documentary evidence to indicate that Taitt lived up to his promise. Regardless of Alexander McGillivray's rank among white men, he tried to please the British—for a time. Later he served the Spanish. Always he aimed at getting revenge for the way in which the patriots had treated his Loyalist father.

When Scottish trader Lachlan McGillivray moved into Indian country, he took as his mate Sehoy of the Tribe of the Wind. Reputedly beautiful, she was the daughter of French-born Captain Marchand and an influential Creek woman. Their son, Alexander, hence had Scottish, French, and Indian blood in his veins. Until early adolescence, he lived at his father's trading post, and in the year that patriots clumsily disguised as native Americans dumped tea into Boston harbor, young McGillivray went to Charles Town to study under his cousin. Despite his mixed blood, he was universally treated as a Creek.

Charles Town, the only major city south of the Potomac River, fired the imagination of the adolescent. Very early, he decided that he would like nothing better than to enter the service of the king of England. At every ceremony in which officials took part, the boy was watching from close range.

At a time not precisely noted, he moved to Savannah to study under another tutor. "Georgia is the most loyal of all the colonies," he reported to his father in a letter. "Here, I see the king's governor on the streets almost daily. The town is alive with activity; if rebels are out looking for trouble, they will find their fill of it in Georgia!"

His appraisal was accurate. Partly because the colony was the youngest of Britain's original thirteen, and partly because it lay in the great southwest with an open frontier stretching to the Mississippi River, the colony seemed to be dominated by Tories. But as the "little brush fire of rebellion" flared into armed revolt, patriots seized more and more power. They established their own government, and for a time the royal governor had to withdraw from the colony. Whigs eventually became so strong that they were able to confiscate the property of known Loyalists.

Lachlan McGillivray's vast domain lay in what is now Alabama, which was then claimed by Georgia. When stripped of his possessions, the trader returned to Scotland; simultaneously, his son returned to his boyhood home among the Creeks. It was there that he eagerly accepted David Taitt's offer after having pressed for a colonel's commission.

Whether or not he actually became a colonel, Alexander McGillivray took up arms in the service of King George III. He led two or three raiding parties, although always insisting that he fought much better with words than with weapons. Broadening his power base by exploiting factions produced by the Revolution, he emerged as "autocrat of the Creeks" after Chief Oconostota was deposed.

McGillivray fashioned a confederacy that included the Upper Creeks, or Red Sticks, along with the Seminoles and the Chickamaugas. At the height of his power, he boasted that he could put ten thousand warriors into the field. If that estimate was accurate, he commanded more fighting men than any American except George Washington.

From the chaos of war, McGillivray emerged as an astute diplomat who managed to exploit European ambitions and the growing nationalism of the one-time colonies. Always protesting his undying loyalty to Britain, he bargained for months with Esteban Rodriguez Miro and eventually signed a treaty with the Spanish governor of East Florida. In a single transaction, the Spanish furnished him with five thousand pounds of powder, ten thousand pounds of ball, and great quantities of flints and other military gear. Glowing from this triumph, he sent runners to the north with a message for George Washington: "Alexander McGillivray is willing to talk peace."

To Washington, that promise meant hope for the future. Perhaps the man of mixed blood who had been reared as an Indian would stop raging at Whigs and patriots. Perhaps he would even call a halt to frontier warfare aimed at forcing white men to return vast amounts of land to the Indians.

Indian agent Benjamin Hawkins, later a U.S. senator, is believed to have encouraged Washington to invite McGillivray to visit him after the war. When the two sat down to parley in New York, Washington found the terms of the chieftain to be very steep. Never having served the Continental army for a day, the Creek was awarded a pension of $1,200. Reputable scholars insist that he was also made a brigadier general. In turn, he repudiated his treaty with the Spanish and agreed to make concessions in the matter of land boundaries.

Logically, that should have ended the career of the Indian leader who served the British and the Spanish before becoming an ally of George Washington. But in the case of the Red Stick Creek who claimed ownership of three vast plantations and more than sixty slaves, logic did not prevail. Widely called "an American Talleyrand," the largely self-taught master of intrigue went back to the Spanish with a copy of the American treaty in his pouch. In return for a Spanish pension three times as large as that granted by the Americans, he repudiated the treaty made in New York.

Successfully making use of mutual distrust among the British, the Spanish, and the Americans, Alexander McGillivray accumulated holdings far greater than those confiscated from his Tory father. He took part in no significant military engagement of the war, but he made himself the most powerful man on the southwestern frontier.

Largely forgotten today, in spite of his immense power, McGillivray had a Mohawk counterpart far to the north. Reared among white men and known by them as Joseph Brandt, the native American leader Thayendanegea offered his services to the British at the outbreak of armed hostilities.

Tradition holds that as soon as the chieftain was accepted as a British ally, he promised each of his warriors an opportunity "to feast on a Bostonian and to drink his blood." General Sir Guy Carlton, commanding officer of forces in Canada at the time, wanted nothing to do with butchery; so he agreed only to employ forty or fifty men as scouts. Colonel Daniel Claus, who was present at negotiations between British and Mohawks, reported, "The Indians were somewhat disgusted" when told they would not immediately go on the war path.

Later, however, Thayendanegea and his warriors saw plenty of blood

Benjamin Lincoln helped persuade George Washington to meet with McGillivray.

flow. Leading a force of approximately one thousand braves, the Mohawk leader fought at Fort Stanwix, New York, in 1777 and saw his forces take a terrible beating.

When an opportunity for revenge presented itself the following August, Thayendanegea and his men swooped upon the frontier settlement of Cherry Valley in western New York, and destroyed it. From that time forward, Americans on the northwestern frontier regarded the Mohawk with execration.

At war's end, however, Thayendanegea became a northern counterpart of Alexander McGillivray. Like the Creek leader, he had a lengthy personal meeting with George Washington, after which he claimed to have received one thousand guineas as down payment and promise of an ultimate reward of twenty thousand pounds for "arranging a peace with the Ohio Indians."

Thousands of native Americans fought against patriots during the long-drawn struggle, and most served under British officers who tried to maintain a degree of control over them. Rank-and-file warriors usually got extra food and a blanket or two, and many managed to slip into the woods with a splendid British musket as a trophy for brief service. However, McGillivray and Brandt, both of whom understood the white man's ways, used the conflict for personal profit on a scale matched by few white-skinned patriots.

40

Printing Presses Worked Overtime Turning Out Paper Money

Philadelphia 9 Oct. 1779

The press stops at 200 Millions, which I believe will be expended in December. Out of the 60 Millions which was heretofore called for from the states, only 3 Millions have been received. How the war can be carried on after December, I know not.

I do not expect the Treasury can possibly be supplied by the States 15 million per Month; North Carolina, I am confident, cannot supply her Quota Monthly. I dread the consequences, but, as you say, "we must take events as they happen."

For God's sake come on to relieve me in Nov., but at the furthest the very beginning of December. In fact I cannot live here. The price of every necessary has advanced 150 times since we parted. I shall return indebted at least £6,000, and you very well know how we lived.

Do not mention this Complaint to any person. I am Content to sit down with this loss and much more, if my Country requires it. I only mention it to you to guard you against difficulties which you must encounter on your return here, unless the Gen. Assembly make suitable provision for yr. expenses, at least.

Your affectionate and obedient ser't,
CORN HARNETT

As a delegate to the Continental Congress, Harnett of North Carolina felt compelled to warn Dr. Thomas Burke, who was scheduled to take his place in Philadelphia. Money had been a problem from the start of "the misunderstanding between London and Philadelphia." During the two years that followed Gates's brilliant victory at Saratoga, it became a matter of top priority.

At the beginning of the conflict, "hard money"—gold, silver, and copper—consisted largely of British and Spanish coins, although some issued by Holland, France, and Portugal were also in circulation. Spanish silver dollars were often cut into eight segments or "bits" because coins of small value were scarce. Paper money, or currency, was issued by most of the colonies and by some banks and mercantile establishments.

Never available in quantities adequate to meet the needs of colonial commerce, English pounds—treated as equivalent in value to dollars—were frequently hoarded. Once the supply of European money was cut off, patriots continued for some years to express values in terms of the pound and the shilling; but there were not enough pounds and shillings on hand to fund the war effort, to say nothing of civilian commerce.

Long-standing British policy had enabled the colonies to issue bills of credit. These could be used to satisfy public debts, but they were not acceptable in private transactions. To compound the problem, most colonial currency was intended for use only in the colony of issue. If a pine-tree shilling from Massachusetts surfaced in Virginia, it might be considered worth only a fraction of its value in the Bay Colony.

By the time Corn Harnett wrote to warn his colleague about inflation in Philadelphia, many leaders were saying that it was too late. Presses should have been stopped months earlier, they declared. According to one observer, "The enemy's whole dependence now rests upon our being crushed with the weight of Reams of depreciated paper money." That is, Britain's slow progress upon the battlefield appeared to be more than offset by the speed of colonial printing presses. Because most issues of currency were not promptly supported by taxes, the value of paper money began to shrink almost before the ink was dry.

To make matters worse, most currency issued by the Continental Congress was hastily produced on whatever paper was at hand. Hence it took little skill to produce counterfeits that readily passed in trade. Most spurious bills of this sort were printed even more poorly than the genuine ones they imitated. In New York City, however, merchants and bankers discovered during the spring of 1776 that some "very superior counterfeits" were in circulation.

George Washington took a hand in trying to catch the maker of the New York counterfeits, for the economy of the patriots' cause was threatened by them. Under his order, a military raiding party surrounded a house on Long Island; and soldiers seized printing presses, counterfeit Continental currency, and an engraver named Henry Dawkins.

Dawkins, who had learned to engrave upon metals in London, came to New York about 1753. He was among the earliest engravers to work on copper in America, and consequently the bills produced by him or under his supervision were far superior to ordinary counterfeit notes. After his arrest in May 1776, some evidence was found that suggested he may have been in the pay of British agents who were seeking to undermine the strength of currency issued by patriots.

If that actually was the case, Redcoats were wasting their time and energy; Continental currency collapsed under its own weight. Soon after the North Carolina congressman penned his urgent warning, paper money became all but worthless. In a move aimed at recalling as much currency as possible, Congress agreed to accept it in payments due to the national treasury from the new states; but even this provision was qualified. To be credited with a payment of one thousand dollars made in this fashion, a state had to send bills with face value of forty thousand dollars to Philadelphia. In retaliation, most states began refusing to accept Continental currency in payment of taxes.

English supporters of the king and his ministers gloated at news of desperation in the rebel capital. One newspaper gleefully informed its readers, "The American Congress has fallen into contempt so profound that the army has declared it will not submit to a peace made by Congress. The people who protested the taxation of tea grumble far louder than before, but they are nevertheless obliged to surrender one piece of furniture after another, even their beds, in order to pay their taxes."

Beginning early in 1777, delegates to the Continental Congress from time to time debated trying to prop up their paper money by controlling prices. Although many weeks were devoted to the issue, no legislation was enacted. One desperate delegate told fellow lawmakers that their inaction forced him to lay out "no less than twenty-one pounds for the purchase of buttons for a servant's coat, a price that did not include having the buttons sewn on the garment."

Having no authority to levy taxes, Congress was forced to rely upon the individual states that had been colonies only a short time earlier. Many were proudly resentful of the central authority in Philadelphia; others were in deep financial trouble themselves. So the dismal outlook in North Carolina was little, if any, worse than that in the other twelve states.

In Boston, firebrand Samuel Adams complained that he paid two thousand dollars for "a suit of cloathes and one hat." Colonel Benjamin Hanks of Litchfield, Connecticut, recorded in his diary that

Coppersmith Paul Revere engraved the plates from which this issue of Massachusetts currency was printed.

"the cost of flour has now reached $1,575 a barrel."

James Bowdoin, destined later to become governor of Massachusetts, lamented that he was "required to pay $150 for a haircut and was lucky to get it at that—for soon after, the barber ceased altogether to accept currency and plastered the walls of his shop with it." About the same time, a housewife was forced to pay $375 for "a single pound of rancid salt pork."

When goods became scarce and with paper money abundant, prices sometimes shot up with incredible rapidity. In Boston a merchant sold a large barrel of rum for eight thousand dollars. Six weeks later when the merchant needed an empty barrel, the original purchaser told him he could get back the barrel—minus the rum—for $12,000.

Since neither lawmakers of the confederated states nor their assemblies seemed capable of doing anything to remedy matters, citizens began to take things into their own hands. In actions strangely reminiscent of raids and demonstrations staged in protest of British taxation without representation, bands of patriots took action against merchants whom they held reponsible for the fiscal nightmare.

Abigail Adams, the eloquent letter-writing wife of John Adams, reported to her husband, "It has been rumored that an eminent, wealthy, stingy merchant with a hogshead of coffee refused to sell under six shillings per pound. A number of females, some say as many as a hundred, assembled with a cart and trucks, marched down to the warehouse and demanded the keys.

"When he refused to deliver the keys, one of them seized him by his neck and tossed him into the cart. Upon his finding that no one would come to his aid, he delivered the keys. Thereupon they tipped the cart and discharged him, then opened up the warehouse, hoisted out the coffee themselves, put it into a cart, and took it away."

Inflation proceeded at such a pace that in many localities it took two hundred, three hundred, or even four hundred dollars to purchase what in normal times would have cost one dollar. Continental currency was so depreciated and despised that many citizens came to refer to a piece of it as a "shin plaster." That is, it was worthless except as paper with which to wrap a sore ankle to which salve had been applied. It was also the source of the expression "not worth a Continental," meaning valueless.

Many Londoners rejoiced at an account—probably exaggerated but pointing directly at the Achilles heel of the rebellion—published in the *Royal Gazette*. According to it, "a large body of inhabitants with paper dollars in their hats paraded the streets of Philadelphia" to dramatize the conviction that Congress was bankrupt.

Recalling stories about the way in which British customs officers were sometimes treated, citizens of the American capital were said to have marched "with a DOG TARRED, and instead of the usual appendage and ornament of feathers, the animal's back was covered with the Congress paper dollars." At the rear of the procession, alleged the British newspaper, the city jailor trudged along to protest having been refused a glass of rum in exchange for a handful of Continental currency.

That account, widely circulated in England, may have been fictional; but the problems to which it pointed were real. Throughout the colonies, interest in armed conflict waned as the value of currency dropped to a point that made it virtually worthless. Barter became the standard form of securing food, clothing, and other everyday necessities; and recruitment of fighting men lagged woefully. Many already in uniform refused to be paid with Continental currency, and members of some units deserted in a body when told that the paymaster had nothing else to offer.

Silver that flowed across the Atlantic in the wake of Benjamin Franklin's diplomatic coup in Paris made it possible to hold the Continental army together; but lacking access to hard money from any source, many civilians who counted themselves as stout patriots seemed almost willing to accept taxation without representation in return for a stable economy.

CHAPTER

41

Reputations Suffered When Things Went Awry

Was Liet. Colo. Paul Revere crityzable for any of his conduct during his stay at Bagaduce, or while he was in or upon the River Penobscot?"
"Yes."
"What part of Liet. Colo. Revere's conduct was crityzable?"
"In disputing the order of Brigadier General Wadsworth respecting the boat & saying that the Brigadier had no right to command him or his boat."
"Was Liet. Colo. Revere's conduct justifyable in leaving River Penobscot and repairing to Boston, with his Men, without particular orders from his Superior officer?"
"No."

Questions and answers recorded by the clerk of a court of inquiry on November 16, 1779, enraged Paul Revere. Remembered today as a famous courier who spread the alarm that the British were coming, the Boston silversmith and engraver considered his horsemanship unimportant; he badly wanted to be known as a valiant soldier.

Before opening his Boston shop, he took part in a colonial expedition against Crown Point, during which he served as a lieutenant of artillery. That brief, seldom-remembered stint, he later insisted, qualified him for the thing he most wanted in life: a commission as an officer of the Continental army.

Paul Revere never got that coveted commission. His only other military service was in the Massachusetts militia. Fighting for his colony, he took part in two expeditions, one a failure, the other a comic-opera fiasco.

Having managed a powder mill and briefly commanded Castle William, a fortification in Boston Harbor, Revere argued that he deserved to wear an officer's insignia. After colleagues yielded to his pleas and made him a lieutenant colonel of artillery, his first term of active service took him to Rhode Island in 1778, where the expedition led by General John Sullivan accomplished nothing.

A few months later, he rejoiced at being included in the Penobscot expedition, one of the biggest and most costly operations mounted by any colony. Aimed at a peninsula near the mouth of Maine's largest river, it set out from Boston in July 1779. Long called Penobscot, but later renamed Castine, the only settlement of importance in the region had been seized by the British in June, a move that threatened Boston's vital shipping industry. Since Maine was then a part of the Massachusetts Bay Colony, patriots there began organizing the Penobscot expedition just nine days after the enemy took control.

General Solomon Lovell commanded the land forces, while the commodore of the Massachusetts navy, Dudley Saltonstall, was in charge of nineteen armed vessels used to transport fighting men and their equipment. As commander of artillery, Lieutenant Colonel Revere was in charge of three nine-pound guns and field pieces of lighter weight.

When more than two thousand men had crowded aboard Saltonstall's warships, many units of militia still stood on shore. The transport vessels were already loaded with nine tons of flour, ten tons of rice and salt beef, and twelve hundred gallons of rum. However, cargo was shifted, additional vessels were called into service, and nine hundred more fighting men were jammed into many of the twenty-four additional transport vessels. Since the expedition included only "about five hundred stand of arms," only about one militiaman in six had any weapon except his own.

When the colonists reached their target on July 25, 1779, and managed to effect a landing, naval forces were so poorly coordinated that the badly outnumbered British managed to hold out until four vessels of their own force arrived on August 13. As a military engagement, the fight that followed was a comic-opera disaster. Most of the forty-one ships in the Massachusetts flotilla were sunk or captured, costing the colony an estimated £1,739,000 and considerable humiliation. The patriots naturally created a court of inquiry "to examine into the behavior of those responsible for the disgrace of the Penobscot" and to assess blame.

Thomas Carnes, a captain of marines aboard the warship *General Putnam*, did not wait for official proceedings to begin. On September 6 he filed lengthy charges that began: "Being requested to Lodge a complaint against Lt. Colonel Paul Revere, for his behavior at

General Charles Lee at Monmouth Court House. [MONMOUTH
COUNTY HISTORICAL ASSOCIATION]

Penobscot, let it be know that . . ." Captain Carnes then detailed five
specific charges which collectively constituted an accusation of insubordination and cowardice.

Relieved of his command and "placed under close arrest at his residence," Revere was freed after three days. Claiming to be the victim of
a campaign for revenge by high-ranking officers with whom he had a
long-standing feud, he conducted his own defense.

That may have been a mistake, for when official findings were an-
nounced on October 7 the name of the midnight rider was not cleared.
He demanded another hearing, during which the testimony given
November 16 (quoted above) went into the record.

Throughout the two formal hearings, Revere insisted that he was being used as a scapegoat. Someone had to suffer for the Penobscot failure, he said, and the axe fell on him because he had for months been saying that vessels of the Massachusetts navy were ineffective. Captains of these ships had long wanted to silence him, Revere told the court, and the Penobscot expedition gave them the opportunity for which they had been waiting.

Smarting at the damage done to his reputation, the now-famous patriot demanded a formal court-martial. Such a military trial would take precedence over the two separate civil hearings that had ended in disappointment to Revere. But Captain Carnes, who had brought the initial charges, was already out of Boston. So was Major William Todd, who supported and amplified accusations leveled at the lieutenant colonel of artillery.

It took five formal demands before Paul Revere got his court-martial nearly three years later. Lengthy charges of disobedience, unsoldierlike behavior, and cowardice had by then been reduced to two specific allegations. One was based upon his alleged "refusal to deliver a certain Boat to the order of General Wadsworth when upon the Retreat up Penobscot River." A second count, which did not include the word *cowardice*, condemned "his leaving Penobscot River without Order from his Commanding Officer."

One general flanked by twelve captains sat in judgment. Although official records and Revere's own diary supported the basic facts of the first charge, the officers dismissed it because the boat he refused to deliver was eventually used during the general retreat. Evidence pointing to cowardice and desertion under fire was tempered, said the court, by the fact that "the whole army was in great Confusion and so scattered and dispersed that no regular Orders were or could be given."

Therefore the court ordered that "Lieu't Colo. Paul Revere be acquitted with equal Honor as the other Officers in the same Expedition." With his reputation among his contemporaries damaged beyond repair but with his name officially cleared, the goldsmith-rider-soldier resumed his earlier practice of wearing a military uniform as his daily attire in civilian life.

Irish-born Thomas Conway was not so fortunate. Made a brigadier general by Congress soon after having come to America under the auspices of Silas Deane, he was recommended for promotion to the rank of major general for gallantry in action. George Washington, who did not like him, blocked the promotion on the grounds that it was unfair to native-born officers.

Furious at this treatment, Conway resigned his commission. Influential members of Congress who were disappointed that Washington was suffering one defeat after another refused to accept the resignation and, against the protests of their commander in chief, made Conway a major general.

In this climate of distrust and power politics, General Horatio Gates seems to have concluded that his brilliant victory at Saratoga should cause him to replace Washington as commander in chief. Gates, incidentally, never admitted that unauthorized leadership by Benedict Arnold may have been a decisive factor at Saratoga.

Secret correspondence between Conway and Gates, some of it criticizing Washington, fell into the hands of General James Wilkinson. Transmitted to the commander in chief, the letters were interpreted to mean that high-ranking officers were engaged in a plot to oust him.

Immediately reassigned to a subordinate role, Conway again resigned within the year. This time Congress accepted the resignation, and his name was permanently smeared by adoption of "The Conway Cabal" as a name for "a most malicious plot" that may actually have been nothing more than indiscreet remarks by some of Washington's jealous, ambitious subordinates.

British-born General Charles Lee, for a period the ranking major general of the Continental army, was often at odds with the commander in chief. They clashed frequently, but Lee's value as an officer was not officially questioned until June 1778. After the chaotic battle of Monmouth, New Jersey, Lee was charged with having ordered a retreat that was halted only when Washington gallantly rode into the line of fire and managed to cause the contest to be called a draw.

Like Paul Revere, Lee was the subject of a court-martial, but not because he requested it. This time it was the commander in chief who brought charges. Suspended from command for a year, Lee subsequently put in writing his contempt for Congress; so he was dismissed from service. Some military analysts—still a minority—now hold that Charles Lee was made a scapegoat for bungling leadership on the part of George Washington.

Regardless of his guilt or innocence, any man against whom charges were filed saw his name permanently blackened. In the turbulent years that began with near-desolation of the Continental army at Valley Forge, fighting was desultory and often ineffective. Brave fighting men managed to relieve their tedium somewhat by telling and retelling stories about patriots who happened to be caught in the middle when plans went awry. That they habitually did so is an index of the low level to which morale fell in the time when the only really dramatic victory by patriots was the diplomatic one engineered by Benjamin Franklin in distant Paris.

42

"Our Vaunted Allies Have Made a Great Display of 'French Courage'"

"**C**harles Town is vulnerable."

"Yes, both of us long ago understood that."

"But if the British move on Charles Town from Savannah in our present state, capture of the city could end our entire enterprise."

"Of course, Governor Rutledge," agreed General Benjamin Lincoln. "We have had little cause to rejoice since Saratoga."

Governor John Rutledge nodded and, as though his colleague were not familiar with them, began reciting a list of engagements.

"Despite the claims of our commander in chief, Monmouth was a draw," he said. "We got nowhere at Newport [Rhode Island], and the Redcoats took Savannah—led by a mere colonel."

"Wayne was our one source of exultation," interrupted Lincoln. "As long as men talk of war, they will remember his bayonet charge at Stony Point [New York]."

"You are right," Governor Rutledge agreed, "but that smashing victory centered upon an installation of no great significance. Savannah is different. If we do not dislodge the enemy soon, they will use it as a base from which to move upon Charles Town and thence northward. God alone knows where."

"Our own forces are not adequate to storm Savannah," General Lincoln responded. "And in light of what he failed to accomplish at Newport, I am not sure that we should put our faith in d'Estaing."

"Newport or not, Count d'Estaing and the French are our only hope," Governor Rutledge insisted. "I beg of you that we today conclude upon a course of action; if we do not, the hurricane season will be upon us. Why not invite Monsieur Plombard to give us his counsel?"

Count d'Estaing, later emperor of Haiti, was among those recruited by the French.

Benjamin Lincoln agreed that they could do little, if anything, without the warm approval of the French consul at Charles Town. Consulted, Plombard said that the recent capture of Granada by the French made it possible to hope that the fleet of Count d'Estaing could be employed against Savannah. "I will dispatch a swift vessel at once, if you wish," he offered. "We will hear from the count soon enough, I warrant."

South Carolina officials heard nothing until lookouts on the coast reported the sighting of five sets of sails, big ones not wholly familiar in contour. They proved to belong to three French frigates and two sister ships sent by d'Estaing to Charles Town so that their commanders could help plan the projected operation.

Soon the troops commanded by General Lincoln were in action, slowly making their way toward their Georgia target. Many patriots considered it to be a good omen that a corps commanded by Count Pulaski, who happened to be in Carolina, readily joined them. Meanwhile, other vessels in the French squadron converged and plotted their course. As a result, the royal governor of Georgia, James Wright, having returned after being briefly ousted by patriots, received alarming news on September 8, 1779.

Early that day, eleven French frigates, two fifty-gun warships, and twenty ships of the line appeared off Tybee Island a few miles from the Georgia capital on the Savannah River. According to estimates of veteran observers, the French fleet carried at least five thousand soldiers, perhaps many more. If Wright and his Loyalists and the British commander and his Redcoats expected to hold the town, they would have to move with lightning speed.

Previous sporadic sightings of occasional French vessels had not alarmed General Sir Augustine Prevost, but the approach of a fleet was another matter. A horseshoe battery, already under construction, was hurriedly completed and provided with arms stripped from small gunboats then in the Georgia port. Four large British vessels were stationed in the Savannah River at such a point that if they failed to stop an advance upon the town, they could retire up the river. Capitalizing on the experience gained at Fort Sullivan, the British commander impressed gangs of blacks and put them to work throwing up redoubts of palmetto logs that were interfilled with sand, while other slaves were worked around the clock to complete a network of trenches. An old ship, the *Rose*, was sunk in the channel with the hope that it would effectively bar the progress of enemy vessels.

Count d'Estaing's men quickly captured the fifty-gun British warship *Experiment*, along with the twenty-four-gun *Ariel* and two or three supply ships. Small craft sent from Charles Town moved readily in waters too shallow for battleships, carrying more than 3,500 French troops to a point within three hours' march of Savannah. Since it would take days to drag heavy guns to forward positions, it was decided to act without them. As soon as the French units were in position to attack, Count d'Estaing pointed out his overwhelming numerical strength and demanded that General Prevost surrender the town and his forces "to the arms of the King of France."

Prevost responded that it was ungentlemanly to demand an unconditional surrender and suggested that they discuss terms—in a successful bid for twenty-four more hours in which to prepare his defenses. During this truce, advance forces of Continentals under General Lincoln made contact with French troops in spite of the fact that Redcoats and Loyalists had destroyed all bridges and obstructed all roads and trails. Simultaneously, however, Redcoats from outlying positions, led by Lieutenant Colonel Maitland, joined the defenders of Savannah. So strengthened, Prevost peremptorily declined to give up the town.

Feints, skirmishes, and sporadic use of heavy guns constituted the only action for several days. General Prevost then sent a messenger under a flag of truce, asking permission to evacuate women and children. After consulting with General Lincoln, Count d'Estaing summarily rejected the request.

By this time, veteran sailors reckoned that the hurricane season was about to begin. If gales should catch the French fleet in unprotected waters, many ships would likely sink; so with time running out, the

*Modern Savannah includes an imposing monument to Count Pulaski, who died try-
ing to take it from the British.*

attackers must strike soon or abandon their effort. Hence commanders selected officers and units calculated to be best able to rush fortified positions and swarm over them to victory.

On October 8 the Americans and their French allies made the long-
awaited strike. More than 200 members of the Charles Town militia
were in the forefront, along with 600 or more Continentals whose
ranks include the corps led by Pulaski. The main body of attackers
consisted of more than 3,500 French veterans and a contingent of
black recruits from islands of the Caribbean. At the suggestion of Lincoln, many members of the attacking force fastened bits of white paper to their hats so that their comrades could distinguish them from
enemies.

Troop movement began as planned at 4:00 A.M., an hour that may
have played a decisive role in the battle. Not familiar with the terrain,
the French officer responsible for leading a diversionary attack stumbled through the swamps and lost his way. Eager to start the action
before defenders could see to use their weapons, d'Estaing signaled for
the assault to begin before the main body of his troops were in position.

The Redcoats, earlier warned by Loyalists of Georgia, were prepared for the predawn assault. Instead of relying upon muskets, they

loaded their cannon with grapeshot and poured such heavy fire upon the attackers that three separate waves of them broke and retreated. General William Moultrie of Fort Sullivan fame later reported that French and American fighting men, crowded together in a narrow space, were under constant heavy fire from well protected British troops. "Our men were so crowded in the ditch and upon the beam," Moultrie wrote in a summary of the action, "that they could hardly raise an arm. While they were in this situation, huddled up together, the British loaded and fired with deliberation at no danger to themselves."

During a long, bloody morning, the South Carolina flag planted beside the French flag in a redoubt was shot from its position. Sergeant Jasper, who had won fame by rescuing a similar flag at Fort Sullivan, again raced to retrieve the colors of his state. He managed to restore the flag to its position, but in doing so he received a mortal wound. General Casimir Pulaski, who led his men directly toward a strong British position, took a direct hit and soon died. By the time d'Estaing was twice wounded, it was clear that the assault could not be sustained.

Before the French commander ordered a general withdrawal, almost one thousand of his troops lay dead. With the exception of Bunker Hill, no other battle of the war produced so many casualties in so short a time.

Soon after leaving their positions before Savannah, vessels of the French fleet encountered a violent storm that caused four frigates to fall into British hands. Count d'Estaing dispatched most of his remaining vessels to the West Indies but himself returned to France. With Charles Town suddenly more vulnerable than it had been prior to the Battle of Savannah, General Sir Henry Clinton sent 7,500 men aboard frigates and ships of the line to plant the British flag.

General Moultrie blamed the disaster upon delay. "Had the French and Americans marched upon Savannah immediately upon arrival," he wrote, "they would have carried the town very easily." In Moultrie's judgment, d'Estaing's refusal to take prompt action permitted the enemy to complete defensive works so strong that a force two or three times as large would have had no greater success.

Cynical patriots who had voiced objection to an alliance with a Catholic nation whose citizens did not speak English, were quick to reply "I told you so." According to them, talk about delay was merely an excuse. "At Savannah our valiant allies," said these folk, "have made a great display of 'French courage,' which folk who speak a proper language call by a name that is more readily understood: *cowardice*."

Part Seven

The World
Turned
Upside Down

Patriots having suffered a humiliating defeat at Savannah, their foes turned to the South to bring the struggle to a speedy end. To their consternation, Loyalists in the region proved less effective than expected, and Continentals fought with fresh fury. A series of smashing engagements came to a climax at Yorktown, where combined American and French forces defeated the British. A handful of rebels had turned the world upside down.

DeKalb, prone, was saved by his personal aide.

43

DeKalb's Title Was Fake but His Zeal for Freedom Was Genuine

Perspiring freely and running unsteadily because they had eaten nothing except green corn and green peaches, American scouts reached advance units and panted an account of what they had found. A huge force led by General Charles Cornwallis, believed to be made up largely of Tories from the North, was proceeding directly toward Continental lines. The Americans had intended to launch a surprise attack on the morning of August 16, 1780, but apparently their foes had made identical plans and were on the way to implement them.

Word of this sudden development impelled General Horatio Gates to call a hasty council of his general officers. When all thirteen aides had assembled, the hero of Saratoga soberly informed them that his plan of battle could not be followed. "Gentlemen," he said, "outline a wise move for us now, and do not bite your tongues."

Otho Williams of Maryland cleared his throat, hesitated, glanced at his comrades, and blurted out a suggestion that the army make an orderly retreat. "Seek out a strong defensive position," he suggested, and "there await the British attack that is sure to come."

Gates shook his head. What would the world think, to learn that the man to whom Burgoyne delivered his sword had turned tail and run? "That is not all," he mused. "Someone must make up for our humiliation at Charles Town."

Their commander's objection left his officers momentarily speechless. After a long silence, Edward Stevens of the Virginia militia said what he knew Horatio Gates wanted to hear.

"It is too late to retreat," he said. "Therefore we have no option except to fight like veterans and die on the field if we must."

No other general officer nodded assent, but Gates signaled that the battle council was over. His aides returned to their units, made up largely of volunteers with little training. Far worse in the opinion of some, a long march from North Carolina to upstate South Carolina had left most of them exhausted and sick. True, they had received comparatively good food during the last day or two, but while on the march rations became so scarce that those officers who still carried a supply of hair powder had used it to thicken their soup.

British forces, rapidly approaching at an angle that indicated they were likely to come into direct contact with Americans on the narrow Charlotte road just outside Camden, South Carolina, were reliably said to outnumber their opponents by nearly two to one. Most of the fighting men led by General Cornwallis were veterans who were about equally divided between Redcoats and well-trained provincials; and Banastre Tarleton's feared Royal North Carolina Loyalist Regiment was known to be in the army, along with Francis Lord Rawdon's Volunteers of Ireland. Gates commanded Maryland and Delaware units of the Continental army, and militia units from North Carolina and Virginia.

"You sir, are to have the honor of the field today," General Gates told Major General Johann DeKalb. That meant command of the vulnerable right wing, protected only by seven pieces of small-bore artillery for which gunners did not have adequate powder and balls.

As six-foot DeKalb strode to his position, he reflected about his variegated career that had brought him into a Carolina field on a scorching August morning. Reared in Huttendorf, Germany, he saw no opportunity in his village, so he became a mercernary for France at about age sixteen. During a decade in uniform, he showed unusual skill in handling men; and more than once he proved to be a competent strategist. Advancing in rank with unusual speed, he was eligible to become a brigadier general before age twenty-six. Only one barrier existed to the eagerly sought post; France, like all European nations, reserved top military positions for men of aristocratic birth.

Realizing that the son of obscure Bavarian peasants would be passed over without consideration of his record, the ambitious soldier of fortune purchased false papers—or penned them himself. Thus he simultaneously became Baron Jean de Kalb and a general officer of the French army.

Selected by the French government for a secret mission, he came to North America in 1762 wearing civilian clothing. Many colonists were already angry at the mother country, but most were reluctant to do more than mutter threats. DeKalb's mission was to assess the military strength of known rebels and to encourage them to take up arms. Anything that hurt Britain would help France.

British warships transported eight thousand men who made up the force that stormed Charles Town.

Back in Paris and again in uniform, it was General DeKalb who introduced American agent Silas Deane to nineteen-year-old marquis de Lafayette. When Lafayette went to the new United States, he chose DeKalb for his traveling companion.

Lafayette received a royal reception, while little interest was shown in his companion. Attitudes soon changed, however, when Americans discovered that DeKalb was one of the few veterans of European wars who spoke good English. It was linguistic skill, not his military record, that persuaded Congress to give de Kalb a commission as a major general. After accepting it on September 15, 1777, he was placed under the immediate command of George Washington. Six months later he was sent to New Jersey and Maryland for a two-year stay. From his base there, he led an abortive attempt to invade Canada.

By March 1780 the situation in the South was becoming desperate. Men under General Benjamin Lincoln had returned from Savannah and were bottled up in Charles Town. There an overwhelmingly superior British force was besieging the port city and was clearly on the verge of a major victory.

At Washington's orders, DeKalb was riding hell-for-leather for Charles Town when the city fell. At Lynchburg, Virginia, where he learned the news, the German waited for fresh orders. It was there that

General Horatio Gates, newly appointed (by Congress, without consulting Washington) as commander of all patriot forces in the South, joined him. They proceeded to North Carolina, where Gates devised a scheme to hit the British unexpectedly "some place far from the coast," to win a victory comparable to that of Saratoga.

DeKalb and his fellow general officers knew that the victory all of them wanted was not likely to come on a road between two fields of corn. Almost as soon as the engagement began, one unit of patriots after another was overwhelmed. Soon less than six hundred men were facing bayonet charges from forces three times as large.

"Retire from the field while you still can!" DeKalb shouted to his officers. Although his head was bleeding profusely from a saber cut, the Bavarian ignored Gates's battle plan and stepped in front of his men to lead a charge.

A stout Redcoat who brandished a bayonet at DeKalb was cut down only seconds before the big soldier of fortune fell, mortally wounded. Most of his men who were able to do so scattered into the swamp; almost all the rest lay dead or wounded on the field. Only the chevalier de Buysson, personal aide to the Bavarian, remained at his side.

British soldiers who swarmed over the battlefield to use their bayonets to finish off the wounded were delighted to find a man in a general's uniform. As one of them raised his weapon, de Buysson threw his own body over that of DeKalb. "Stop!" he shouted. "Your general must decide this man's fate!"

The British dragged DeKalb to a half-demolished wagon, propped him up against one of its wheels, and waited for Cornwallis to appear. At a glance the British commander recognized him. "Get a litter! Quickly!" he ordered. "Take this man into the town and send for surgeons."

British physicians examined DeKalb, then shook their heads. "He has taken sabers, bullets, and bayonets," one of them observed, "eleven big wounds altogether."

South Carolina tradition insists that the British commander visited DeKalb at least twice during the three days he lay dying. Having discovered that his enemy was—like himself—a Freemason, Lord Cornwallis made arrangements for the funeral. Thus the bogus baron, who was a genuine freedom fighter, was the only high-ranking Continental army officer to be buried by his enemies with full military and Masonic honors.

CHAPTER

44

With No Holds Barred, Whigs and Tories Fought to the Finish

Denard's Ford, Broad River
October 1, 1780

Gentlemen:

Unless you wish to be lost in an inundation of barbarians who have begun by murdering an unarmed son before his aged father, and afterwards lopped off his arms, and who by their shocking cruelties and irregularities, give the best proof of their cowardice and want of discipline: I say if you wish to be pinioned, robbed, murdered, and see your wives and daughters in four days abused by the dregs of mankind, in short if you wish or deserve to live, and have the name of men, grasp your arms in a moment and run to camp.

If you choose to be degraded forever and ever by a set of mongrels, say so at once and let your women turn their backs on you, and look out for real men to protect them.

PAT FERGUSON,
Major 71st Regiment

Published in broadside form as an open letter, that appeal by a distinguished British officer was circulated throughout North Carolina. Having been in the colony for some time, Ferguson realized that General John Burgoyne was right in his judgment that Tories were strongest and most fervent in the South. It was here, not exclusively but more notably after the fall of Charles Town to the British, that Whigs and Tories waged true civil war.

There were no pitched battles and only a few full-scale skirmishes. Most action was taken by individuals and by small bands of vigilantes. Whigs burned the cabins of Tories, slaughtered their livestock, ruined their crops, and drove their women and children away. Tories hanged Whigs, rode them on rails, leveled their homes, destroyed their fields, and taunted women and children as they fled into the forest.

Major James Wright, son of Georgia's royal governor, once voiced what appears to have been a fairly accurate assessment of the southern mood. "Take the first three men you meet upon the streets of Savannah," Wright said, "and demand a statement of loyalty. One will profess undying devotion to king and country. Another will declare that only Whiggery can survive and will boast that he spent last evening at the Liberty Pole. But the third will profess no allegiance at all and say he would not give a pinch of snuff for the difference between a Whig and a Tory."

About one-third of the settlers in the region—Whigs, or patriots— really did vow that they would settle for nothing less than independence. Their Tory neighbors, or Loyalists, were about equal in number and were fervent in seeking to preserve relationships between the mother country and her colonies. People who had no strong feelings were caught in the middle.

Because frontier warfare was localized and sporadic, neither London nor Philadelphia had more than vague awareness that, especially in the Carolinas and in Georgia, divided and polarized settlers fought one another savagely.

Patrick Ferguson's appeal to civilian Tories may have stemmed from actions of a band of Cumberland County Whigs who beat an aged settler blamed for having served as a piper to call Tories to assemble. From the piper they got names of men who answered his call; and when they had rounded up their victims, the Whigs sent them one by one before a squad of horsemen. As each captive came within reach, a rider raised his blade and split the skull of the victim.

Daniel McMillan, not captured with the initial group, was targeted for special punishment. According to a contemporary account, "He came into the house begging for his life, with the blood streaming from his side, his hunting shirt on fire, where he had been shot in the shoulder, his wrist cut and broken by a sword, his arm shattered and torn by a musket ball, two or three musket balls having passed through his body; but revenge was not yet satisfied, and another ball through his breast near the left shoulder, soon put an end to his suffering."

What Major Ferguson failed to say in his appeal to citizens loyal to the king was that Whig atrocities were committed in revenge for the cold-blooded murder of about half a dozen of their number at Piney

Bottom, a branch of Rock Creek. There regional lore insists that Tories seized Whigs and tied them to trees as a prelude to "administering the blacksnake whip until the bare bones showed," then shooting their victims and leaving their bodies dangling from the trees where they died.

Once Charles Town became a British stronghold, Tories of the region went on a rampage. Even in the city, many civilians were treated for a time as prisoners of war. In the countryside, where all semblance of law and order long ago had vanished, plantations were systematically looted and destroyed. Horses and cattle were usually spared from death but seized as prizes of war. Any field dry enough to burn was likely to get the torch, along with barns, sheds, and houses.

David Fanning's North Carolina Loyalists were charged with having encouraged Catawba Indians to kill and scalp nearly a dozen men

Where they were dominant, Tories lynched patriots; and where patriots were in control, they lynched Tories.

wounded in a frontier clash. Tories, in turn, reported that prisoners held by a band of Whigs were told that if they wished to avoid starvation, they would have to pay for their rations. "Men were compelled to give thirty-five Continental dollars for a single ear of Indian corn and forty for a drink of water; when fording a stream, they were not allowed to drink from it."

At a settlement on Waxhaw Creek, which meandered back and forth between North and South Carolina, Colonel Banastre Tarleton's band of well-trained and heavily armed Tories caught up with a unit headed by Colonel Abraham Buford. Most of Buford's force consisted of Continental infantry from Virginia, along with an artillery squad that hauled two six-pounders through the rough terrain.

Greatly exaggerating the strength of his force, Tarleton demanded unconditional surrender. That message was followed by a threat: "If you are rash enough to reject my terms, the blood will be upon your own head." Buford did not ponder his reply but immediately responded, "I reject your terms, and we will defend ourselves to the last extremity."

Refusal to accept his terms caused the Tory leader to unleash his civilian-volunteers with such fury that their foes were soon overpowered. Once Buford's men threw down their weapons and raised their hands in surrender, a Whig account declared that "there commenced a scene of indiscriminate carnage never surpassed by the ruthless atrocities of the most barbarous savages. Not a patriot was spared; once all lay upon the ground, Tories walked about the field and systematically plunged their bayonets into every man that exhibited the least sign of life."

Tarleton then turned his attention to a village whose settlers had given food and shelter to Buford's men. Those males able to do so had fled, so the Tory leader rounded up old men, small children, and women of every age. Forty or so prisoners were herded into the tiny Waxhaw meetinghouse.

When one of Tarleton's dragoons noticed a boy of about fourteen in the group of captives, he signaled for the youngster to come to him. Pointing to his boots, he demanded that they be cleaned. "No, sir," responded the boy. "I am a prisoner of war and claim to be treated as such."

Furious, the Tory drew his sword. Simultaneously, the boy lifted his arm to protect his head and received a glancing blow to his head, but a more serious wound to his arm. Bleeding profusely, he was forced to march to Camden, where he was jailed until his mother came with money to purchase his release.

No one knows how many widows and orphans were among the horde of homeless refugees—Whigs and Tories alike—produced by

Young Andrew Jackson was slashed and jailed for refusing to clean the boots of a Tory.

civil war on the southern frontier. Most remained nameless, and their stories have not survived even in oral tradition; but the adolescent whose head and arm were slashed swore a solemn oath that he would some day get revenge.

Years later, the world was stunned when the man from the Waxhaws won a smashing victory over the British in the Battle of New Orleans. As he received the plaudits of his countrymen, British-hater Andrew Jackson must have rejoiced. At last he was striking a blow for every civilian Whig who had learned the meaning of Tory fury during the turbulent closing years of the American Revolution!

45

Over-the-mountain Men Shot Holes in British Strategic Plans

"**O**ur Colonial strategy is flawed."

"Events suggest that you are correct, but what changes would you propose to make?"

Sir Henry Clinton leaned forward, gesturing to emphasize the points he wished to impress upon the British ministers and their top aides. "Our forces have been too widely scattered," he said. "Draw several small bodies together into an army big enough to crush any rebel force in the field. Then select major objectives—towns, cities, and fortified installations of strategic value—and move upon them, one by one."

Hours of discussion centered upon the proposals outlined by the son of an early colonial governor of New York. Although many of Britain's top leaders agreed with him, they were reluctant to take action that might displease commanders already on the field in the colonies. In the end, Clinton's proposals were shelved shortly before he was sent to America in 1775. His brilliant victory over Washington in the Battle of Long Island brought him glory and knighthood.

"We must take a fresh look at Sir Henry's suggestions about strategy," insisted a war department aide when London received word that General Sir William Howe was asking to be relieved of his command; but weeks of discussion ensued before Howe's request was approved. Dispatched in November 1777, formal word from the king and his ministers did not reach the commander of all British forces in America until the following April. By then it was generally known that Clinton had been picked to succeed the man weary of fighting far from home.

With the approval of London, Clinton immediately began planning to implement the strategy he had proposed years earlier. Savannah was already back in British control after a time in American possession. Clinton reasoned that West Point controlled access to much of New

Because he moved in and out of terrain few British could utilize, General Francis Marion was called the "swamp fox."

York, and Charleston was the key to the entire South. When his force of six thousand men failed to take West Point, the British commander entered into negotiations expected to lead to its surrender by Benedict Arnold. While that plan was maturing, he gathered an immense fleet with which to transport eight thousand or more men to the South.

His easy capture of Charles Town in May 1780 meant that 5,400 Americans were made prisoners at a cost of only 255 British casualties. Clinton and his superiors in London hailed the victory as the most significant of the war.

"With Savannah and Charles Town in our hands," Clinton reasoned, "we will take our time about moving forward to other vital centers. As we progress, they will topple under their own weight, much like dominoes arranged in a row. North Carolina has enough Loyalists to keep the rebels in that colony busy; we will push on to Virginia before the start of winter."

According to his plan, villages, settlements, and entire sections of the frontier were of little importance. A few units of regulars and bands of hard-hitting American-born Loyalists should have no trouble in keeping thinly populated frontier regions under control. Except that guerrilla fighting was much more frequent and widespread than had been expected, things went about as Clinton had expected until some of his finest commanders made a series of small mistakes, each seemingly unimportant in itself.

Following the orders of General Cornwallis, many of his regulars remained in Camden after the battle to take possession of property held by rebels. Most male Whigs had fled, knowing that death was the penalty for those who had received protection by, and later failed to keep their oath of allegiance to, England. Since some captured militia were also scheduled to be hanged, it took some time to complete the cleanup action after the British victory in which de Kalb died.

Delays at Camden were annoying, but not significant. Somewhat more troubling was the discovery that the Waxhaw region was bare of foodstuff; back-and-forth movements of fighting men had stripped it bare. That meant that men headed by Tarleton, Ferguson, and Cornwallis himself had to send foraging parties to sweep the countryside for many miles to get even meager supplies. Meanwhile, in Georgia Colonel Elijah Clarke and his riflemen managed to swarm over the outpost at Augusta. At that site the long-established fort was not essential to defeat the southern rebels, but loss of it was one more source of annoyance and frustration.

Marching along the border between North and South Carolina, Major Patrick Ferguson discovered that patriots were on his trail. He requested from Cornwallis an additional three hundred or so troops, "enough," he wrote, "to finish this business. This is their last push in this quarter; they are extremely ragged." Casting about for a defensive position that could not be stormed, the professional soldier born in Scotland selected Kings Mountain.

He did not realize that Isaac Shelby and veteran Indian-fighter John Sevier actually led a sizeable army of hardened volunteers. Almost all of their men were experienced woodsmen who were expert with their long rifles and were at home in rough terrain. Many of them gave affectionate names to their weapons. "Hot Lead," as its proud owner called it, was said to be capable of throwing a ball at least three times as far as the best British musket. Many other rifles were of comparable power.

As over-the-mountain men converged upon their quarry holed up in what Ferguson considered an impregnable position, some of Sevier's scouts captured a British messenger. When the fellow delivered his documents, Nolichucky Jack Sevier roared with laughter at reading the terse message: "I hold a position on King's Mountain that all the rebels out of hell cannot drive me from."

The patriots picked about nine hundred of their most experienced men to storm the natural citadel selected by Ferguson. Approximately one mile long, it rises above the surrounding countryside as a rocky summit that the Scottish-born leader considered too steep to be scaled. He was right in believing that attackers would expose themselves to musket fire, but wrong in failing to see that his men could fire only when they stepped into open spots. Skilled hunters who were accustomed to taking down squirrels, 'possums, deer, cougars, and

Long rifles of skilled woodsmen proved too much for entrenched British.

other fast-moving animals turned their long rifles upon the exposed Tories and mowed them down relentlessly.

Men who were at Kings Mountain that crisp October day in 1780 said that the action was over in less than an hour. More than twenty patriots lay dead, and another sixty or seventy were wounded. But at least 150 of Ferguson's men—dedicated and well-trained Tories who made up some of the finest units under British control—had been killed. More than 150 others were so badly wounded that the victors concluded that it would be futile to try to evacuate them, so they left them lying in their own blood. Nearly 700 of the king's finest threw down their muskets and raised their hands in surrender.

Major Patrick Ferguson is now famous for the twentieth-century discovery that at Brandywine he had George Washington in his gun sight but failed to pull the trigger. "It would not be gentlemanly to shoot a man in the back of his head," he confided as the Continental commander in chief wheeled his horse and rode away. Over-the-mountain men, who knew nothing of Ferguson's encounter with Washington or his splendid military record, were less sporting. Ferguson was killed while directing the fire of his men.

Although the British loss hardly exceeded one thousand men, news of it triggered bonfires and street dancing in cities held by patriots. Better even than in London, where the consequences were acknowledged as being enormous, Americans instantly recognized that it would take 100,000 or perhaps even 200,000 troops to police the vast regions west of the well-populated coast. While the British might hold major towns and cities indefinitely, they had no hope of subduing the countryside short of putting ten times as many men in the field as they counted in units of regulars and Loyalists.

Better than most analysts, General Clinton sensed that Kings Mountain meant that his long-planned strategy was badly flawed. Pondering news of the battle, he called the victory by the patriots without military training "the first link of a chain of evils" that he feared might lead to collapse of the entire British movement to suppress rebellion.

Individual leaders of patriots interpreted Sevier's victory at Kings Mountain as a signal to turn their own irregular forces loose. Thomas Sumter and Francis Marion, already considered gadflies by their foes, began to sting and to bite more deeply. Elijah Clarke set out to use newly captured Augusta as a base from which to harass every British military force in Georgia. Patriots not already under arms stepped up their assaults upon Tory neighbors and began making plans to establish new and independent political structures. General Cornwallis weighed alternatives and decided that in the light of Kings Mountain, he should fall back upon Charles Town rather than press forward through North Carolina into Virginia as planned.

During a single hour at an improbable place, over-the-mountain men had effectively shot Britain's strategic plan full of holes.

46

Greene Resolved to Clothe His Men, Regardless of Cost

"Sir, I believe we have found the man you've been looking for."

Major General Nathanael Green, selected by Washington to replace Gates as commander in the South, looked up from the map over which he was bending. "For what service?" he demanded.

Surprised, his aide responded, "Why, sir, for the service you have listed as essential to victory—procurement of clothing for your troops."

"Splendid!" responded his commander. "I thought perhaps you referred to the matter we discussed yesterday—the need for someone to persuade our wagoners that we cannot meet their demands."

"No, sir, that is still pending; they threaten to leave the service before accepting forty shillings. I sincerely hope that they do not mean what they say. But a factor in Charles Town, John Banks, vows that for a price he can take care of the urgent matter of clothing. Supplies in the city are said to be plentiful, and Banks has the confidence of the British commander."

"Bring him to me as soon as possible," directed Greene.

In a series of brief meetings with Banks, the Continental leader became satisfied that he could do as he promised. Over and over, Greene had promised his officers, "We will have no Valley Forge or Morristown in this department."

He did not have to explain his meaning. Every man in Continental uniform knew that Washington's army suffered even more dreadfully at Morristown, New Jersey, during 1779–80 than at Valley Forge earlier. Although the relatively mild climate of Georgia and the Carolinas promised that bone-chilling weather would not trigger mutiny as it had at Morristown, affluent Nathanael Greene had always insisted to anyone who would listen that "A fellow with nothing but a ragged shirt

Alexander Hamilton, secretary of the treasury.

over his gaunt belly cannot fight well, no matter what his convictions." Having suddenly been elevated to a post second in importance only to that of Washington, the Rhode Islander intended to field an army whose men were properly equipped and provisioned.

Having served for more than a year as quartermaster general, he was familiar with purchasing procedures. Even before departing for the South shortly after having presided over the court martial that condemned Major André, he began sending urgent bulletins to Philadelphia. Immense quantities of all kinds of stores, clothing in particular, were immediately needed in order to press forward to victory in his new assignment, he insisted.

Greene was not surprised at the failure of officials to act promptly, but he became increasingly exasperated as days dragged into weeks. As frost on November mornings warned that winter was not far away, he realized that even in the South, half-clad men who spent many of their days wading through swamps and most of their nights sleeping without tents were sure to become ineffective as temperatures dropped.

This man Banks, who vowed that he could smuggle from under the eyes of the British any quantity and quality of clothing desired, represented a golden opportunity. To wait for decisive action in Philadelphia would be folly that well might consign the South to years of British domination.

Reasoning in this fashion, sleep eluded Nathanael Greene many nights during which he tried to calculate his own worth and to estimate what he could borrow from his good friend Lafayette. Robert Morris probably could be counted upon to lend him money as well, and though Alexander Hamilton might have little cash to spare, his influence would help to hasten decision-making processes in Congress and the army.

Private letters also suggest that General Greene was influenced in reaching a rash decision by his knowledge that George Washington was serving without salary. If his commander in chief could sacrifice so dearly for freedom, how could Nathanael Green do less than pledge his own holdings for the sake of his men?

Nathanael Greene's friend Robert Morris is often termed "financier of the Revolution."

Having no idea that George Washington would later submit a co-lossal expense account that more than made up for his lack of salary, his close friend and admirer authorized John Banks to procure "all essential goods with which properly to outfit our entire fighting force." As a result, individual wagons that began to file out of Charles Town at rapid intervals formed wagon trains that wound their way to Greene's scattered units.

Merchants with whom Banks dealt readily accepted Greene's prom-issory notes. Most such paper was discounted by banks and held to be collected as soon as the commander received reimbursement for his outlay on behalf of his men.

Alexander Hamilton was the first to warn Nathanael Greene that reimbursement—expected to be slow—might never come. Sadly, re-ported the future U.S. secretary of the treasury, penny-pinching law-makers were inclined to throw out claims for purchases made before having been formally authorized. It made little difference that money had been spent to help win the fight for freedom; requisitions lying on desks of fiscal officers should have been approved before money was spent.

Hamilton's early assessment proved to be accurate. Greene's well-clothed and generally well-fed troops performed superbly, but Con-gress refused to repay their commander for what he had spent on be-half of his men; and once-wealthy Greene was therefore deeply in debt when fellow countrymen celebrated the end of the conflict. South Car-olina tried to help Nathanael Greene by giving him title to land seized from Tories—potentially valuable but not yet turning a profit. Georgia did the same thing, making him master of Mulberry Plantation, where Eli Whitney later invented the cotton gin.

Broken in spirit and in health by misfortune bred of patriotism, Greene died at age forty-four. Some years passed before Andrew Wayne, Henry Knox, and other top Continental leaders intervened on behalf of his widow. By a margin of only nine votes in the House of Representatives, lawmakers in 1792 agreed to reimburse Greene's es-tate in the sum of $47,000.

Alexander Hamilton personally wrote out a U.S. treasury depart-ment check for $23,500. Simultaneously, he prepared for the widow of the man who was bankrupted while clothing his men a second docu-ment with which she was all too familiar: a $23,500 promissory note, payable in three years.

47

Ex-wagoner Daniel Morgan Scrapped Conventional Battle Plans

When astonished but delighted comrades in arms congratulated Brigadier General Daniel Morgan on his brilliant victory at the Cowpens in South Carolina, he professed humility. "Clearly, the army faced a crisis," he said. "Had we retreated across the Broad River, half my men would have slipped away in the night. That left no choice except to face the Redcoats as best we could. Without quite realizing it, I think I must have reverted to my days as a wagoner."

Those who listened to Morgan's account of the all-important battle knew what he meant. It was standard military strategy to use a swamp or flooded woodland as a defensive "anchor." At the Cowpens he selected open ground that seemed to invite bayonet charges from veterans under the command of Lieutenant Colonel Banastre Tarleton.

"I would not have a swamp in view of my militia as they began to smell powder," he later wrote. "It calls to men to make for it; once there, even the bravest are likely to turn it into a refuge. That—next to retreat—was the last thing I wanted."

Morgan viewed retreat as so disastrous that he said he wished that Loyalists under Tarleton would surround his units and make retreat impossible. Since such a course of action was highly improbable, he deliberately scrapped time-tested battle plans. Lacking a swamp as an "anchor," he placed his least-experienced men in the front line. Behind them he stationed his Continental troops and a few experienced Virginia militia. "Hold your ground at all cost," he ordered their leader, Lieutenant Colonel John Howard. "When the Redcoats strike, the Old Wagoner will crack his whip, I promise."

At his rear, Morgan placed his cavalry on a low ridge not exposed to British fire. Their leader, a relative of George Washington, is said to

Daniel Morgan, as he is believed to have looked when in "battle uniform." [NEW YORK PUBLIC LIBRARY]

have protested the unorthodox stance; normally, a commander tried to arrange for his finest and most experienced men to receive the enemy and brace for the first assault. It was taken for granted that green recruits would be useless for this role.

"The Old Wagoner has a new idea," Daniel Morgan told young Washington. "Last night, I went among the militia and secured their promise to fire two volleys before thinking of retiring. They solemnly promised me that they will take careful aim at the epaulets and then pick off those who display them; I believe they mean it. Whether they do so or not, our lives depend upon them."

Expecting to fight in standard fashion, Tarleton ordered his finest units to lead the assault. With fixed bayonets, they advanced against American positions. At a distance of about one hundred yards, men in Morgan's front line released a lethal volley that caused many officers to fall. After having fired a second volley, Americans in the front line moved to their left, leaving seasoned men of the second line facing the enemy.

These battle-hardened veterans momentarily wilted as the British advanced, then fell back under orders. Smelling victory, Tarleton signaled for his men to go forward on the double. They obeyed but broke ranks to do so. As they raced in disorder toward Americans, Morgan suddenly commanded his line to halt, face about, and charge with bayonets. Simultaneously, the small but powerful force of patriot cavalry raced to prevent slow-moving Loyalist dragoons from making a retreat.

Although the terrain was completely different from that at Kings Mountain, the end results were about the same. Less than an hour after the first shot was fired, individual Redcoats began to surrender. Soon entire units threw down their weapons and cartridge boxes, hoping to flee faster if not impeded. Only a handful reached the safety of the swamp. At the cost of a few casualties, another small army of mostly inexperienced men had decimated a highly experienced band of British supporters who lacked nothing in weapons, equipment, and supplies.

When General Cornwallis received news of the disaster that had befallen still another of his strike forces, he began to ponder a new course of action. Perhaps it would be well, he reasoned, soon to abandon the Carolinas entirely. If made promptly, a move into Virginia would not be interpreted as a retreat. Instead, London could well as-

In fierce hand-to-hand fighting at the Cowpens, mostly untrained patriots defeated seasoned British veterans in less than an hour.

Moored for months at Wallabout, Long Island, the British prison ship Jersey *was the most infamous vessel of a fleet in which eight thousand captive patriots died of disease and starvation.*

sess it as a bold strike at Virginia, now recognized as the heartland of the enemy. Earlier, he had boasted that he would send from the South so many captives that the prison ship *Jersey* "would sink to her gunwales under the weight of Continental officers."

Now less confident after the humiliating defeat at the Cowpens, Cornwallis was careful to report to superiors in London that "the disaster of the seventeenth of January can not be imputed to any defect in my conduct—for the detachment sent was clearly superior to the force against which it was dispatched."

Loyalists, he pointed out, had been of considerable value in the campaign to master the South but were less numerous than he had been led to believe. Of all bands of settlers, he reported, Scottish highlanders were most ready to enlist and fight for the king, a strange turn of events since Scots had earlier supported Bonnie Prince Charlie in his abortive attempt to seize the English throne.

Tarleton's legion, the finest body of Loyalist fighting men in the Carolinas if not in all of North America, could not be rebuilt for many months, if ever. Lamentably, Tarleton concluded, "only a very inconsiderable number of settlers could be prevailed upon to fight with us or to exert themselves for us in any form whatever."

That verdict confirmed the conclusion reached by those who analyzed accounts of the action at Kings Mountain. Instead of being inconsequential to overall strategy, it was obvious that poorly trained patriots who volunteered for a short time could more than hold their own when given a chance to fight on familiar ground.

When General Cornwallis voiced these conclusions, he did not know that the victor at the Cowpens was among once-despised "soldiers for a season" whom he earlier thought professionals could master without half trying. Weary of congressional inaction and more than half sick, Morgan resigned his Continental commission in July 1779 and gave full time to building his mansion, Saratoga, in Virginia. He only reentered the Continental army in response to Washington's insistent pleas, going south largely because he considered Horatio Gates an incompetent braggart.

His foe did not know it, but for his southern tour of duty Daniel Morgan really was among the ranks of short-term soldiers. Having answered Washington's call and having made a lasting innovation in strategy, he took off his buckskin "uniform" and returned to his Virginia plantation. "This much is certain," he told neighbors upon arriving home. "The complexion of the war has changed. Cornwallis faces decisions far more difficult than he anticipated."

CHAPTER

48

A Pyrrhic Victory Pushed Cornwallis into Virginia

Few fighting men on either side had time or energy to make detailed notes about day-to-day occurrences. Sergeant R. Lamb of the Royal Welsh Fusiliers was an exception. Even on long forced marches he recorded impressions in his "Journal of Occurrences." His account of action of March 15, 1781, one of the few eyewitness reports about that momentous day, preserves a story not included in official reports sent to London:

> I saw Lord Cornwallis riding across the clear ground. His Lordship was mounted on a dragoon's horse—his own having been shot. Saddle bags under the creature's belly much retarded his progress, due to the immense quantity of underbrush that was spread over the ground. His Lordship was evidently unconscious of his danger.
>
> I immediately laid hold of the bridle of his horse, and turned the animal's head. Then I mentioned to His Lordship that if he had continued as he was going, he would have been surrounded by the enemy and, perhaps, cut to pieces or captured.
>
> I continued to run along side of the animal, keeping the bridle in my hand, until His Lordship gained the safety of the 23rd Regiment which was then drawn up in the skirt of the woods.

That may have been the narrowest escape experienced by the British nobleman during his long stay in North America. On the day that Lamb claimed to have saved his commander, great numbers of Redcoats were not so fortunate.

Determined to restore the balance of military power after the humiliation of Cowpens, the British leader reread in his favorite books a number of detailed accounts of European campaigns. Inspired by what great strategists had done earlier, he decided upon a drastic course of action. To pursue and smash fast-moving patriots, his forces

Although his countrymen blamed Cornwallis for having lost the war, many analysts consider him perhaps the ablest British commander who fought in America.

would have to move much more rapidly, but they could not do this while impeded with great quantities of gear.

Accordingly, settlers in the North Carolina back country soon scanned the sky with wonder when they saw great clouds of smoke. Those close to the British position realized that the dragoons had rolled most of their wagons together, then piled them high with tents and empty rum kegs before setting them afire. When the blaze became intense, all provisions except what men could carry on their backs were thrown into the flames to prevent the possibility of the rebels' making use of them.

Stripped of all baggage, the Redcoats were ready to serve as a strike force of light troops. Simultaneously, Cornwallis authorized leaders of other bodies to issue new calls for civilian Loyalists to enlist as fighting men.

Meanwhile, moving with extreme speed over terrain that was familiar to some of his men, Nathanael Greene retreated into Virginia, drawing the British behind. Once his army crossed the Catawba River, Cornwallis breathed a bit easier; then he discovered that the Yadkin, the Deep, and the Dan still lay ahead. At the Virginia border, the patriots made an easy crossing. They then took every available boat to the opposite shore so they could recross with speed.

When Alexander Hamilton received an account of Greene's leadership, he became almost poetic in praise. "To have effected a retreat in the face of so ardent a pursuit, through so great an extent of country, through a region offering every obstacle and affording scarcely any resource," wrote Hamilton, "with troops destitute of every thing, who a great part of the way left the vestiges of their march in their own

General "Light Horse Harry" Lee commanded American cavalry at Guilford Court House.

blood—to have done all this, I say, without loss of any kind, may without exaggeration be hailed as a masterpeice of military skill."

Weary from chasing rebels and now short of food, Cornwallis had to move back toward his base of supplies. Venturing daringly close to Redcoats but always remaining beyond reach, Greene seems to have set out to wear the enemy down.

Meanwhile, Colonel John Pyle led a band of about four hundred fresh Loyalists toward the main body of British soldiers. However, some of his recently recruited pickets mistook a rebel band for British soldiers (the uniforms they wore were similar). The result was that nearly two hundred Loyalists were killed or wounded in less than ten minutes.

When news of the carnage reached Cornwallis, no one needed to interpret its significance for him. "All hope of doubling our forces from the ranks of faithful Loyalists is now gone," he lamented.

Earlier outnumbered about three to two, Greene was reenforced by 3,000 Virginia militia and members of other small units. That gave him about 4,500 battle-ready men against 2,400 or so in British ranks. For the first time ready to fight, Greene drew up a battle plan based upon Morgan's victory at Cowpens and took up a position at Guilford Court House, North Carolina.

It was in this rough, wooded spot that Cornwallis might have dashed into the hands of patriots, had it not been for Sergeant Lamb's quick thinking. Far from being a conventional, coordinated struggle,

Nathanael Greene and aides prepare to cross the Dan River.

Guilford Court House quickly broke up into a series of small engagements. In this melee, not even the commanders had any idea how the battle was going until American units began to withdraw from the field.

Measured in strategic terms, the badly outnumbered Redcoats were victorious. They dislodged patriots from a prepared position and held the field, but the cost of victory was high: one man in four killed, wounded, or captured. When word of the engagement reached London, Charles James Fox spoke for many members of Parliament who were already weary of the war far away. "A few more such victories," said Fox, "would destroy the British Army."

It did not take that verdict to persuade the British commander that it was time to act upon his contemplated change in plans. He decided to leave the southernmost colonies in the hands of patriots who now controlled everything except a few centers of population. By moving into Virginia and effecting a speedy confrontation with George Washington and his winter-weary Continentals, there was a chance that Lord Cornwallis could salvage his damaged reputation.

CHAPTER

49

Bernardo de Galvez Led the Spanish Offensive in the West

"**G**uns of Fort George pose little danger."

"Agreed; but those of British frigates do—and in order to escape them, vessels must go over sand bars on which they will be trapped."

"Nonsense!" scoffed thirty-three-year-old Bernardo de Galvez, governor of Louisiana. "Come! I will show you!"

Standing on the deck of his flagship, the captain-general of Cuba—Galvez's immediate superior—watched as the colorful young official climbed aboard his own vessel and began gesturing to seamen. Soon the *Galveztown* was under way, picking up speed as she maneuvered with the wind. Dashing over the sand bar considered dangerous to the Spanish fleet, the ship turned gracefully and came back to her original position.

Far more effective than any number of arguments, this demonstration launched the long-planned Spanish attack upon Pensacola in May 1780.

Galvez considered the position crucial to his plan to drive the British from the Gulf of Mexico. Long before Spain declared war upon Great Britain in 1779, the Council of the Indies favored his proposal to take advantage of the American rebellion. Many of its members, including Galvez, argued that Spain's longtime enemy was virtually shackled by her involvement in the North American conflict. That meant, they said, that they had a splendid opportunity to redeem their honor that had been so badly tarnished when England's Royal Navy trounced the Grand Armada of Philip II in 1588.

King Charles III was as eager to humiliate and defeat the English as were his ministers. Yet he wanted to make sure that his nation did not become entangled in "the infectious plague of rebellion against monarchy" that had erupted in the British colonies. He refused to join

France in her alliance with the emerging United States and waited to take action at what he considered an appropriate time.

It came in 1779 when Charles III declared war upon Great Britain, carefully abstaining, however, from use of language that would require Spain to fight for the defense of Americans. In Paris, Benjamin Franklin expressed disappointment at the terms of the Spanish decision. Months later when it became known in Louisiana, Governor Galvez rejoiced that it would permit him to pursue with new vigor his long-established goal of striking hard at the British in the far west.

A veteran of military service in Portugal, Mexico, and Algiers, Galvez reached Louisiana as a colonel in charge of a regiment of foot soldiers. Influential relatives persuaded the Spanish king to name him royal governor of the province in 1776; and soon after he took office the following January, he issued an order by which the vital port of New Orleans was opened to American shipping.

During his first year in office, the thirty-one-year-old vented his long-standing animosity at the British by seizing eleven frigates. When warships appeared to support a demand that the vessels and their cargoes be released, Galvez agreed to talk with enemy leaders. As they climbed aboard his own ship—the appointed meeting place—he welcomed them. Then he pointed to row after row of barrels of gunpowder on the deck. "I received them with match-rope in hand," he reported to Havana, "in order to forestall any notions of violence."

Although the frigates were released after payment of what their captains protested as exorbitant charges, the governor of Louisiana lost none of his zeal in harassing the British. He gave the freedom of the city to a Continental army agent, Oliver Pollock, and frequently entertained the American at his own table. It was Galvez who turned over to Pollock $75,000 to purchase the supplies without which George Rogers Clark's incursions into Illinois could not have been launched.

It was natural for Galvez to seize upon his sovereign's declaration of war as an opportunity to strike rapidly and hard. His first target, the British outpost of Manchac on the lower Mississippi River, was not formidable; so he devoted only a fraction of his own resources—perhaps six hundred men—to an expedition against it. Spanish and Indian fighting men had a special ally in James Willing, who called himself "Captain in the service of the United Independent States of America." Actually an officer in a unit of the military service that became the U.S. Marines, Willing and his Americans moved up the river with Galvez and helped to capture Manchac late in the first year of Spain's new war with her old enemy.

To truly rule the region, Galvez knew that he must take Baton Rouge, Natchez, Mobile, and Pensacola. So he moved against Baton Rouge so swiftly that British resistance crumbled when Spanish forces

Spanish soldiers at Pensacola.

appeared. Having captured the town without firing a shot, Galvez turned toward Natchez and took it just two weeks later.

He and the Americans, who were his informal allies, were under no delusions; Mobile would not be so easy, and Pensacola was one of the strongest fortified positions on the continent. Only a large combined land and sea operation would have a chance of success there.

Governor Diego Joseph Navarro of Cuba was not enthusiastic when called upon to provide most of the ships deemed necessary for the planned expedition. He considered St. Augustine the most important British installation south of the rebellious colonies and wanted to form a joint American–Spanish force to move against the oldest city on the continent. Pressed hard by Galvez, Navarro reluctantly committed himself to providing thirteen vessels for the Pensacola expedition.

Expecting the fleet from Havana to join his own small flotilla, Galvez put 750 men aboard his small ships and set sail on January 14, 1780. When the expected rendezvous had not taken place after nearly sixty days, the governor of Louisiana decided to proceed alone. Nine eighteen-pound guns landed more than a mile from Fort Charlotte, which guarded Mobile. From there they were hauled through the dense woods, a feat that many artillery experts would have considered to be impossible. A few hours after they opened fire, the defenders of the British installation hoisted the white flag.

That left the British holding only Pensacola on the entire Gulf of

Mexico. Because of its massive fortifications, Galvez refused to move against Pensacola until he had assembled at Havana what he considered a suitable force. Some of the four thousand fighting men who crowded aboard sixty-four ships were Indian warriors led by Alexander McGillivray. Others were American volunteers, ex-slaves, and Creole recruits; but most of his soldiers were veterans of Spanish wars and conquests. They entered Pensacola Bay on March 8, 1781.

In the fortress that the British had renamed Fort George in honor of their sovereign, the commander was confident that he could hold out against a frontal assault. A prolonged siege would be another matter, and news that Galvez had persuaded the Spanish admiral to bring his big ships into the bay spelled potential disaster for the defenders.

Skirmishes and artillery duels on land, along with an occasional brief fight between warships, ended when an additional one thousand Spanish troops debarked late in the month. After lengthy conversations with Galvez and his generals, British officers capitulated and began to evacuate the fort and the town it defended. That meant that the Spanish now held control over all of West Florida.

To complete the cleanup operation in the far west, Galvez put a strong garrison at St. Louis. An expedition aimed at moving overland to Detroit to seize that installation failed, but news that Spanish warriors had penetrated what is now southern Michigan gave Sir Henry Clinton a severe jolt.

Few influential persons in London were greatly interested in the Gulf of Mexico or the Mississippi River; some had never heard of Pensacola. Consequently, King George III did not protest at peace terms under which both East and West Florida were ceded by England to Spain in exchange for the commercially lucrative Bahama Islands.

Surveying the American Revolution, in which Spain's involvement was late and indirect, some analysts have concluded that the importance of the Pensacola victory has often been overlooked. Spain, not Britain, was now dominant in the western hemisphere, and Britain lost an opportunity to secure the Americans between pincers whose prongs were Canada on the north and Florida on the south.

Bernado de Galvez, whose name is not well known in the United States, rejoiced, not because he had helped the cause of American independence but because he had struck a mighty blow against Britain. Professing humility he never exhibited in his actions, the man who led the assault against the British in the far west said he didn't deserve the honor that was his when his grateful sovereign rewarded him by making him Viscount de Galveztown.

CHAPTER

50

"My God, It Is All Over!"

Important news from the colonies reached London on Sunday, November 25, 1781. At the Pall Mall residence of Lord George Germain, the expression on the face of a courier from Falmouth revealed that he knew his tidings to be very bad. Germain hastily scanned messages prepared nearly six weeks earlier, then hurried to Downing Street to share their contents with Prime Minister North.

When handed the official documents, North read only a few lines before "nearly falling to the floor, as though he had taken a ball in his breast." Waving his arms wildly and pacing up and down the room, the chief spokesman for King George III repeatedly cried, "My God, it is all over!"

His emotional reaction stemmed from a curt dispatch informing British leaders that on October 19, General Sir Charles Cornwallis had surrendered his men and their weapons to George Washington at Yorktown, in the colony of Virginia.

Having moved into the rebel heartland from Wilmington, as he planned to do after a series of humiliations, Cornwallis at first harried the countryside almost at will. When growing numbers of patriot units began to converge upon the region, the British commander sent scouts to seek a suitable location at which to erect a fortified camp.

Pondering the alternatives, he selected a site on the south bank of the York River as a spot at which defensive works could easily be built. Desirability of the place was enhanced by the ease with which warships could evacuate his force from it, if necessary.

Once scouts reported that a huge enemy army seemed to have holed up near the coast, patriot leaders faced a dilemma. Should they ignore Cornwallis and proceed with plans, long ago formulated by George Washington, and concentrate upon New York? Or should they turn aside to strike at the large army of Redcoats and Germans whose distance from supply depots might make them vulnerable?

Early in the discussion, Lafayette insisted that sea power—not in-

Victorious George Washington, as depicted in a widely-circulated engraving.

fantry units and field guns—would prove decisive. Washington questioned that verdict but listened patiently as his young French subordinate repeatedly went over the reasons for his judgment.

"Sea power aside, the relative strength of the two defensive positions must be considered," argued the comte de Rochambeau. A veteran of the Seven Years' War, the fifty-five-year-old Frenchman had brought four picked infantry regiments to America with him and was highly respected. He considered New York to be at least three times as strong as Yorktown and urged that the allies concentrate upon the more vulnerable target.

Still eager to drive the British from America's second largest city, Washington abruptly changed his plans when he learned that a French expedition was on its way from the Caribbean to help them. Commanded by François Joseph Paule de Grasse, marquis de Grasse-Tilley, the fleet had three thousand troops aboard. Moving up the Atlantic coast, on September 5, 1781, de Grasse encountered a British fleet commanded by Admiral Thomas Graves. With a numerical advantage—twenty-four ships of the line against nineteen—the French closed in. Both fleets suffered heavy losses during an indecisive battle, after which they sailed along parallel courses for four days without renewing the fight.

Sir Henry Clinton, whose huge force of veterans was just seven days away when Cornwallis surrendered.

While de Grasse still had the British vessels in sight, Lafayette sent him an urgent message by packet: "Move at once into the mouth of the York River. Your presence will prevent the escape of a splendid British army now under siege."

With Washington and Greene having joined forces with Lafayette and Rochambeau, the siege of Yorktown—never resembling a pitched battle in the field—was already under way. Elaborate sets of trenches were being dug by both sides, and allied forces expected to use heavy artillery to batter the British into submission. Vessels of the French fleet would prevent Cornwallis from taking to the sea to escape.

With food supplies running low, Cornwallis realized that he could hold out for only a short time. Writing in cipher to Sir Henry Clinton, his commander in chief, he pointed out that a semicircle had been formed by "Americans on the right and French on the left, leaving no good avenue of escape on the landward side." He was being pounded hourly, he reported, by heavy artillery and mortars. The English general concluded: "I have only to report that nothing but a direct move to York River, which includes a successful naval action, can save me."

Clinton assembled troops with all speed and persuaded his colleagues of the navy that rescue of Cornwallis and his army should take priority over all other missions, but they got under way too late. An

French Admiral de Grasse, whose fleet came to the aid of Washington's Continentals.

attempt to cross the York River to escape into the countryside having failed because of bad weather, Cornwallis directed an officer to move toward allied lines with a white flag.

Under his proposal, a twenty-four-hour cease-fire would prevail while representatives of the two forces met at a farm house to discuss terms of surrender. Washington, who knew he had the advantage of superior numbers, haughtily replied that he would consent to a cessation of hostilities for no more than two hours.

Cornwallis countered with a request that all prisoners of war be returned to their native lands. Washington replied that he could not consent to such terms; he would grant the British and the Germans no more concessions than Americans had been given at the surrender of Charles Town. That meant all defeated officers would be permitted to keep their side arms and personal gear, and senior officers would be permitted to return to England. After Charles Town, many of those soldiers not exchanged were shipped to the *Jersey* and other prison ships. Americas had no such "floating hells," so Washington directed that most prisoners go to internment camps for the duration of the conflict.

With hostilities due to be resumed in two hours, Cornwallis capitulated and agreed that at 2:00 P.M. his garrison would march out "with shouldered arms, colours cased, and drums beating a British or German march." American and French forces lined up to receive the surrender were stretched on both sides of the road for more than a mile. With drummers reportedly beating to the cadence of a song that was used in the aftermath of the conflict at Cambridge, weeping Redcoats marched to the tune of "The World Turned Upside Down."

Reporting himself indisposed, Cornwallis detailed General Charles O'Hara to present the ceremonial sword of surrender. General Washington had learned in advance that Cornwallis would not personally lead the ceremony, so he delegated acceptance of the sword to Benjamin Lincoln, his own second in command.

On the day of the surrender, not even Washington and Cornwallis realized the ultimate consequences of the events taking place. Cornwallis expected to recoup his military fortunes, and Washington did not realize that the surrender would elevate him to a new high in esteem. He had enjoyed no significant personal victory since the battles of Trenton and Princeton more than six bitter years earlier.

Both men expected the six-year struggle to continue. Hence Washington was "put into a fury" when De Grasse summarily rejected his suggestion that the French fleet go to the relief of Charles Town. In New York, Clinton began drawing up fresh plans to pull together the estimated 34,000 troops scattered throughout the rebellious colonies, the Floridas, Nova Scotia, Providence Island, and the Bermudas.

London was under no such delusions as those harbored by Cornwallis and Clinton. Better than anyone else, Lord North realized that the staggering defeat would lead to demands for peace by his war-weary constituents and that his own ministry would come to a quick end.

Yorktown meant, too, that France and Spain would rise in power during the era in which Britain's dominion over the seas would be fast drawing to an end. After Yorktown, thirteen once-important colonies newly formed into a confederation were poised to replace the mother country as the dominant power of the West.

A More Perfect Union

Far from being overjoyed at the conclusion of the surrender cere-monies at Yorktown, George Washington was somber. In a per-sonal letter he confessed his apprehension "lest the late important success, instead of exciting our exertions, should produce such a re-laxation in the prosecution of the war, as will prolong the calamities of it."

When he and other patriots saw that British leaders actually in-tended to effect a gradual withdrawal of all forces in the New World, attention was focused upon Paris. There Benjamin Franklin, John Jay, and John Adams wrangled and bargained for months to arrive at a peace treaty.

Adopted on September 3, 1783, the Treaty of Paris recognized the independence of Britain's thirteen former colonies. Boundaries of the new political entity—often called The United States of North Amer-ica—were clearly stipulated. Florida marked the southern limit, while the Great Lakes lay at the northern edge. At the west, the Mississippi River was the boundary.

Much of this vast territory was inhabited only by native Americans. Immense tracts had not yet been carefully explored by white men. Hence, leaders of thirteen states that had reluctantly come together in a loose confederation began to quarrel over western land.

Squabbles over land, militia quotas, paper currency, and numerous other issues soon multiplied. The former colonies were free, but they faced almost insurmountable problems. Although keenly aware of them, George Washington rejoiced that he did not have to solve them. Having reached Mount Vernon on Christmas Eve 1783, he let it be known that he was more than ready for the quiet life of a Virginia squire.

His tranquility lasted only a short time. Virginia Governor Edmund Randolph informed the former commander-in-chief that a federal convention would be held soon. Delegates would face the tremendous task of revising the Articles of Confederation that had created a loose and often chaotic central government.

"I beg of you, Excellency, to do one more thing for Virginia," Randolph wrote. "Virginia needs you at the convention, which will convene shortly in Philadelphia."

Knowing that it violated his promise to himself, Washington reluctantly said "Yes" in April 1787. He reached Philadelphia on May 13, where church bells pealed in honor of his arrival. On the next morning, he walked to the State House (now Independence Hall) for the opening of the convention. To his chagrin, he found that only two delegations—Virginia and the host state of Pennsylvania—were on hand.

It was an omen of things to come.

Ex-colonies differed widely in their backgrounds and expectations. Size was a major difference, too. Delaware had fewer than 60,000 citizens, while Virginia's population topped 750,000. Mutual suspicion was as widespread as mutual ignorance.

Seven states were required for a quorum, which was reached after an eleven-day delay. The first order of business was the election of a presiding officer. Financier Robert Morris nominated Washington, who was elected by acclamation.

Soon he found himself presiding over a badly divided body seldom numbering more than forty delegates. Representatives of each state were out to get what they could for their own constituents. Rhode Islanders, who wanted nothing to do with the conclave, never did send delegates to it.

Weeks of secret deliberations, often stormy, did not produce the planned revision of the Articles of Confederation. Instead, an entirely new document was shaped. We know it as the Constitution of the United States of America.

Nearly all members of the convention signed the new document on September 17, 1787. Then they voted to submit it to citizens of the several states, asking them, "the *source of all sovereignty*, to ratify it or reject it."

Strong supporters of the doctrine of state sovereignty immediately attacked the new document. It would not take effect unless and until ratified by nine states, and those who opposed a strong central government fervently hoped to persuade a majority of their citizens to vote against it.

Delaware ratified the Constitution of the United States on December 7, 1787. Pennsylvania, New Jersey, Georgia, Connecticut,

Massachusetts, and Maryland soon followed. South Carolina's vote was affirmative in May, and New Hampshire ratified it on June 21, 1788.

Once the requisite nine ratifications were made, the Constitution became operative. Under terms of the initial agreement, the new government was launched on March 4, 1789. George Washington, whose dreams of leisurely years on his planatation had been shattered by plans for the convention, was the unanimous choice as the first head of the new nation.

At his inauguration, he headed a strong central government, but he was president of only eleven states. North Carolina did not ratify the Constitution until November 1789, and Rhode Island held out until the following May.

In spite of hold-out states, the victories won by Washington and his comrades on battlefields had produced political results not envisioned during years of conflict. Adoption of the Constitution meant that there were no longer thirteen semi-independent states. Instead, each former colony gave up some of its own sovereignty for the sake of the strength that comes from unity.

Ratification of the Constitution and the inauguration of an elected president showed that long-range results of the American Revolution were even greater than imagined during years of struggle. However difficult it was to overcome sectional differences and to persuade all colonies to accept it, once ratified, the document shaped in Philadelphia took on a life of its own:

> WE, THE PEOPLE OF THE UNITED STATES, in order to form a more perfect union, establish justice, insure domestic tranquility, provide for the common defense, promote the general welfare, and secure the blessings of liberty to ourselves and our posterity, do ordain and establish this constitution for the United States of America.

Not simply within the nation created by it, but throughout democracies around the globe, the document that represented the culmination of the American Revolution has shaped the modern world.

Index

Adams, John, 17, 37, 38–42, 99, 111, 125, 130, 133–138, 144, 198, 230; **39, 41**

Adams, Samuel, 40, 42, 55–59, 62, 172, 231; **54**

Albany, New York, 163

Allegheny, 112

Allen, Ethan, 96–100; **97**

Andre, John, 217–220, 260; **219, 222**

Appalachian Mountains, 49

Arnold, Benedict, 96, 121–125, 149, 151, 191–194, 217–223; **219**

Attucks, Crispus, 36, 40

Baldwin, Abraham, 171

banishment, 198

Barker, Penelope, 76–79; **77**

Beaumarchais, Caron de, 204–205

Bennington, Vermont, **190**

Bernard, Francis, 18, 21, 29, 34–35

Boone, Daniel, 9–10, 115–120, 173; **119**

Boonesborough, Kentucky, **117**

Boston, Massachusetts, 17, 26, 28, 33, 43, 56–59, 68, 72, 91–95, 110, 129, 233–237; **35, 37, 41, 63, 67, 70**

Boston Massacre, 33–37, 38–42, 89, 135; **37**

Boston Tea Party, 43, 66–70; **67**

boycott, 79

Braddock, Edward, 55

Brandt, Joseph, 226–227

Breed's Hill, 93–95

Brown, John, 43–48, 55, 73; **44**

Bunker Hill, 21, 93–95, 100, 145, 184; **92, 93**

Burgoyne, John, 91, 139, 160, 188–194, 249

Burke, Edmund, 80–81; **81**

Burr, Aaron, 123

Bushnell, David, 144–148; **145**

Caldwell, James, 168–169

calendar, 104

Cambridge, Massachusetts, 58, 106–107, 113, 129

Camden, South Carolina, 246–247, 255–256; **244**

Canada, 110, 114, 119, 121–125, 139, 151, 189, 218, 247

Caribbean Sea, 18

Carleton, Guy, 122, 226

Carroll, Charles, 136

cartoons, 69–70, 72, 79; **25, 69, 73, 78, 93, 109, 128, 180**

Castle, William, 31, 68, 164, 234

Charles II (England), 18; **20**

Charles III (Spain), 272–273

Charles Town, South Carolina, 25, 32, 70, 79, 102, 139–143, 224–225, 238–242, 251, 254–255; **247**

Charlotte, North Carolina, 101–105

Cherokee Indians, 117–118

Church, Benjamin, 130

Clark, George Rogers, 10, 168, 173–177, 273,

Clarke, Elijah, 256

Clinton, Henry, 139, 205, 207, 211, 219–220, 242, 254, 275, 278; **278**

Colonials, 9, 11, 20, 26, 45, 102, 197–200, 249–253; **86, 88, 109, 114, 134, 162, 169, 171, 189, 193, 203, 251**

combat, **86, 159, 212, 257, 265**

Common Sense, 113; **56**

communication, 32, 36, 46, 49, 58–59, 62–63, 78, 105, 174, 254, 276; **57**

Concord, Massachusetts, 89, 184; **162**

Congress, Continental, 10, 71–75, 97–100, 109–110, 111, 121–122, 133–138, 153, 171, 185, 192, 194, 209, 218, 229–232, 236–237; **75**

Conway, Thomas, 236–237

Corbin, Margaret, 211–212
Cornwallis, Charles, 143, 150, 165, 245–248, 255–258, 265, 268–271, 276–280; **269**
Correspondence, Committees of, 58–59, 70–71, 102; **57**
Cowpens, South Carolina, 263–267; **265**
currency, 112, 228–232; **231**

d'Estaing, Jean Baptiste, 205, 217, 238–242; **239**
Daggett, Naphtali, 169–170
Darragh, Lydia, 215–216
Dartmouth, Earl of, 101–102
de Galvez, Bernardo, 272–275
de Grasse, François Joseph Paule, 277–280; **279**
DeKalb, Johann, 150–151, 245–248; **150, 244**
Deane, Silas, 150–151, 202, 247
Declaration of Independence, 32, 127, 136, 160, 167, 171; **134**
Dickinson, John, 21, 100, 111, 134, 135–136
distance, 18, 53, 62–63, 78, 111, 200
Dockyards Acts, 47
Dudingston, William, 45–46

East India Company, 66–70
Edenton, North Carolina, 76–77; **78**
Emerson, William, 170

Ferguson, Patrick, 249–253
flags, 184–187
Fort Ticonderoga, 10, 96, 129, 190; **97**
Fort William and Mary, 85–88
Fort Sullivan, 139–143, 183; **141**
Fox, Charles James, 82–83, 271; **83**
France, 121, 149–153, 182, 187, 201, 243, 276–280
Franklin, Benjamin, 23, 25, 60–65, 68, 113, 135, 149–154, 181, 201–206, 207, 237, 273; **61, 73, 209**
Franklin, William, 207–210; **208, 209**

Gage, Thomas, 40, 55, 65, 72, 85, 122, 130, 165, 172
Gaspee, 43–48, 55; **44**
Gates, Horatio, 132, 192–194, 218, 237, 245, 248
George III, 23, 49–50, 63, 80–84, 97, 112, 114, 123, 127, 134–135, 207, 224, 275–276; **112, 114**

Gibault, Pierre, 168
Green Mountain Boys, 96–100
Greene, Nathanael, 150, 223, 259–262, 269–270; **271**
Grenville, George, 22, 61
Guilford Court House, North Carolina, 270–271; **270**
gunpowder, 87

Hale, Nathan, 147; **148**
Hamilton, Alexander, 222, 261–262, 269; **260**
Hancock, John, 29–32, 37, 98, 172; **31**
Harvard College, 56, 58, 107, 164
Hayes, Molly, 211–216; **212**
Henry, Patrick, 19, 24, 71, 75, 84, 98, 111; **78, 99**
Hopkinson, Francis, 148, 185
Howe, Richard, 145–146
Howe, William, 129, 139, 149, 158, 191, 254
Hutchinson, Thomas, 18–19, 55, 57, 60, 64, 66, 68

Indians, 116–120, 173–177, 190–191, 224–227; **175, 189**
inflation, 232

Jackson, Andrew, 253; **253**
Jasper, William, 142; **187**
Jefferson, Thomas, 24, 103–105, 135, 223; **103**
Jones, John Paul, 178–183, 186; **179, 180, 183**

Kaskaskia, Illinois, 175
Kentucky, 115–120, 173–177
Kings Mountain, North Carolina, 256–257, 266–267; **257**
Knox, Henry, 129, 159, 180, 262
Kosciuszko, Thaddeus, 149–154, 192

Lafayette, Marquis de, 151–154, 276–278; **152**
Lake Champlian, 96, 110, 149
Laurens, Henry, 25, 140
Lee, Charles, 152–154, 237; **235**
Lee, Ezra, 146–148
Lee, Richard Henry, 102, 133, 140–143; **137, 270**
Lexington, Massachusetts, 9–11, 88, 89; **169**
Liberty Pole, 250; **171**

Lincoln, Benjamin, 238–242, 247, 280; **227**

Livingston, Dicey, 215

London, 18, 27, 33, 42, 46, 49, 51, 55, 57–58, 60, 64, 80–84, 111, 127, 136, 139, 143, 145, 179, 200, 209, 223, 232, 249, 250, 254, 265

Louis XVI, 182, 194, 200

Loyalists (Tories), 9, 10, 19, 23, 26, 61, 74, 84, 160, 190; 194, 197–200, 219, 224–225, 240, 243, 245–248, 255–258, 266; **196, 215, 251**

lynching, **251**

Marion, Francis, 258; **255**

McCrea, Jane, 188–191; **189**

McGillivray, Alexander, 224–227

Mecklenburg Declaration, 101–105, 135–136

medicine, military, **131**

Merrill, Nancy, 214

Monmouth, New Jersey, 211; **212, 235**

Montague, John, 43

Montgomery, Richard, 122–123

Morgan, Daniel, 123, 177, 192–193, 263–267; **193, 264**

Morris, Robert, **261**

Morristown, New Jersey, 259

Motte, Rebecca, 214–215

Moultrie, William, 140–143

Muhlenberg, Frederick, 170

Muhlenberg, John Peter Gabriel, 167

Murray, John, 49

Narragansett Bay, 43–48

New Bern, North Carolina, 50

newspapers, **27**

New Hampshire, 85–88

New York, New York, 55, 68, 70, 93, 107, 129–130, 131, 139, 144, 146–147, 149, 158, 219–220; **114**

North, Lord, 36, 67

Nova Scotia, 199

Olive Branch Petition, 100, 113–114, 127

Otis, James, 9, 17–21, 26, 58, 67, 73; **16**

Paine, Thomas, 113–114; **56**

Parliament, 18, 19, 22, 27, 33, 36, 67, 80–84, 113

Penn, William, 111–114

Pensacola, Florida, 272–275; **274**

Philadelphia, Pennsylvania, 68, 71, 94, 102, 113, 136–137, 150, 174, 182, 215, 217, 220, 229; **75**

Pitcairn, John, 92–93

Pitt, William, 22, 84

Plessis, Marduit de, 151

Preston, Captain Thomas, 35–37, 38–42

Princeton College, 102

Princeton, New Jersey, 160

Prison ship, *Jersey*, 279; **266**

Providence, Rhode Isand, 43–48, 73, 85

Pulaski, Count, 185; **153, 241**

Putnam, Israel, 146

Quartering Act, 34, 36; **70**

Quebec Act, 69

Quebec, Canada, 121–125

Quincy, Samuel, 39

Quincy, Josiah, 39

Rahl, Johann Gottlieb, 156–160

Reed, Joseph, 106, 157

Regulators, 50

Revere, Paul, 36, 38, 85–86, 91–95, 172, 233–236, **35, 63, 90, 94, 231**

Richmond, Virginia, 98

Ross, Betsy, 184–185

Rutledge, John, 238

Saratoga, New York, 160, 165, 192–194, 204, 245; **193**

Savannah, Georgia, 154, 195, 225, 238–242, 243; **187, 241**

Schell, Zelma, 213–214

Sevier, John, 50–52, 256, 258; **51**

Shipley, Jonathan, 83–84

smallpox, 129–132; **128**

smuggling, 18, 30

Sons of Liberty, 30, 40, 68, 75, 83, 88, 93

Spanish, 272–275; **274**

Stamp Act, 20, 23, 27, 61, 73, 111–114

Stark, John, **190**

Steuben, Baron von, 153–154

Sullivan, John, 85–88, 94

Sumter, Thomas, 258

Tarleton, Banastre, 246–247, 263–267

taxes, 18, 23, 56, 67–68, 112; **25**

tea, 66–70, 76–79; **23, 67, 69, 78**

Thomson, Charles, 134, 136
Thruston, Charles M., 170
Tories. *See* Loyalists
Townshend, Charles, 66–67
Townshend Acts, 29, 67
Transylvania Company, 118–119
treason, 131, 217–223
Trenton, New Jersey, 137, 155–160; **157**
Trumbull, Jonathan, 34
Tryon, William, 50, 107, 209

Valley Forge, Pennsylvania, 151, 195, 206; **205**
Vincennes, Indiana, 168, 175–177
Virginia Resolves, 25

Walpole, Horace, 22
Warren, Joseph, 58, 94; **36**
Washington, George, 10, 32, 106–107, 113, 122, 129–132, 136, 140, 144, 145, 146, 148, 149, 151, 154, 155–160, 180, 184–185, 195, 206, 209, 211, 226, 247, 257, 262, 276–280; **12, 100, 128, 135, 157, 277**
Watauga Association, 49–52
West Point, New York, 150, 211, 254
Whately, Thomas, 60–65
Whigs (Patriots). See Colonials
Whipple, Abraham, 45–48; **47**
Wilderness Road, 120
Wilkes, John, 82–83; **84**
Williamsburg, Virginia, 49, 73–74, 76
Witherspoon, John, 170
women, 211–216; **78, 212, 215**
Wright, James, 9, 250

Yale College, 144, 171
"Yankee Doodle," 163–166; **162**
Yorktown, Virginia, 10, 154, 243, 276–280

Zane, Elizabeth, 213

Boldface entries indicate illustrations.